THE AFRICAN AMERICAN ODYSSEY

Item 9-10

Ebony, May 1965.

General Collections. Reproduced by permission of EBONY Magazine © 1965, Johnson Publishing Company, Inc.

The African American
ODYSSEY

AN EXHIBITION AT THE LIBRARY OF CONGRESS
FEBRUARY – MAY
1998

EDITED BY
Debra Newman Ham

• LIBRARY OF CONGRESS •
WASHINGTON • 1998

The exhibition and catalog are made possible through the generous support
of Anheuser-Busch Companies, Inc., The Morris and Gwendolyn Cafritz
Foundation, CITIBANK, Fannie Mae Foundation, Home Box Office,
and the James Madison Council.

Library of Congress Cataloging-in-Publication Data
Library of Congress
    The African American odyssey : an exhibition at the Library of Congress,
February 1998 / edited by Debra Newman Ham.
        p.   cm.
    Includes bibliographical references and index.
    ISBN 0–8444–0954–5 (alk. paper)
____ _____Z663.A75   1998
        1. Afro-Americans—History—Exhibitions.   I. Ham, Debra Newman,
1948–   . II. Title.
E185.53.W3L53   1998
973' .0496073' 0074753—dc21   97–47582
                                                          CIP

♾ The paper in this publication meets the requirements for permanence established
by the American National Standard ANSI/NISO Z39.48–1992, Permanence of Paper
for Publications and Documents in Libraries and Archives.

Exhibition curator: Debra Newman Ham
Exhibition director: Carroll Johnson
Catalog editor: Debbie Hardin

Catalog design: Caesar Jackson

For the Library of Congress:
Irene Chambers, *Head, Interpretive Programs Office*
Carroll Johnson, *Exhibit Director, Interpretive Programs Office*
Ralph Eubanks, *Director of Publishing*
Evelyn Sinclair, *Editor, Publishing Office*

Contributing curators of the Library of Congress:
Maricia Battle, *Prints and Photographs Division*
Samuel Brylawski, *Motion Picture, Broadcasting, and Recorded Sound Division*
Adrienne Cannon, *Manuscript Division*
Ronald Grim, *Geography and Map Division*
Alan Jabbour, *American Folklife Center*
Ardie Myers, *Humanities and Social Sciences Division*
David Parker, *Motion Picture, Broadcasting, and Recorded Sound Division*
Rosemary Fry Plakas, *Rare Book and Special Collections Division*
Wayne D. Shirley, *Music Division*
Brian Taves, *Motion Picture, Broadcasting, and Recorded Sound Division*

Photography: Roger Foley

Contents

"Books Are Weapons: Read about—The Negro in National Defense, Africa and the War, Negro History and Culture—at the Schomburg Collection of the New York Public Library."
Federal Art Project poster, ca. 1943. Color silkscreen. Prints and Photographs Division.

Foreword

JAMES H. BILLINGTON
Librarian of Congress

For more than one hundred years the Library of Congress has been collecting materials by and about African Americans. The pioneering builder of the Library's unparalleled African American collections was Daniel Alexander Payne Murray, who began his long career in the Library in 1871 as assistant to Librarian of Congress Ainsworth R. Spofford. Daniel Murray devoted a large part of his career at the Library to building this collection, believing that "the true test of the progress of a people is to be found in their literature." In 1925, he bequeathed to the nation his personal collection of nearly fifteen hundred books and pamphlets that demonstrate the achievements of African Americans in all fields of endeavor. Over the years, the Library has also acquired an extraordinary amount of unique material in many forms on many aspects of African American life—through copyright deposit, institutional and individual bequests, and purchase.

In 1993 the Library of Congress published *The African-American Mosaic: A Library of Congress Resource Guide for the Study of Black History and Culture*. Along with its related exhibition *Selections from the African-American Mosaic*, excerpts from this publication have been available on the Library's much-visited Web site and have generated considerable scholarly attention. The electronic exhibition has had more than a million viewers and describes the extensive collection of materials in all media that the Library has amassed.

Late in 1992, I had decided to mount a major exhibition on the subject of African American history to be displayed in all three of the Library's buildings on Capitol Hill. The subsequent success of the resource guide and the electronic exhibition confirmed the desirability of mounting this comprehensive exhibit, which will be the largest exhibit on African American history and culture ever undertaken by the Library.

The African American Odyssey documents the history of slaves stolen from Africa and brought to colonial America. The exhibit also highlights abolition and the Civil War, Reconstruction, the world wars, and the 1960 civil rights era. Most of the materials in *The African American Odyssey* and additional related items will soon be available electronically to people all over the world. Although an exhibition allows us to display only one or two pages of a document or book at a time, on-line technology will enable us to show the entire text.

We at the Library hope that *The African American Odyssey* and its subsequent on-line counterpart will both ease the work of researchers in remote locations and induce readers and viewers to come in person to explore the collections of the Library. As Americans become increasingly aware of the many vital threads that constitute the fabric of our national life, our common memory is enriched and our horizons are widened. We trust that this exhibition will increase knowledge and understanding among all Americans. In so doing it should help not just to break down racial barriers caused by prejudice and ignorance but also to build up interest in the richness and complexity of the still only partially studied primary materials constituting an important part of our shared national history.

"Battle Hymn: A new play about John Brown of Harpers Ferry."
Works Progress Administration (WPA), Federal Theatre Project poster, ca. 1935–39.
Prints and Photographs Division. B WPA NYG 6551

At the house dinner was served and about 20 of us
was. . .[called] up to the house door and set free.
Amen. Amen. Amen.

HOUSTON HARTSFIELD HOLLOWAY
Memoirs of a former Georgia slave

Preface

DEBRA NEWMAN HAM

A mosaic is formed by inlaying small bits
of colored stone, glass, or tile in mortar to create a picture
or design. Although each piece could stand alone, its collective message tells far more than each individual tile. This
exhibit is about the intricate mosaic of Library of Congress
collections relating to African American history and culture.
The image embraces more than one continent. The social,
economic, and demographic composition of Africa, Europe,
and the Americas has been vastly altered over the past four
centuries as a result of the slave trade and the economy
that slave labor spawned. The picture also involves more
than one race. A most compelling aspect of this collage is
that along with the struggle of the slaves and their descendants are a host of white allies and others who worked
with them to throw off the galling yoke of servitude.
Finally, the details of this mosaic take us through several
hundred years and a wide variety of absorbing documentation including books, pamphlets, prints, photographs,
music, films, sound recordings, and maps.

The purpose of the exhibition is to provide observers
with an appreciation of the size and scope of the body of
African American materials at the Library of Congress
and, perhaps, encourage some to do more in-depth study

of what they observe. Even for those of us who are somewhat familiar with the Library's African American holdings, the discovery of the fine details of these collections is ongoing. Each new research project and exhibit acquaints us with materials that we did not know existed.

This catalog accompanies an exhibition intended to provide an overview of African American history from slavery through the civil rights era. Nine chronological sections of the exhibit in the Library's Thomas Jefferson Building model the timeline of *The African-American Mosaic: A Library of Congress Resource Guide for the Study of Black History and Culture.*[1] Here we provide a brief chronological history of the fate of the African in America since the colonial period, illustrating examples of Library of Congress holdings for each era since the founding of this nation. *The African-American Mosaic* and this exhibit demonstrate that there are few aspects or periods of African American history and culture that are not amply documented by the Library's collections.

A few years ago the doyenne of African American bibliography, nonagenarian Dorothy Porter Wesley, stated that *The African-American Mosaic*—the three-hundred page guide that prompted this exhibit—introduced her to a world of Library resources that were hitherto unknown to her.[2] Because by 1994 Wesley had regularly consulted the Library of Congress collections for seventy years, she found this discovery amazing indeed. As developer and director of the Negro Collection at Howard University in Washington, D.C., Wesley had an ardent interest in the preservation of materials relating to African American history and culture at Howard and elsewhere. As the first black graduate of Columbia University's School of Library Science and long-time resident of Washington, D.C., it seemed natural that she often found herself collaborating in projects at the Library of Congress.

Wesley helped to organize and describe the Booker T. Washington collection donated to the Library in 1943 by Tuskegee Institute in Alabama. In 1969 after a brief stint in residence at the Library she prepared a bibliography titled *The Negro in the United States.*[3] In the 1969 *Annual Report of the Librarian of Congress,*[4] Archibald MacLeish discusses "the surge of interest in Negro affairs" that resulted in a flood of research requests at the Library. One of the ways that the Library met this deluge was by contracting with Wesley—then called Dorothy Burnette Porter (who was

known even then as "an eminent authority" in African Americana)—to prepare this bibliography.

About the same time the Library's Manuscript Division specialist for the national period, John McDonough, responded to a late 1960s request for information about African American resources in the division. During these years, partly because the anticipated commemoration of the 350th anniversary of arrival of Africans at Jamestown, Virginia, in 1619, and partly because of the Library's acquisition of the vast archives of the National Association for the Advancement of Colored People (NAACP) in 1964 and the National Urban League (NUL) records in 1966, McDonough began to collect information about the division's manuscript resources for black history. He presented a paper about the subject before the 1969 annual meeting of the Association for the Study of Negro (later Afro-American) Life and History in Baltimore. He subsequently expanded the paper for an extensive article in the *Quarterly Journal of the Library of Congress*[5] titled "Manuscript Resources for the Study of Negro Life and History." This excellent and comprehensive essay provided the first collective discussion of Manuscript Division resources on this subject.

In late 1993 when Wesley received galley proofs for *The African-American Mosaic* several weeks before the symposium, she called Prosser Gifford, the Library's director of scholarly programs, to chastise him. Why? She explained that she had a million things to do but when these proofs arrived, she started reading and could not put them down. She marveled at the comprehensiveness of *The African-American Mosaic* and noted that it was the first major attempt since her bibliography and McDonough's article to try to inform researchers about the wide array of materials relating to African American studies at the Library.

During the 1994 symposium, Wesley also bemoaned the fact that *The African-American Mosaic* informed her—to her dismay—that she had traveled to England to consult records available only minutes from her home on microfilm in the Library collections. Wesley and other scholars on the panel—Fisk University librarian Jessie Carney Smith, film historian Thomas Cripps, and African American museum director John Flemming—discussed the days when only card files or library specialists could help the researcher navigate the vast wealth of African American resources. They rejoiced that computer catalogs and guides such as *The African-American Mosaic* could provide them with so much help.

During the preparation of the resource guide, Library of Congress staff members were excited by the discovery of pockets of materials in other divisions of the Library. Among the eight subject or medium specialists and one former staff member who participated in the project were experts in manuscripts, maps, the general collections, rare books, prints, photographs, music, film, and recorded sound.[6] Discovering resources about which we knew very little made each of us eager to uncover additional corresponding resources in the collections under our own purview. Those of us who had little familiarity with the Prints and Photographs Division were fascinated to learn about hundreds of trade cards, cartes de visite, and stereographs with images of blacks. The typed poems with editorial marks and several books autographed by Langston Hughes in the Manuscript Division were seen alongside the many volumes Hughes published. Hughes's lyrics set to music from the Music Division and prints and portrait photographs of the great poet from the Prints and Photographs Division complement the tapes that allow us to hear what he sounded like at various times in his life. Literary maps from the Geography and Map Division show us where famous black literati lived and worked in the United States. Each aspect of the subject became richer and fuller as specialists from the various Library divisions worked together.

Pulitzer Prize-winning author David Garrow, who spoke at the same *African-American Mosaic* symposium during which Wesley made her delightful and insightful remarks, provided evidence of our success. Garrow commented that he had carefully culled Library of Congress books and manuscripts relating to the civil rights movement while preparing his biography of Martin Luther King, Jr.,[7] but he was not aware—before reading *The African-American Mosaic*—of the Library's vast treasures relating to the subject in photographs, recordings, sheet music, maps, and film. Other users have made similar comments.

At the time of the publication of *The African-American Mosaic*, and in addition to the one-day symposium, the Library of Congress mounted a small exhibit in the James Madison Building called *Selections from "The African-American Mosaic."* Although the exhibit was relatively popular during its several-month showing, it has more recently become a "best-seller" on the Library's Web site. Our statistics show that hundreds of thousands of people have visited the exhibit on-line.

Librarian of Congress James H. Billington announced to the staff in February 1994 that the Library planned to mount a major African American history exhibit. Four years later, this exhibit, *The African American Odyssey*, signals the fruition of that plan. It is mounted in the beautiful, newly renovated Thomas Jefferson Building. The exhibit traces the African American quest for freedom and full citizenship in all areas of American life. Though it focuses primarily on the political and social arenas, many items also highlight the African American pursuit of free literary and artistic expression.

This exhibit represents only a rivulet of the sea of collections the Library holds relating to African Americans. Even a brief listing of every item relating to the subject would probably take many several lifetimes to complete. But not all of the materials in the Library are supportive of African Americans. Many documents, in fact, tell a story of hatred and foster old stereotypes. Derogatory caricatures, buffoonery, unpronounceable dialect, racial epithets, and degrading studies and literature abound. During the period between the Civil War and World War I there are literally thousands of copyrighted plays, musical scores, drawings, and books poking fun at the newly freed race or longing for the old days when African Americans were enslaved. Minstrels and blackface are abundant. There are probably few places on earth that provide resources for a more comprehensive study of institutional racism than the collections here. The years between emancipation and World War I are especially revealing in this regard. Library materials for this period indicate that many ill-wishers predicted that African Americans would not be equal to the liberty for which they had longed, prayed, and fought. Those racists were wrong.

There is another side to the story of African Americans in the Library's collections. This exhibit is about that other side, the side in which courage triumphs over adversity, patience over hatred, right over wrong, and freedom over slavery. African Americans, though victimized by slavery and racism for several centuries, have demonstrated the ability to face the adverse circumstances in which they found themselves and overcome immense odds to fully participate in all aspects of American society. They have used the resources at their disposal to break the bonds of servitude and become full-fledged citizens of the United States. African Americans have fought and died in every American war, toiled to build the nation's economy, and tirelessly agitated for color-blind citizenship in the United States. Library resources abundantly attest to the African American freedom struggle from the colonial period to the present. That is the heart of the mosaic: The bits and pieces of evidence available in the Library of Congress that, taken together, provide unquestionable documentation of the African American quest for full citizenship in the nation, from the colonial period through the twentieth century.

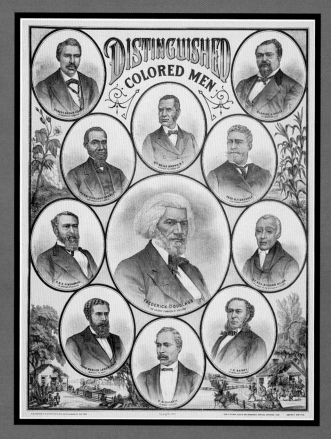

Item 5-10
George F. Crane. "Distinguished Colored Men." New York: A. Muller & Co., 1883.
Hand-colored lithograph. Prints and Photographs Division.

As for luxuries outside of meat and bread
there was none and we wanted none for we was free.
Glory to God was our daily cry.

HOUSTON HARTSFIELD HOLLOWAY
Memoirs of a former Georgia slave

Introduction

DEBRA NEWMAN HAM

The resiliency among the people kidnapped from the African continent begins to emerge even from the earliest books and documents held in the collections at the Library of Congress. These resources show people of color not only as victims of a cruel system of slavery and oppression—and they certainly were—but as actors who found effective ways to cope with or escape from the confines of enslavement. Even on board the vessels of their captivity from the seventeenth to the mid-nineteenth centuries some enslaved Africans mutinied and took command of the ships that held them. For those who survived the rigors and the pestilence of the passage from Africa to America and found themselves auctioned to the highest bidder, freedom was still a watchword.

Documented by the exhibition are a few of the famous slave mutinies and revolts that dispel the view that African slaves were docile and content with their lot. Fear of slave revolts was quite common in the American colonies and in the early years of the nation. A perusal of any colonial newspaper indicates that runaways, acts of slave resistance, and fears of slave rebellions were widespread. Especially after the successful rebellion of Afro-Haitians over the

French at the turn of the nineteenth century, white Americans experienced a widespread dread of slave reprisals against their owners. As cultivated lands increased in acreage, the size of the slave population sometimes grew to equal or exceed the number of whites in some southern states. Slaveholders realized that a unified revolt by those held in bondage could signal doom for the owners.

It is not surprising that emancipated or runaway slaves who wrote or dictated their memoirs often discussed freedom. Houston Hartsfield Holloway, formerly a Georgia slave, wrote, after his emancipation, that although his master was not too harsh or his work too arduous, he and others formerly enslaved on that plantation greeted each new day of freedom with the cry, "Glory to God!" He explained that the black folks did not know how to be free and that the white folks did not know how to have free blacks around them but that these factors were not a deterrent in the freepersons' enjoyment of their liberty.

The Slave Narrative Collection in the Manuscript Division includes transcripts of interviews with former slaves conducted in the 1930s. The interviews document the slaves' longing for freedom and illustrate the coping methods they used while they were treated as chattel, or property, by the perpetuators of the *peculiar institution,* as the American slave system was called. These records document how eagerly these people of color embraced first the hope and then the reality of freedom.

The nation witnessed the work of creative blacks such as poets Phillis Wheatley and Jupiter Hammon; scientist and astronomer Benjamin Banneker; abolitionist, orator, and statesperson Frederick Douglass; and scholar and activist W. E. B. DuBois, all before the dawn of the twentieth century. Introductory letters published in Wheatley's book *Poems on Various Subjects, Religious and Moral*[1] at the time of its publication in 1773 served as affidavits that an African-born woman with classical training did indeed write the contents. It was necessary to print such affidavits because few whites believed that blacks were capable of learning or creativity.

Of the thousands of African American slaves who ran away, some formed their own communities and marketed their own services. Other escapees indentured themselves or their children

to white masters. Some served at sea on American and European vessels. Several thousand gained their freedom serving alongside their owners during the Colonial war. Thousands more fled to freedom behind the British lines during the Revolutionary War and the War of 1812. Continental Army Commander and later the first president, George Washington, who was himself a slave owner, mulled over the possibility of allowing blacks to serve as members of regular troops in the Continental Army. Ultimately, free blacks and slaves fought on the side of the Americans, although many more fled to and aided the British.

Those servicemen who were formerly enslaved gained their freedom as a result of their military service in the Continental Army. In addition to their freedom as a repayment for services rendered, the British took former slaves with them to Canada, Jamaica, and England. In 1787 concerned British citizens repatriated hundreds of Africans from each of these regions to West Africa where they established Sierra Leone. Beginning in 1820, with the aid of the American Colonization Society, several thousand African Americans from various states returned to Africa and founded Liberia. Other black migrants made their way into the American West.

Blacks within and without the shackles of bondage were successful at a variety of business ventures and credited with numerous inventions. Harriet Beecher Stowe, author of *Uncle Tom's Cabin,*[2] even argued that it was not Eli Whitney but a black slave who developed the little machine to separate the seed from the cotton—known as the cotton gin. That process revolutionized cotton production in the United States. In addition to this disputed claim there is documented evidence of a number of scientific inventions patented by blacks since emancipation.

The small free black population during the period up to 1860, however, aided by sympathetic whites, were most outspoken—and most creative—in their protest against slavery, an institution many of them knew from firsthand experience. The Library collections include hundreds of African American books, poems, speeches, and sermons that echoed a call for liberty not unlike that of the American colonies from their perceived oppressor in the eighteenth century—Great Britain. Wheatley wrote that some who perused her "song" would wonder from where her "love of freedom sprung." She explained that she "young in life" had been "snatch'd from Afric's fancied happy seat." Wheatley's position as a "pampered" Boston slave would have been enviable to many slaves who endured physical and emotional abuse, but that did not squelch her longing for freedom. With the Declaration of Independence, doctrines of equality and the inalienable rights of life, liberty, and the pursuit of happiness reached the ears of the free person and slave alike, and the oppressed longed to throw off the oppressor.

Hundreds of thousands of whites allied with free blacks to aid in the destruction of the peculiar institution. Quakers, for example, were speaking, writing, and petitioning in legislatures against slavery from the eighteenth century. In addition to formal methods of protest, grassroots networks emerged to fight against slavery. Members of both races acted as conductors on the Underground Railroad, which was, in truth, neither underground nor a railroad. It was a series of secret travel routes and hiding places established for the purpose of guiding runaways from the slaveholding states to the North or Canada. Library of Congress holdings comprise a virtual avalanche of materials relating to antislavery efforts, including personal papers of great abolitionists such as Frederick Douglass, Susan B. Anthony, Henry Ward Beecher, Salmon P. Chase, Theodore Weld, and many more. Antislavery and proslavery political debates divided the nation, led to local violence and, ultimately, to war.

During the Civil War black soldiers demonstrated that detractors who said they would flee in terror in the midst of a battle were wrong. Black soldiers proved as able to wield a gun as a plow, hoe, or harness. They worked behind the scenes as well as on the front lines with the Union troops. African American civilians proved that they cared about their families in spite of claims that they were too negligent and immoral to care for their own homes. For example, Union chaplains and Freedmen's Bureau officials wearied themselves aiding free people in legitimizing their marriage vows. A letter in the Manuscript Division indicates that in 1863 white Union chaplain Asa Fiske once performed simultaneous wedding ceremonies for 119 African American couples who had fled to safety behind Union lines. For African Americans, the right to have a family, protect spouses and children, earn an honest living, and dwell in peace became one of the driving desires for freedom.

As Union soldiers and northern teachers, preachers, businesspeople, and missionaries traveled into defeated sections of the Confederacy, they discovered aspects of slave life and culture hitherto unknown to them. African American spirituals, folk songs, and churches and African traditions and linguistic traits caused many

northern observers to reassess their views about blacks. Because masters and mistresses feared literate slaves, every slaveholding state passed laws forbidding African American education. This accentuated a longing for learning that impressed almost every chronicler of the South in the period during and after the Civil War. Old and young free people of color sat together in classrooms. The old often clutched their Bibles longing to be able to read its pages for themselves on this side of heaven. One-room schoolhouses, poorly paid teachers, and nascent institutions of higher education sprang up throughout the South. The 1900 census reports indicates that in the period between the Civil War and the turn of the century, the majority of the African American population broke the bonds of illiteracy.

The immediate post-Civil War period saw the passage of the Thirteenth, Fourteenth, and Fifteenth Amendments to the Constitution, which abolished slavery and granted citizenship and male suffrage. Although this seemed to promise a new era of freedom for African Americans, troubles soon set in. Gains in civil rights legislation and political representation in state and local legislatures and in the U.S. Congress were eroded in several decades. Congressional reports in the Library holdings chronicle the Ku Klux Klan death threats to those blacks who dared to participate actively in the political and economic arenas of the South. Tenancy, sharecropping, and peonage bound many poor African Americans in a new kind of bondage from the 1870s through the turn of the twentieth century. Blacks had to begin anew to strive for social and political rights in their homeland.

In spite of setbacks, by the turn of the twentieth century a race formerly barred from literacy by law was largely literate and had published thousands of books, pamphlets, plays, and music pieces. Nevertheless, in 1896 the U.S. Supreme Court dealt a crushing blow to the struggle for freedom by declaring in the *Plessy v. Ferguson* case that it was legal to provide "separate but equal" accommodations for blacks on public conveyances. The concept of racial separation crept through the fabric of American life, North and South. Historian Rayford Logan, whose diaries are among the Library's holdings, called this period the nadir of the historical experience of free blacks. Race riots and other types of racial violence ushered in a reign of terror in much of the South.

The voices of the nation's black citizens were not silenced by the onslaught of racial repression. Black journalists such as Ida B. Wells Barnett and William Monroe Trotter, scholars such as W. E. B. DuBois and Carter G. Woodson, and educators such as Booker T. Washington and Nannie Helen Burroughs spoke out against lynching, other forms of violence, bigotry, segregation, and racial discrimination. White neoabolitionists and their African American allies formed the National Association for the Advancement of Colored People (NAACP) and the National Urban League (NUL) to fight against racism in the political, economic, and social arenas of American life.

Even while African Americans were pre-occupied with the status of their citizenship they were assisting the nation in wars against Native Americans, Mexicans, and the Spanish in Cuba and the Philippines. The blood of African Americans was spilled in defense of the nation in every war, but the battle for equal treatment under the law continued unabated. African American military units were generally segregated and black soldiers were often used as supply troops rather than fighting men. During World War I African American soldiers and home-front workers fought for democracy abroad as well as at home. From World War I through World War II, employment and educational opportunities in the North and racial repression in the South prompted many blacks to migrate to the north-ern urban areas or southern industrial centers.

This intense period of rapid urbanization led to social, religious, political, and cultural move-ments in the burgeoning black communities. Polit-ical activists such as Marcus Garvey, religious leaders such as Father Divine and Daddy Grace, and entrepreneurs such as Madame C. J. Walker and C. C. Spaulding and others converged on major urban centers to sell ideas and products to a growing African American population. In New York African American artists and writers began to show their genius in a movement known as the Harlem Renaissance, although artistic innovations were not limited to any one locale. Howard University philosophy professor Alain Locke described the 1920s as the era of the "New Negro." It was a period when African Americans sought to define themselves and articu-late their own objectives and needs rather than have them defined by others.

Through the Depression, African Americans, who were already among the poorest groups in the country, sought relief for both their urban and rural communities. New Deal programs offered under President Franklin Delano Roosevelt's administration did provide economic relief for some and artistic outlets for others. It was during this period that the Works Progress Administration

conducted hundreds of interviews with elderly people who were formerly enslaved and preserved some of their recollections for posterity. The Federal Writers', Federal Art, and Federal Theatre Projects afforded talented blacks the opportunity to demonstrate their abilities to a wide audience. The Harmon Foundation, an organization whose records are among the holdings of the Manuscript Division, awarded prizes and grants to many of these creative African Americans.

By the time that the United States entered World War II African Americans were becoming increasingly out-spoken about contradictions in American life. How could blacks fight with the U.S. military to abolish the monster of Aryan racial supremacy in Europe while they battled with a similar specter in the United States? Black newspa-pers hammered home the issue until they were silenced by censors. Professional and political groups composed of African Americans demanded desegregated military units, black officers and pilots, infantry rather than supply duty, equal opportunity for employment in home-front industries, and the end of racial discrimination in America. African American labor leader A. Philip Randolph, whose personal papers are among the holdings of the Manuscript Division, threatened in 1941 to lead one hundred thousand blacks in a March on Washington, D.C. In the face of this chal-lenge, President Roosevelt issued Executive Order No. 8802 forbidding racial and religious discrimination in defense industries.

African Americans found that the Roosevelts— especially Eleanor—were important allies in their cause. Working through political avenues in several unsuccessful attempts to pass federal antilynching legislation, through labor unions with leaders such as Randolph, and through economic pressures, African Americans attempted to make the big changes that were promised in the post-Civil War era but that were not yet reality almost a century later. Protests were coming before state and federal legislatures and courts from every side. Blacks were just plain tired of mistreatment in their homeland. They did not want to be "second-class" citizens. They wanted the same opportuni-ties available to others.

Pressures from protest groups, particularly the NAACP, were slowly providing workable strategies for ending segre-gation in housing, education, transportation, employment, and business. A series of major Supreme Court cases began to seriously erode the pillars of discrimination. The most renowned case brought by the NAACP and argued in 1954 by Thurgood Marshall was *Brown v. Board of Education of Topeka, Kansas.* This was the key victory in the legal battle to dismantle segregation in the United States. When Marshall and the other Legal Defense Fund lawyers presented their arguments in *Brown,* they cited cases relating to segregated schools in various parts of the United States so that the "separate but equal" doctrine could be challenged in a variety of settings throughout the country. The Court heard the case twice before ruling unanimously that separate schools were inherently unequal, thus paving the way for future decisions declaring unconstitutional all racial segregation.

Along with legal triumphs the civil rights movement gained momentum in 1956 and 1957 during the Montgomery, Alabama, bus boycott led by two ministers, Martin Luther King, Jr., and Ralph Abernathy. In 1958 President Dwight Eisenhower sent federal troops into Little Rock, Arkansas, to enforce school desegregation at Central High School. Two years later, in 1960, four students from North Carolina Agricultural and Technical College in Greensboro sat down at a local lunch counter and refused to move until they were served. They were not served. Young people around the country were stirred by the bravery of the Montgomery boycotters and Greensboro student sit-in. Without an organized effort white and black citizens—especially students—began to stage sit-ins in other parts of the South and in chain stores throughout the country. A variety of organizations began to participate in the movement with marches, freedom rides to desegregate public transportation, voter registration drives, boycotts, and publicity campaigns. As the press closely documented the movement, many in the nation were horrified by the severe repression of the movement, especially the violence meted out to peaceful demonstrators and the bombing and murder of civil rights activists.

The movement culminated with the August 28, 1963, March on Washington, during which an estimated 250,000 blacks and whites of many faiths marched together demanding voting rights and an end to segregation and job discrimination, as well as equal opportunity in all other areas of American life. Several centuries of struggle culminated in the passage of the Civil Rights Act of 1964, the Voting Rights Act of 1965, and the Fair Housing Act of 1968. The passage of these laws did not end bias but they did reaffirm the African American right to equal protection under the law. Because of the records of the National Association for the Advancement of Colored People, the NAACP Legal Defense Fund, the National Urban League, the Brotherhood of Sleeping Car Porters and Maids, the Leadership Conference for Civil Rights, and personal papers of many of the movement's leaders, documentation relating to the civil rights movement is probably more extensive in the Library of Congress than any other research repository in the world.

The civil rights movement opened doors for African Americans in politics, the sciences, sports, fine arts, media, business, higher education, and a wide variety of professions that had previously barred their participation. Although racial prejudice and discrimination continue, such practices are not legal. Perhaps the African American experience demonstrates the effectiveness of the American system to a degree unparalleled in the experience of the nation.

Item 2-13
Illustration from Henry Bibb, *Narrative of the Life and Adventures of Henry Bibb, an American Slave*
(New York: The Author, 1849).
Rare Book and Special Collections Division.

The merchandise of gold, and silver, and precious stones, and of pearls, and fine linen, and purple, and silk, and scarlet . . . and wine, and oil . . . and horses, and chariots, and slaves, and souls of men . . . .

REVELATION 18:12–14

1 Unwilling Immigrants of Sable Hue: African Americans in the Antebellum Period

DEBRA NEWMAN HAM

A few aspects of the Atlantic slave trade from the seventeenth to the nineteenth centuries can be compared to today's illicit drug trafficking. First, the trade was extremely lucrative. The proceeds from the successful transport of even one shipload of African captives to the New World could yield enormous profits, which ultimately were divided among shipbuilders and shipowners, suppliers of goods (such as "Negro cloth," shoes for slaves, and so on) and services including African merchants and European crews, and plantation owners, who would benefit for generations from the toil of unpaid laborers. Second, like the drug trade today, the slave trade victimized millions of Africans by destroying families; stigmatizing black coloration; obliterating historical, cultural, and linguistic ties; and instituting perpetual servitude. American slavery placed an intolerable burden on its unwilling African immigrants. Africans were also victimized because they could not market their own labor, and free white workers were harmed economically as they encountered difficulties competing with the unfree labor force.

Third, those guilty of aiding and abetting the heinous slave traffic were of every race, color, and religion—just like drug dealers. They were poor and rich, both literate and unlearned, statespersons and criminals, female and male, black, white, red, and brown. Fourth, millions have lost their lives in the slave and drug commerce. African victims and the European crews who stole them together succumbed to terrible plagues and violence. And fifth, just as world governments have expended millions of dollars to eradicate the illegal drug trade, herculean international efforts were necessary to stave traffic in humans.

Slaves and Souls of Men (Revelation 18:14)

People of different races have been enslaved over thousands of years of human interaction. African slavery existed for many centuries before the European discovery of the Americas and the onset of the Atlantic slave trade. Before the European domination of the New World, African war captives were held in bondage by their African captors or sold within Africa. Some were traded to foreign buyers on the Maghrib, marketed across the Mediterranean or Red Seas or over the far reaches of the Indian Ocean. Scholars often refer to this dispersion of Africans and their occasional return to the continent as the African diaspora.

African domestic slavery resulted from a variety of unfortunate circumstances. Vanquished warriors, women captured because of the value of their labor or their beauty, and the poor, weak, and defenseless often found themselves owned by another African or, after the eighth century, sold by their African captors to Muslims who in turn sold them to various parts of the world.

Slavery is cruel regardless of the nationality, color, or gender of the owner. Yet for all its cruelties, the African and Islamic slave trade never equaled the sheer volume of the Atlantic trade. By the fifteenth century European navigational skill began to eclipse that of other nations, ushering in an era of exploration and discovery that would change the face of the world. Early explorers such as Christopher Columbus opened up the Western hemisphere to hardy European settlers seeking their fortunes. Ideally, to be maximally exploited by immigrants, the vast American territory needed agricultural laborers who could be bound to the land. Early settlers experimented with both Native American and African labor but found that African workers could not escape with the

ease of Native Americans who knew the territory and that African knowledge of tropical agricultural production enabled them to produce bountiful crops of sugar, rice, indigo, cotton, tobacco, and other products.

African traders were more than willing to sell unfortunate African captives to the Europeans and, later, to American merchants, who began to frequent the West African coast. Western traders and their African collaborators ultimately established slave collection depots, called forts, where they could negotiate for their human cargo. Because of malaria and yellow fever—diseases that were not clearly identified until the nineteenth century—only a small percentage of Europeans and Americans could penetrate the African interior and live. The trade only prospered because African raiders and chiefs were willing participants. Europeans, however, fueled avarice and African ethnic rivalries and warfare by providing valued products, weapons, and ammunition to their African allies.

Beginning in earnest in the sixteenth century and ending well into the nineteenth, the Atlantic slave trade swallowed up millions of Africans. Some entire sections of the territory north and east of the West African coast were depopulated. Although speculations have varied widely, no one really knows exactly how many Africans fell prey to the trade. Systematic records were not kept. Language barriers existed, and most of the exploited African societies were preliterate and consequently kept no written records of those who were lost—although African oral traditions document the kidnapping of many kinsmen. Where records for European and American vessels exist they generally give only the names of the ports at which they purchased Africans, the numbers acquired perhaps with separate information about gender, the ports in the New World at which they were sold, and, sometimes, monetary accounts. The slave merchants did not care about the names or the parentage of the Africans, although they began to prefer some of the ethnic groups judged to be less recalcitrant than others.

In 1969 when Africanist Philip Curtin argued that no more than 9 or 10 million Africans were drawn from their homeland, including those who perished in the passage, scholars protested that Curtin's numbers were *far too low!* [1] Some scholars now believe that a figure of 25 million is more accurate. Estimates of deaths on board vessels as a result of disease, murder, and suicide during the thirty-day voyage vary from casualty rates of one-third to one-fifth of all captives. Logs of slavers indicate that vessels carried between 150 to 400 Africans. The vessels were often deliberately overcrowded so that the owners' losses because of deaths on board would not be so severe. The business of slavery was so lucrative that

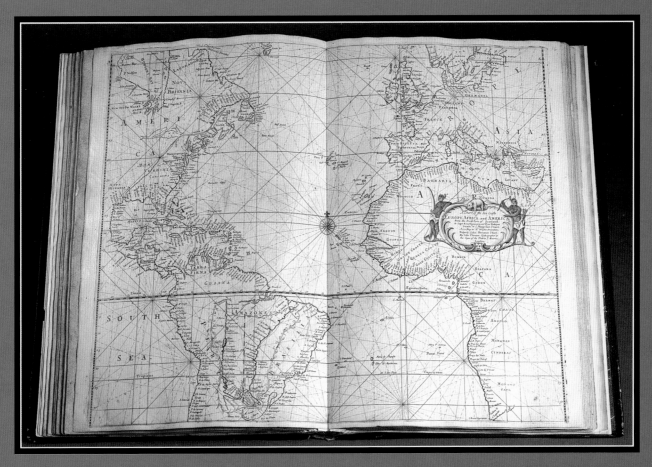

Item 1-11 A

"A Chart of the Sea Coasts of Europe, Africa, and America . . . ." From John Thornton, *Atlas Maritimus, or the Sea Atlas* (London, 1700?).
Geography and Map Division.

Copy

Province of ⎫ The Examination of William Prust
Massachussetts Bay ⎰ now resident in Boston Mariner
1. March 1765

The Examinant saith, that he is about thirty
eight years of age, that he was born in Biddeford
in England, that he served his apprenticeship to
the Sea with Captain George Darracot of Boston
aforesaid, that about a year since or thirteen months
he shipped himself as Chief mate aboard the
Brigantine Hope of New London Gould master but
the Examinant was then in New York, that he
went from New York to New London, and sailed from
thence in the said Brigantine the latter end of
february, for the Coast of Guinea, that having been about
three weeks from New London, he was turned before
the mast, but does not know for what reason,
and George Taggart the second mate was made
Chief mate And a few days after they arrived at
Goree, where the Captain shipped a second mate
one Huntington, who came from a Brigantine one
Campbell master, belonging to New York — after
some time spent in trading at Goree Captain Gould
And Company in the aforesaid Brigantine Hope
went to Gambia, And then returned to Goree and
took in between thirty And forty slaves, and then
went to Senegal And took in two or three more
slaves, but did not go over the Bar, That whilst
they lay there, one day about the 15. May the Captain
was very tyranical And had beat And abused
all the people very much, and the Examinant
received some Blows from him, that about nine
or ten o'Clock at night of the said 15. May

Item 1-1 (left)

"The Examination of William Priest, now resident in Boston . . . ," a handwritten transcript regarding a slave revolt aboard the brigantine *Hope,* March 17, 1765.
Peter Force Collection. Manuscript Division.

Item 8-18 (above)

Prentiss Taylor, *Scottsboro Limited* (P.T. VII), 1931. The trial of nine black youths in Scottsboro, Alabama, in 1931 for the alleged rape of two white women was the subject of Taylor's haunting image conveying the sorrow and outrage that surrounded the trial. A variant was used on the book jacket for *Langston Hughes's Scottsboro Limited: Four Poems and a Play in Verse* (New York: Golden Stair Press, 1932), and this print is inscribed to Hughes by the artist.
Lithograph. Prints and Photographs Division. Courtesy of Roderick S. Quiroz.

vessel owners were able to insure their cargo, build shipyards for the construction of slave ships, and have special clothing made and food grown for the needs of the slaves.

African Resistance

Involuntary African immigrants who were sold in the New World protested their condition from the outset. They fought with their captors, attempted to escape from collection points, mutinied on board slave-trading vessels, or tried to commit suicide. Rioting and suicides on board vessels became so common that Western traders eventually discontinued the practice of allowing captives to come to the upper decks for fresh air. As the trade became increasingly profitable, shipbuilders began to construct specially outfitted vessels with decks from two to three feet high. Africans had to sit or lay on the low decks chained together for the entire voyage. Thus, Africans came to the Americas longing to be free from the degradation and humiliation of their captivity and enslavement because of the treatment that they had already experienced before and during the voyage to bondage. One African, Olaudah Equiano, who became literate after his capture and sale, wrote about his experiences in a book first published in 1789. He related that when he looked around the slave ship he saw "a multitude of black people chained together." He described the terrible stench, floggings of the captives by the crew, and "shrieks of the women and groans of the dying" that rendered the slave ship "a scene of horror almost inconceivable." He wrote that he was so sick, miserable, and scared that he envied the freedom of the "inhabitants of the deep."[2] Equiano related that the crew confronted violence by the Africans on board with severity, and that Africans who tried to commit suicide by drowning were dragged from the water and returned to their chains if they survived.

The *Amistad*

Probably the most famous mutiny of captured Africans was aboard the Spanish vessel *Amistad*. After the sale of Africans in the Caribbean in 1839, those on board the schooner *Amistad* succeeded in murdering all the white crew members

except a few who were ordered to steer the ship back to Africa. About fifty Africans led by a warrior named Cinque forced the crew to comply during the day but at night they sailed west, landing off the coast of New York where the Africans were captured by local authorities. The case became a cause célèbre, and several important and volatile issues presented themselves. Should the U.S. government collaborate in the slave trade by returning the Africans to the owners of the vessels? Should the government hold the slaves and thereby become a slave owner? Should it sell the slaves and consequently become a slave merchant? Or, most controversial of all, should the United States free the slaves and thereby become an emancipator?

Southerners and northerners debated the issue of slavery at great length during the Constitutional Convention in 1787. The case remained an explosive issue during ensuing years in Congress as the controversy over human property led to passionate arguments on both sides of the issue. The case went all the way to the Supreme Court. John Quincy Adams served as the sixth president of the United States from 1825 to 1829 and as a member of the House of Representatives from 1831 to 1848, where he tirelessly affirmed the right of abolitionists to air their cause. Because of this, he was asked to defend the *Amistad* Africans. In his memoirs for May 1841 Adams discussed revising his arguments in the case for publication. He deliberated about the "danger, the insurmountable burden of labor to be encountered in the undertaking to touch upon the slave-trade" and lamented,

> No one else will undertake it; no one but a spirit unconquerable by man, woman or fiend can undertake it but with the heart of martyrdom. The world, the flesh, and all the devils in hell are arrayed against any man who now in the North American Union shall dare to join the standard of Almighty God to put down the African slave-trade, and what can I, upon the verge of my seventy-fourth birthday, with a shaking hand, a darkening eye, a drowsy brain, and with all my faculties dropping from me one by one, as the teeth are dropping from my head—what can I do for the cause of God and man, for the progress of human emancipation, for the suppression of the African slave-trade? Yet my conscience presses me on; let me but die upon the breach.[3]

The former president presented a series of arguments so cogent that the Court freed and repatriated the Africans.

The Peculiar Institution

Peculiar institution, an expression for slavery that came into popular use during the early nineteenth century, referred to the distinctive nature of chattel slavery in the American South. By the time that the *Amistad* decision was rendered by Chief Justice Roger B. Taney in 1841 much had happened to change the plight of the African in America. Even though Africans were enslaved in other parts of the New World by the sixteenth century, the first arrival in the British colony of Virginia as indentured servants is recorded in 1619. Traders sold the heaviest concentration of Africans in the southern territory of the North American colonies, but they were also bought and sold in most other settled areas in the seventeenth and eighteenth centuries.

In the North slaves generally worked as household servants, as workers on small farms, in mines, or as craftspersons of various sorts such as seamstresses, caulkers, coopers, smiths, and cooks. In the South owners used slaves in a wide variety of duties for the maintenance of small farms and large plantations. Many of the papers of early national leaders clearly evidence their involvement—often to the point of preoccupation—with slavery and the slave trade, particularly their dependence on slave labor to make large land holdings maximally productive. Edwin Morris Betts, editor of Thomas Jefferson's *Farm Book,* stated that Jefferson was never able to eliminate slaves from his economy "because to have done so would have destroyed the chief support of all of the activities of his plantation." The papers of both Jefferson and James Monroe demonstrate that they often needed to sell or hire out slaves to meet their financial obligations. One receipt in the Carter G. Woodson collection in the Manuscript Division of the Library is for the 1809 sale of a Jefferson slave to James Madison.

> I hereby assign & convey to James Madison President [Uni]ted States, the within named servant, John . . . for the remaining term of his service . . . for the consideration of two hundred and thirty one dollars 21 cents. . . .

Woodson acquired the bill of sale from a descendant of the servant.[5]

The Library holds many collections relating to slavery in the South that yield insight into the lives of the slave owners and some information about the work of the slaves, if not the substance of their lives. A few journals in the Manuscript Division written by slaves—such as the handwritten thirty-odd pages by Fields Cook pertaining mostly to his soul's salvation and his providential protection from death—and the memoirs of former

Georgia slave Houston Hartsfield Holloway render first-hand accounts of the peculiar institution. Slave narratives and life histories from the New Deal Federal Writers' Project describe enslavement from the vantage point of the slave.[6]

By the time of the Civil War more than half of the population of Virginia was made up of African Americans. In South Carolina the slave population was just more than 400,000 and the white population was fewer than 300,000. The 1860 census indicates that the total number of African Americans in the United States was 4,441,830—3,953,760 of whom were slaves and 488,070 free—and that there were 26,922,537 whites. Whether we look at Virginia plantations such as Westover, Mount Vernon, or Monticello, or large estates in any other state in the South does not matter. The landed, monied aristocracy of the old South held humans in bondage, and it was African Americans who were responsible for the construction of those lovely plantation houses with their sturdy outbuildings, well-manicured gardens, and productive fields.

Although most African Americans did labor in the fields, W. E. B. DuBois wrote in *The Negro Artisan* that a small percentage of both slaves and free blacks in Virginia also worked as artisans who toiled in "tobacco factories, ran steamboats, made barrels," labored as masons, and specialized in many other areas.[7] Although male slaves who were trained as artisans usually used their skills on their owners' plantations, they also were often "hired out" to other plantations. They performed various services such as blacksmithing, carpentry, hostelry, and coopering.

An interesting document in the Library's Manuscript Division is the "List of Negroes belonging to the estate of William Byrd Esq. on Roanoak [sic] River taken July 7, 1757." It was probably compiled by an overseer. Some of the black men on this Virginia plantation are listed by first name and occupation. Bob, Riger, Cudgo, Prince, and Tomy were carpenters; Daniel and Dick worked as shoemakers; and David and Sippo were listed as coopers. Blacksmiths included Aron and Jack and wagoners were Orrery, Batt, Moses, and Emanuel. Wager was the name of the slave who worked as a miller. Simon and Sadler—also listed under the heading "miller"—were "hired at Williamsburg." Those who hired the bondsmen gave their master payment for the slave's service but the artisan usually also received a small sum. Female slaves could be hired out but it was far more common among men.

Many industrious slaves would scrupulously save the small amount they received until they had earned enough to purchase their own freedom at an amount stipulated by their owners. Female slaves were hired out, but it was far more common among men. The men would then subsequently purchase their wives and children. Sometimes, because the children followed the legal status of the mother, the men would purchase their wives first, and then themselves and their children. But the slave had no rights, a truth Chief Justice Taney reinforced when he stated in the 1857 *Dred Scott* decision that blacks had no rights that whites were bound to respect. An owner did not have to agree to sell or to give the slave a percentage of the wages.

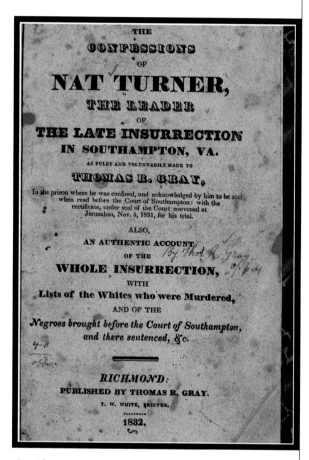

Item 1-8
The Confessions of Nat Turner, the Leader of the Late Insurrection in Southampton, Va. (Richmond: Thomas R. Gray, 1832). Rare Book and Special Collections Division.

Even a cursory perusal of colonial newspapers during the period before the American Revolution or indeed in any period before the Civil War testifies to the reluctance of the enslaved to be content with their lot. Advertisements and features include reports about runaway slaves, crimes of those enslaved against their owners, and slave plots and revolts or rumors of uprisings. The press documents white antislavery and proslavery sentiment and reflects religious outrage—especially among the Quakers—against the mistreatment of slaves and the family devastation that resulted from the trade in humans. Equiano's *Interesting Narrative* briefly describes a scene of the anguish expressed by brothers who most probably would never see one another again as they were sold off in different directions. He also discusses the indignities of the slave auction where humans were shamelessly treated like cattle.[8]

Nat Turner Insurrection

Small-scale slave revolts and plots were relatively common. Occasionally, however, revolts reached alarming proportions. This was particularly true with the Nat Turner insurrection in Southampton, Virginia, in 1831. Turner, who felt that God revealed to him the method of liberating the slaves, told only a few trusted companions about his plan because he understood that rebellions often failed because someone informed the authorities. Turner's strategy was to go to one household at a time, kill all the whites, free the slaves, and thereby add to the numbers of those who were in his rebel brigade. Before the whites stopped Turner and his followers about sixty whites had lost their lives. Subsequently, the terrified state of Virginia hanged Turner, but not before he dictated his confessions.[9]

Many analyzed the reasons for the uprising and the methods that should be used to prevent similar bloody occurrences. Every state in the South that had not already done so passed laws forbidding anyone to teach African Americans to read and write. A black North Carolinian who became a U.S. senator (1870–1871), Hiram Revels wrote the following in an autobiographical sketch:

> Prior to the Nat Turner insurrection, in the state of Virginia, the state of North Carolina was noted for its mildness toward its free colored people, who they allowed to vote, discuss political questions, hold religious meetings, preach the gospel together some educational advantages. But after that insurrection, they changed their policy in regard to free Negroes. For at the first meeting of the legislature, laws were passed depriving them of all political, religious, and educational privileges.[10]

Slaves' freedom of movement was further curtailed. They had to carry passes and could be interrogated by whites who saw them on the roads. The manumission of slaves became illegal in many states, and blacks who were already free found it even more difficult to live in peace in the United States.

Item 1-21

"Long Time Ago" (Baltimore: John Cole, 1833). Also known as "Shinbone Alley,"
this song is one of the few genuine African American tunes published before the
Civil War. Performer Thomas ("Daddy") Rice (1808-1860), whose signature song
"Jim Crow" gave the name to segregated accommodations in the twentieth century,
stands in blackface costume at the head of the music.
Music Division.

The governor of South Carolina, James Hamilton, Jr., wrote to his counterpart in Virginia, Governor John Floyd, asking him to explain the reasons for the Turner uprising. In a four-page letter Floyd discussed his opinions about the causal factors. First, he blamed the "spirit of insubordination" on the "Yankee population" in general and Yankee peddlers and traders in particular. He said that this group began by sharing Christianity with the slaves and teaching them that God is not a respecter of persons, that blacks are as good as whites, that all are born free and equal, that they cannot serve two masters, and "that white people rebelled against England to obtain freedom, so have blacks a right to do."[11]

In addition, Floyd argued that preachers, particularly northern ones, were persuading many to conform to a true Christian lifestyle. As a result, many women were "persuaded that it was piety" to teach their bondpersons to read the scriptures. He explained that many of these very respectable women took their mission seriously, becoming "tutoresses in Sunday Schools and pious distributors of tracts from the New York Tract Society."[12]

Then, the governor explained, the people of the state began to ignore the laws that forbade people of color to meet in large groups. Owners allowed African American religious meetings with numerous participants to take place. Next, he wrote, "commenced the efforts of the black preachers." Floyd noted that the preachers read a variety of tracts and pamphlets from the pulpit followed by the "incendiary publications" of David Walker, William Lloyd Garrison, and others. Hymns that spoke of the longing for freedom often accompanied the services.[13]

Both of the men Floyd referred to were Bostonians. Garrison was a militant white abolitionist who published a newspaper, the *Liberator*. He advocated both the abolition of slavery and the complete social and political equality of the races. David Walker wrote a pamphlet titled (in part), *Walker's Appeal, in Four Articles: Together with a Preamble to the Coloured Citizens of the World*. The pamphlet called for blacks to rise up and overthrow their oppressors. Walker argued,

> The man who would not fight under our Lord and Master Jesus Christ, in the glorious and heavenly cause of freedom and God—to be delivered from the most wretched, abject and servile slavery, that ever a people was afflicted with since the foundation of the world, to the present day—ought to be kept with all of his children or family, in slavery, or in chains, to be butchered by his *cruel enemies*.[14]

Floyd asserted that he was "convinced that every black preacher in the whole country east of the Blue Ridge" was a participant in the Turner plot. He placed the blame for masterminding the plan on the leaders of the church, but he believed that all the discussions about freedom and equality prepared the mass of African Americans for the uprising. Walker's pamphlet circulated widely even after being banned by the United States Congress and outlawed in every southern state.

Floyd reiterated that he believed that he was "fully justified . . . in believing that northern incendiaries, tracts, Sunday Schools, religion and reading and writing" were the primary causes of the revolt.[15]

Finally, in order to prevent another such occurrence, Floyd planned to ask the Virginia legislature to confine slaves to their masters' estates, prohibit black preachers, "absolutely drive from this state" all free blacks, and institute a gradual emancipation procedure by which slaves could earn funds to purchase their freedom. He noted that he would have to broach the last point "tenderly and cautiously."[16]

The most important aspect of Floyd's letter is that it so thoroughly documents the yearning for freedom on the part of the slaves. Although many would not describe them as Americans, they felt themselves to be an integral part of the nation and heirs to the promise of freedom articulated in its founding documents. Virtually every African American who became literate and articulate expressed this belief. Petitions from literate blacks to colonial legislatures as early as the seventeenth century reiterate this truth.[17]

As slavery became increasingly profitable the complications mushroomed. Abolitionists became more outspoken, militant, and recalcitrant. They wanted slavery abolished forever. Southerners, convinced that they had a right to own property—even human property—contended that no one should be able to deprive them of their rights. The nation, divided by a free democratic system for whites while blacks suffered both in bondage and freedom, experienced growing pains that threatened to rend it in two.

Item 3-15
John Greenleaf Whittier, "The Branded Hand" [Philadelphia, 1845?]. The abolitionist poet immortalized the deeds of Massachusetts sea captain Jonathan Walker (1790-1878) who was apprehended off the coast of Florida while attempting to carry fugitive slaves to freedom in the Bahamas, jailed for more than a year, and branded with initials signifying "slave stealer." Broadside publication of a poem, with woodcut illustration. Rare Book and Special Collections Division.

THE BRANDED HAND.

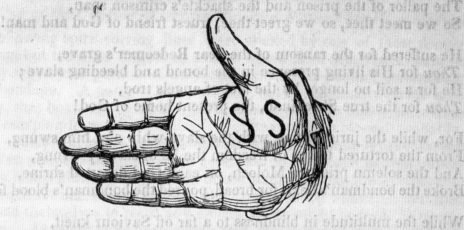

Walker resided in Florida with his family from 1836 until 1841. He then removed to Massachusetts because he would not bring up his children among the poisonous influences of slavery. While in Florida, the colored people whom he employed were treated as equals in his family, much to the chagrin of the slaveholders of that region. In 1844 he returned to Pensacola in his own vessel. When leaving, seven of the slaves who had in former years been in his employ, and were members of the church with which he communed, begged to go with him. He consented. When out fourteen days, a Southern sloop fell in with and seized them. Prostrated by sickness, he was confined in a dungeon, chained on a damp floor without table, bed or chair. He was in the pillory for an hour, pelted with rotten eggs, branded S. S.—slave stealer—in the palm of his right hand, by Ebenezer Dorr, United States Marshal, fined $150, and imprisoned eleven months.

THE BRANDED HAND.

BY JOHN G. WHITTIER.

Welcome home again, brave seaman! with thy thoughtful brow and gray,
And the old heroic spirit of our earlier, better day—
With that front of calm endurance, on whose steady nerve, in vain
Pressed the iron of the prison, smote the fiery shafts of pain!

Is the tyrant's brand upon thee? Did the brutal cravens aim
To make God's truth thy falsehood, His holiest work thy shame?
When, all blood-quenched, from the torture the iron was withdrawn,
How laughed their evil angel the baffled fools to scorn!

They change to wrong, the duty which God hath written out
On the great heart of humanity too legible for doubt!
They, the loathsome moral lepers, blotched from foot-sole up to crown,
Give to shame what God hath given unto honor and renown!

Why, that brand is highest honor!—than its traces never yet
Upon old armorial hatchments was a prouder blazon set;
And thy unborn generations, as they crowd our rocky strand,
Shall tell with pride the story of their father's BRANDED HAND!

182857

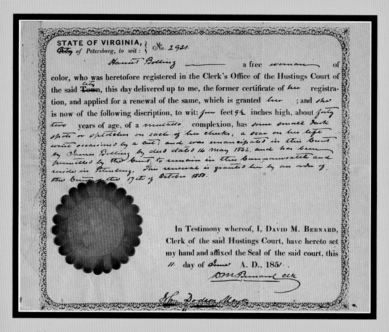

Item 2-2

Certificate from the State of Virginia certifying the freedom of Harriet Bolling,
Petersburg, Virginia, 1851.

Carter G. Woodson Papers, Manuscript Division.

Free People of Color

Various factors began to complicate the legal status of African Americans in North America even as early as the colonial period. The foremost was emancipation or manumission. Because of conscience, affection, gratitude, financial agreements, or guilt, owners began to free their slaves. Some freed only small numbers. For example, on his death former President Thomas Jefferson freed only five slaves, whereas George Washington emancipated 164 of his Mount Vernon slaves. Other masters developed romantic or sexual liaisons with their bondswomen and the resulting offspring—bound in slavery because the mother was enslaved—were often granted their freedom. Sometimes the mothers were also manumitted and granted property and small sums of money.

Men were usually granted their freedom if they served in the military aiding in battles with state militia against Native Americans, or if they became part of the Continental and U.S. armed forces. In every colonial conflict, it seems, as many blacks if not more joined their owners' enemies than those who fought alongside their owners. The last quarter of the eighteenth century marked an important transition period for blacks in the United States because many thousands obtained their freedom in this way.

From 1775 to 1783 the American colonies fought the War of Independence against England. The protracted war afforded thousands of blacks the opportunity to gain their liberty. Black and white Americans were well aware of the incongruity of a government that, on one hand, sanctioned the institution of slavery, and on the other hand, drafted the Declaration of Independence proclaiming that "all men are created equal." This dichotomy caused enough political ferment to hasten the emancipation of blacks in many states. In fact, by the end of the Revolutionary War *every* northern state had passed laws to free their slaves.[18]

Both the British and the Americans used African Americans as military and political pawns during the war. American military leaders were reluctant to allow black men to join their armed forces on a permanent basis, even though black men had fought with the Continental Army, distinguishing themselves at the battles of Concord, Lexington, and Bunker Hill. Certainly it was a contradiction to allow black men to fight for the freedom of others without being given true freedom for themselves. Ultimately, both the British and the Americans promised freedom to African Americans who joined their ranks.

The Americans generally honored their promise of freedom to black Revolutionary War soldiers, as did the British. In 1783, when the war ended with the defeat of the Red Coats, many African Americans left the United States with the British soldiers to go to the West Indies, Canada, and England. The papers of the Continental Congress indicate that slaves of both George Washington and Patrick Henry made their way to the British lines

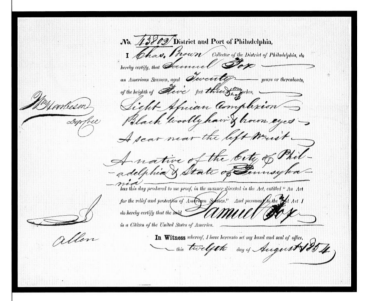

Item 2-6
Samuel Fox's certificate of citizenship, August 12, 1854. Fox was a black seaman who obtained this certificate in Philadelphia.
Black History Collection, Manuscript Division.

where they were granted their freedom. During the war era many blacks took up residence among Native Americans, particularly among the Seminoles in Georgia and Florida.

Although the vast majority of African Americans remained enslaved until the Civil War, a small free black population emerged in every region of the country. By 1860 one out of every eight African Americans was free. Free people of color, however, did not usually enjoy the same citizenship rights as whites. They could vote in a few areas, hold property, and work. Often they were not allowed to testify in court against whites, bear arms, assemble in large numbers, or receive benefits from local institutions such as public schools, even though they paid taxes.[19]

A Pivotal Year: 1787

In the face of discrimination, people of color began to form their own churches, schools, civic organizations, and fraternal groups. The year 1787 marked some important movements relating to African Americans. In that year the members of the Continental Congress addressed themselves to the questions of whether blacks should be counted as people rather than property for the purpose of representation in the United State legislature, whether the African slave trade should continue, and whether territories allowing slavery should be extended. A series of compromises between northern and southern legislators resulted in three-fifths of the black population being counted for purposes of representation in Congress, the prohibition of slavery in the Northwest Territory, and the cessation of the African slave trade after 1807. Americans realized that these measures presented only temporary solutions to important racial problems in the United States. Many members of Congress began to observe the results of the Sierra Leone experiment to see if colonization of freed slaves in Africa would present one workable solution to U.S. racial problems.[20]

Some free blacks also watched the development of Sierra Leone closely. The year 1787 also saw important organizational movements among free blacks in the United States: In Philadelphia Richard Allen and Absalom Jones organized the Free African Society, a mutual aid association, and they began an independent black church movement; and Prince Hall, a black man originally from Barbados and a veteran of the Revolutionary War, was successful in obtaining a charter for an all-black Masonic Lodge from the Grand Lodge in England in 1787.

Free people of color began to form literary, missionary, colonization, and abolition societies as well as musical groups, lending libraries, and a wide variety of businesses and self-help associations. African Americans started to write and publish sermons, newspapers such as David Ruggles and Samuel Cornish's newspaper, *Freedom's Journal,* first published in 1827, and histories of their own accomplishments, such as William Cooper Nell's 1855 book titled *The Colored Patriots of the American Revolution.*[21]

Paul Cuffee

Free people of color in their quest for full political rights were extremely articulate in their protests against slavery, but they also began to explore alternative solutions to racial problems. One example was Paul Cuffee, a free man

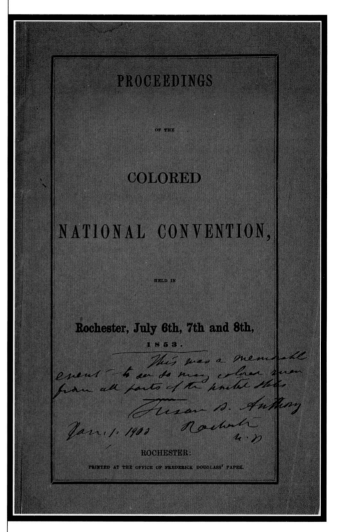

Item 2-17
Proceedings of the Colored National Convention held in Rochester July 6th, 7th and 8th, 1853 (Rochester: Frederick Douglass, 1853). After the passage of the Fugitive Slave Act, black leaders called for the creation of a national council to support a black community outside white society. Susan B. Anthony, a neighbor and friend of Frederick Douglass in Rochester, New York, owned this copy of the proceedings of the 1853 convention.
Rare Book and Special Collections Division.

of African and Native American ancestry, who learned to articulate the doctrines of freedom for oppressed African Americans. Cuffee eventually became an active exponent of African colonization in general and of the Sierra Leonean scheme in particular.

Item 2-20

J. H. Daniels, Bishops of the A[frican] M[ethodist] E[piscopal] Church, 1876. Richard Allen is depicted in the center of this print; also shown are the A.M.E. book depot in Philadelphia, the school in Zeenia, Ohio, and missionaries to Port-au-Prince, Haiti, the black-run nation founded in 1791, after a revolt led by Toussaint L'Ouverture toppled the French government there, that offered inspiration to African Americans.

Lithograph. Prints and Photographs Division.

Born in Massachusetts before the Revolutionary War, Cuffee encountered racism from his earliest years. Nevertheless, he was able to get some education and then found work as a sailor and navigator, a laborer in shipyards, and, ultimately, as a shipbuilder. As he gained navigational skills, he became an entrepreneur who saw opportunities in shipping and seized them. By 1780 he had built a ship of his own and by 1806 he owned one large ship, two brigs, some smaller vessels, and considerable property. He was able to engage very profitably in trade in general, but he refused to be involved with the slave or liquor trade.[22]

In spite of his accomplishments Cuffee still confronted racial prejudice. His wealth continued to grow as did his contributions to the Massachusetts government through taxes, yet he could not vote. Cuffee, realizing that the colonies had railed against Great Britain for taxation without representation, believed that the colonies were guilty of the same injustices by taxing free blacks without letting them reap all the benefits that tax dollars earned for other citizens. In defiance, Cuffee and his brother John refused to pay their taxes. Embroiled in legal troubles because of their stand, they finally decided to submit. They protested their taxation in the next session of the Massachusetts legislature and to their surprise that body decided that from that point on all privileges of citizenship would be granted to free black taxpayers.[23]

Cuffee approached the citizens in his neighborhood about establishing a school for all the children. No one agreed to join him in such a venture. Cuffee decided to finance and build a Quaker school on his own land that he opened not only to black children but to all of the children in his community—gratis.[24]

Even when the Massachusetts courts abolished slavery in 1783, the social, economic, and political problems that blacks encountered remained complex. Cuffee reasoned that the best avenue for African Americans to pursue was to reestablish contact with West Africans for the purpose of colonization and trade. He thought that together Africans and African Americans would be able to make great commercial gains if they could work together to establish a shipping network of their own. In addition, if free people of color felt that the stigma attached to them was too severe, they could move to Sierra Leone. During an 1811 to 1812 visit to West Africa, Cuffee formed the Friendly Society with an African American emigrant named John Kizzell for the purpose of encouraging emigration of free people of color.

Cuffee was unable to interest anyone in financing his Sierra Leonean colonization scheme. Consequently, he determined that he would finance it himself but he encountered a major obstacle. The United States was engaged in the War of 1812 against Britain, and American citizens were not permitted to trade with England or her colonies. After the cessation of hostilities in 1815—at a personal expenditure of $4,000—Cuffee took nine free black families totaling thirty-eight individuals to settle in Sierra Leone. Although he had difficulty marketing his trade goods when he returned, Cuffee became even more determined that black Americans needed to emigrate if they were to achieve true independence and racial dignity. Many free blacks as well as some whites received Cuffee's emigration plan with enthusiasm.[25]

Some white emigrationists began to formulate their own ideas for the colonization of black Americans along the lines that Cuffee planned. Others envisioned trade ventures, and still others wanted to evangelize Africans. Unfortunately, many whites simply hoped to rid the United States of its free black population. Interested whites met in December 1816 to form the American Society for Colonizing the Free People of Color in the United States. Soon, most simply called it the American Colonization Society (ACS). The newly formed society sought to recruit Cuffee to lead their first emigrant expedition, but he died before the plans for the first group of ACS settlers could be fully formulated.

Free black leaders in Philadelphia, led by James Forten, Richard Allen, and Absalom Jones, immediately held a protest meeting. Cuffee, they felt, had been working to help African Americans people, but ACS, they contended, was definitely working against their best interests. ACS founders tried to assure free people of color that the society's motives were not sinister and for a few months protests by African Americans were quieted. Nonetheless, so many of the organizers of the society made their anti–free-black and anti-emancipation views public, few African Americans expressed any willingness to apply for colonization in Liberia, the new ACS West African settlement.[26]

Most free blacks were many generations removed from Africa, its people, language, and culture. African American leaders in Philadelphia insisted that they would not leave the United States because their "ancestors (not of choice) were the first successful cultivators of the wilds of America." Consequently, they strongly believed that they should be entitled to participate in the nation's blessings.[27] They aided in the building and development of the United States, they fought in its wars, and they—albeit unwillingly—had become an integral part of the American heritage. It was their country too, they argued. They were not willing to leave it for lands unknown. They wanted freedom—freedom to be Americans within the borders of the United States of America. They wanted freedom for all slaves and freedom to participate in the nation's government, economy, and educational pursuits.

Colonization

Not all agreed. For example, a free man of color from Illinois, disillusioned with America's prospects, stated that he loved this country and its liberties but rued the fact that his freedom was partial. He was even willing to settle outside of the United States "to open the door of freedom."[28] During the course of the nineteenth century about 12,000 African Americans did emigrate to Liberia but most had no desire to leave the country. Many just hoped to relocate where they could enjoy unrestricted freedom. Many southern states passed laws that forced free blacks to leave their jurisdictions. There were few places where whites welcomed free people of color. Many whites believed that free blacks encouraged slaves to run away or abetted them in their efforts to hide from their owners. In this, they were correct. They also contended that free blacks were often the masterminds of slave revolts. Free people of color were also competitors in the limited job market.

Of the available relocation options, African Americans seemed to prefer Pennsylvania and Ohio to Haiti or Liberia. Indeed, large numbers began to emigrate to these U.S. states, arousing the fears of many whites sensitive to the growing black population. In 1829 local officials in Cincinnati, Ohio, passed a law ordering all free blacks to post $500 good-behavior bonds or to leave the city within thirty days. Blacks leaders asked for a time extension so that they could go to Canada to look for a settlement there. In the meantime, whites rioted, causing some deaths in the black community. On their return, black leaders discovered that more than a thousand blacks had decided to migrate to Canada. Within a few years the Canadian legislature passed several resolutions stating that large groups of black migrants were not welcome there.[29]

Early migrants to Liberia encountered the full force of tropical diseases and many died. This heightened African American reluctance to leave the United States. Reverend Peter Williams articulated the majority viewpoint of the free African American community at an oration on July 4, 1830:

> Though delivered from the fetters of slavery, we are oppressed by an unreasonable, unrighteous, and cruel prejudice, which aims at nothing less than the forcing away of all the free coloured people of the United States to the distant shores of Africa. Far be it from me to impeach the motives of every member of the African [sic] Colonization Society. The civilizing and Christianizing of that vast continent, and the extirpation of the abominable traffic in slaves . . . are no doubt the principal motives which induce many to give it their support.
>
> But there are those, and those are most active and most influential in its cause, who hesitate not to say that they wish to rid the country of the free coloured population, and there is sufficient reason to believe that with many, this is the principal motive for supporting the society. . . .[30]

Most African Americans were not willing to yield their place in America. Refusing to abandon their quest for full citizenship, they were activists on every available front, insisting that the nation's promises of liberty and justice be available to all regardless of hue.

Item 3-7

William H. Johnson, *On a John Brown Flight,* ca. 1945. William Johnson, born in Florence, South Carolina, and active as a painter, printmaker, and teacher, used aspects of modernism, primitivism, and impressionism in his work and celebrated such antislavery activists as Nat Turner, Harriet Tubman, Abraham Lincoln, and Frederick Douglass, as well as John Brown.

Screen print. Harmon Foundation Collection, Prints and Photographs Division.

I am in earnest—I will not equivocate—
I will not excuse— I will not retreat a single inch,
AND I WILL BE HEARD.

WILLIAM LLOYD GARRISON
The Liberator, 1831

2 Harsh as Truth: Abolition, Antislavery Movements, and the Rise of the Sectional Controversy

PAUL FINKELMAN

For African Americans in the North, the antebellum period was one of struggle, frustration, and occasional triumph in the face of prejudice in their own part of the country and unending bondage in the South, where millions of black slaves labored in bondage with little hope of freedom. Their white allies were equally frustrated. Before the Mexican-American War (1846–47), especially, they were likely to face hostile neighbors, frequently found themselves confronting social ostracism, and sometimes had to deal with mob violence. Despite the discouraging reality of a slaveholders' republic, black and white opponents of slavery worked together, and separately, in the struggle against human bondage.

Opposition to slavery did not spring up, full blown, in the early nineteenth century. Rather, it had been building for more than a century. In the late seventeenth and early eighteenth centuries, some Americans rejected slavery on religious grounds. Religion would remain a key factor in white opposition to slavery. Almost all white abolitionists of the antebellum period (roughly 1820–61) came out of a religious Protestant background. Almost all of the delegates to the first meeting of the American Anti-Slavery Society were committed Congregationalists, Unitarians,

Quakers, or evangelicals. The *Declaration of Sentiments* of the society condemned masters for "usurp[ing] the prerogative of Jehovah" and for violating the biblical injunction against being a *Manstealer.* Many of the most important abolitionists were ministers, such as Theodore Dwight

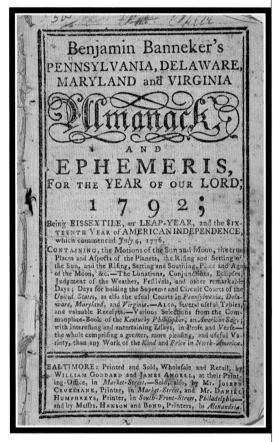

Item 2-14
Benjamin Banneker's Pennsylvania, Delaware, Maryland and Virginia Almanack and Ephermera, for the Year of Our Lord 1792 . . . (Baltimore: William Goddard and James Angell, 1792).
Rare Book and Special Collections Division.

Weld, Henry Ward Beecher, Theodore Parker, Beriah Green, Orange Scott, and Joshua Leavitt. The two most famous white male abolitionists, Wendell Phillips and William Lloyd Garrison, were not men of the cloth but were deeply religious. So too were most of the political abolitionists, such as Salmon P. Chase and Joshua Giddings. Indeed, most abolitionists viewed their cause as part of a holy crusade against sin.

In the last quarter of the eighteenth century, enlightenment ideals came to supplement the religious opposition to slavery. Some opponents of

slavery were persuaded by the natural rights ideals articulated in the Declaration of Independence and other revolutionary-era documents. Some Americans saw the contradiction between slavery and a revolution built on the idea that all people were "created equal" and "endowed by their creator" with rights that included liberty. In the years after the Revolution some northerners also saw slavery as a political threat to the Republic and to the democratic values the Republic embodied. By the antebellum period these strands of anti-slavery thought reinforced each other, although almost always these themes were articulated in tandem with the notion that slavery in the end was sinful and in violation of the biblical injunction to "do unto others as you would have them do unto you."

The antislavery movement was always an amorphous collection of people who to greater or lesser degrees worked to educate the North about the evils of slavery, to stop the spread of slavery into the western states, to break slavery's stranglehold on the national government, to protect fugitive slaves who escaped to the precarious freedom of the North, and to break down the barriers of racial prejudice. Not every antislavery northerner supported all these goals. Ideologically they ran the gamut from pacifists who opposed all forms of violence to gun-toting members of integrated vigilance committees who were prepared to use whatever force it took to protect fugitive slaves. Out of Boston came William Lloyd Garrison's pleas for nonresistance as the key to ending slavery; but from the same city came the African American militant David Walker, who urged in his *Appeal . . . to the Colored Citizens of the World* that slaves kill their masters to gain their freedom. Out of the Midwest came Salmon Portland Chase, who fought the fugitive slave laws in court while building a national antislavery party that could offer a political challenge to the South; but also from the Midwest came John Brown, with his apocalyptic view of the need to violently attack slavery in order to encourage a confrontation that could end the system.

Although differing on tactics and methods, most opponents of slavery agreed on three basic ideas. First, they agreed that American slavery violated the morality of the Protestant Christianity that almost all abolitionists shared.[1] This was true for radical Protestants such as Reverend Theodore Parker as well as for members of traditional and conservative churches. For example, the lawyer William Jay and Chief Justice Joseph C. Hornblower of New Jersey were devout Episcopalians.

Item 3-19 A
William Lloyd Garrison, "Sonnet to Liberty." Boston, December 14, 1840.
Holograph manuscript. Manuscript Division.

Sonnet to Liberty.

They tell me, Liberty! that, in thy name,
 I may not plead for all the human race;
 That some are born to bondage and disgrace,
Some to a heritage of woe and shame,
And some to power supreme, and glorious fame:
 With my whole soul, I spurn the doctrine base,
 And, as an equal brotherhood, embrace
All people, and for all fair freedom claim!
Know this, O man! whate'er thy earthly fate —
 God never made a tyrant, nor a slave:
Woe, then, to those who dare to desecrate
 His glorious image! — for to all He gave
Eternal rights, which none may violate;
 And by a mighty hand th' oppressed He yet shall save

Wm. Lloyd Garrison.

Boston, Dec. 14, 1840.

(1)

ADDRESS OF JOHN BROWN

To the Virginia Court, when about to receive the

SENTENCE OF DEATH,

For his heroic attempt at Harper's Ferry, to

Give deliverance to the captives, and to let the oppressed go free.

[MR. BROWN, upon inquiry whether he had anything to say why sentence should not be pronounced upon him, in a clear, distinct voice, replied :]

I have, may it please the Court, a few words to say.

In the first place, I deny every thing but what I have already admitted, of a design on my part to *free Slaves.* I intended, certainly, to have made a clean thing of that matter, as I did last winter, when I went into Missouri, and there took Slaves, without the snapping of a gun on either side, moving them through the country, and finally leaving them in Canada. I desired to have done the same thing again, on a much larger scale. *That was all I intended.* I never did intend murder, or treason, or the destruction of property, or to excite or incite Slaves to rebellion, or to make insurrection.

I have another objection, and that is, that it is *unjust* that I should suffer such a penalty. Had I interfered in the manner, and which I admit has been fairly proved,—for I admire the truthfulness and candor of the greater portion of the witnesses who have testified in this case,— had I so interfered in behalf of the Rich, the Powerful, the Intelligent, the so-called Great, or in behalf of any of their friends, either father, mother, brother, sister, wife, or children, or any of *that class,* and suffered and sacrificed what I have in this interference, *it would have been all right.* Every man in this Court would have deemed it an act worthy a reward, rather than a punishment.

This Court acknowledges too, as I suppose, the validity of the LAW OF GOD. I saw a book kissed, which I suppose to be the BIBLE, or at least the NEW TESTAMENT, which teaches me that, " All things whatsoever I would that men should do to me, I should do even so to them." It teaches me further, to " Remember them that are in bonds, as bound with them." I endeavored to act up to that instruction.

I say I am yet too young to understand that GOD is any *respecter of persons.* I believe that to have interfered as I have done, as I have always freely admitted I have done, in behalf of his *despised poor,* I have done no wrong, but RIGHT.

Now, if it is deemed necessary that I should forfeit my life, for the furtherance of the ends of justice, and MINGLE MY BLOOD FURTHER WITH THE BLOOD OF MY CHILDREN, and with the blood of millions in this Slave country, whose rights are disregarded by wicked, cruel, and unjust enactments,—I say, LET IT BE DONE.

Let me say one word further : I feel entirely satisfied with the treatment I have received on my trial. Considering all the circumstances, it has been more generous than I expected ; but I feel no consciousness of guilt. I have stated from the first what was my *intention,* and what was not. I never had any design against the liberty of any person, nor any disposition to commit treason, or excite Slaves to rebel, or make any general insurrection. I never encouraged any man to do so, but always discouraged any idea of that kind.

Let me say something, also, in regard to the statements made by some of those who were connected with me. I hear that it has been stated by some of them, that I have induced them to join me ; but the contrary is true. I do not say this to injure them, but as regarding their weakness. Not one but joined me of his own accord, and the greater part at their own expense. A number of them I never saw and never had a word of conversation with, till the day they came to me, and that was for the purpose I have stated. Now I have done.

John Brown

Printed by C. C. Mead, 91 Washington Street, and for Sale at the LIBERATOR Office, 21 Cornhill, Boston.

Most white abolitionists, however, came from Puritan or Quaker roots. The attack on slavery was deeply rooted in the religious culture of America, dating from the 1680s. Abolitionists constantly used religious arguments to persuade northern whites to oppose slavery. Most abolitionists were self-consciously religious, and many were ministers. In black communities the struggle was often centered in the church. Northern black ministers, such as Jermain Loguen, Samuel Ringgold Ward, J. W. C. Pennington, Samuel E. Cornish, and Theodore S. Wright were important organizers at the local and national level. In the South there were religious overtones to the abortive Gabriel's Rebellion and the Vesey Conspiracy. Nat Turner, the leader of the bloodiest slave rebellion in the antebellum South, was a lay preacher.

Second, all opponents of slavery understood that the very existence of the institution contradicted the meaning of America's own revolution for liberty and independence. Wendell Phillips used the heroes of the revolution to argue that opposition to slavery was rooted in America's most deeply held values. Similarly, William C. Nell published a book on black heroes of the Revolution in order to show that African Americans had earned the liberty the slave owners and the U.S. Constitution denied them. David Walker, on the other hand, reprinted the Declaration of Independence in his *Appeal,* making the point that blacks had a right to take their liberty if white Americans would not give it to them. In a famous speech, Frederick Douglass asked what the Fourth of July meant to the slave—only to show that slavery made American liberty and independence into a lie.

Third, most opponents of slavery believed that the institution was a cancer on the body politic of the United States. They believed that at the national level the nation was controlled by a malevolent "slave power" that was conspiring to deny liberty to free blacks and white northerners, as well as to slaves. Although there was no "conspiracy" in any formal sense, it was certainly true that the national government seemed to be firmly in the

hands of the masters and their allies. Between 1801 and 1861 every president but one—John Quincy Adams—was either a slave owner,[2] a former slave owner,[3] or a northern "doughface" who supported slavery and opposed aboli-

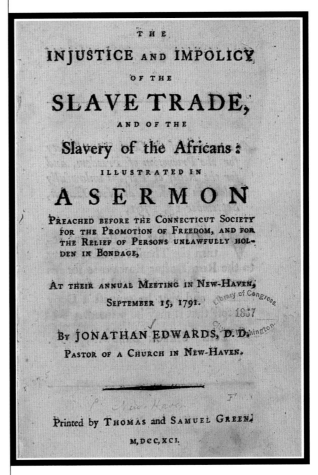

Item 3-2
Jonathan Edwards, *The Injustice and Impolicy of the Slave Trade and of the Slavery of the Africans* (New Haven, Conn.: Thomas and Samuel Green, 1791). Connecticut theologian Jonathan Edwards (1745–1801) invoked the Golden Rule and the natural rights arguments of the era of the American Revolution to support the abolition of slavery in a sermon to a local antislavery group.
Rare Book and Special Collections Division.

tionists.[4] Only two men served as Chief Justice in this period, both—John Marshall and Roger B. Taney—were southerners, and though Roger B. Taney no longer personally owned slaves, he was bitterly proslavery and unalterably opposed to any rights for free blacks. With the exception of a handful of years, the Court always had both a southern majority and a proslavery majority. During the critical three decades before the Civil War only one Justice, John McLean of Ohio, was openly and consistently opposed to slavery. Similarly, in this period almost no one hostile to slavery held cabinet positions or

Item 3-6
John Brown, "Address of John Brown to the Virginia Court, When about to Receive the Sentence of Death" (Boston: C.C. Mead, 1859). Convicted of treason and sentenced to death for his ill-fated attempt to seize the federal arsenal at Harpers Ferry, Virginia, John Brown argued that he intended only to free slaves, not to incite insurrection.
Printed Ephemera Collection, Rare Book and Special Collections Division.

Item 2-18
Charles White, *Frederick Douglass,* **1951.**
Lithograph. Prints and Photographs Division. Courtesy of Heritage Gallery, Los Angeles, California.

Item 3-8
Frederick Douglass, "John Brown," a lecture.
Typescript with autograph notations, 1860. Frederick Douglass Papers, Manuscript Division.

JOHN BROWN.

Not to fan the flame of sectional animosity, now, happily,
in the process of rapid, and, I hope, permanent extinction,--not
to revive and keep alive a sense of shame and remorse for a great
National crime, which brought its own punishment, in civil war, in
loss of treasure, tears and blood,--not to recount the long list
of wrongs inflicted upon the African race by more than two centuries of cruel bondage,--but to pay a just debt long due to a great
historical character of our own times and country--a hero and martyr in the cause of liberty--one with whom I was well acquainted,
and whose confidence and friendship it was my good fortune to share,
is the object of my lecture this evening.   I wish especially to
give you such facts, recollections, and impressions as I have of
him and his raid on Harper's Ferry, as will, I hope, show him entitled to your respect and sympathy, if not your entire approval.

In its bearings upon the question of slavery, the importance
of this raid cannot well be over-estimated or over-stated.   Aside
from the late tremendous war, of which it was, in some sense, the
beginning, I know of no incident in all the thirty years' conflict
with slavery which will be remembered longer, or which will make a
more thrilling chapter in American history, or which tended more
directly to the abolition of slavery than this remarkable raid.
The story of it has been often told and is doubtless still fresh in the memory of
some who now hear me, but for the sake of those who may not have
known it, or may have forgotten its details, and in order to have
the subject more clearly before us at the outset, it may be well
to state briefly the main facts connected with it.

On the night of the 16th of October, 1859, there appeared in
the mountains of Maryland, near the confluence of the Potomac and

1

leadership positions in Congress, and at the same time unyielding proslavery politicians ran Congress and served in almost every presidential administration.

Although opponents of slavery agreed on the political problems of America, they could not agree on either their cause or a possible solution to them. Garrison, Wendell Phillips, and their followers argued that the Constitution was a proslavery compact, "A covenant with Death, and an Agreement in Hell," as Garrison put it.

Garrison and his followers thus refused to participate in electoral politics, in order to avoid the moral stain of voting under a proslavery Constitution. But others, such as Gerrit Smith, James G. Birney, and Salmon P. Chase, participated in the Liberty, Free Soil, and Republican parties in order to challenge slavery at the polls. Black opponents of slavery were also divided over the importance of politics, even as they all agreed on the political evils of slavery. Some, such as the activist William C. Nell, agreed with Garrison that political activity was useless or, worse, corrupting. Others urged blacks to participate in the elections in those states in which they could vote.[5] Alexander Crummell and Henry Highland Garnet, for example, were tireless organizers for the Liberty Party in New York during the 1840s. By the late 1850s, however, both men, along with the Harvard-educated physician Martin Delany, had become emigrationists, arguing that the only chance for blacks was outside of the slaveholders Republic.[6]

Frederick Douglass, on the other hand, though he had initially rejected politics in favor of Garrisonian disunionism, had by the 1850s become a proponent of political activity and was an early black supporter of the Republicans. Douglass understood that black voters, and even the occasional black officeholder, were a profound challenge to the "slaveocracy." By 1860 at least three blacks had held public office, and a few others had run unsuccessfully on the Liberty Party ticket. In 1847 Macon Bolling Allen was appointed a justice of the peace in Massachusetts. In 1855 John Mercer Langston won the office of township clerk in Brownhelm, Ohio, to become the first black elected to public office by popular vote in the United States. In 1855 George B. Vashon ran for attorney general of New York on the Liberty Party ticket. Although a weak third party, the nomination nevertheless signaled the movement of

blacks into statewide electoral politics. In 1857 Thomas Howland was elected to the office of election warden in Providence, Rhode Island. Another black, William Alexander Leidesdorff, served on a California school-board in 1848.[7] It is likely that some blacks served on schoolboards in Ohio and Michigan during this period, because blacks were allowed to vote for those officers where there were separate schools and schoolboards.

These were surely minor offices, but they were significant nonetheless. Black voting and office holding challenged the very core of proslavery thought. They disproved prevailing notions of racial inferiority just as they demonstrated that some northern whites would support black office seekers.

In the end, the success of antislavery would come from the unlikely combination of conventional politics and war. By the late 1850s moderate opponents of slavery had gravitated to the new Republican Party, which had its origin in northern opposition to the spread of slavery into Kansas. Moderate and conservative Republicans were only concerned about keeping slavery out of the territories. But many Republican leaders, such as Senator Salmon P. Chase of Ohio, Senator William H. Seward of New York, and Governor John Andrew and Senator Charles Sumner of Massachusetts, were bonafide political abolitionists. Where they could vote, most African Americans supported the new party, realizing that it was the first serious political party that was rooted in opposition to slavery.

The party's standard bearer, an obscure Illinois railroad lawyer, was publicly enigmatic on the great issues that concerned abolitionists. The abolitionist Wendell Phillips asked, "Who is this huckster in politics...this county court advocate?"[8] Abraham Lincoln was clearly hostile to slavery and believed that blacks were at least entitled to the inalienable rights of life, liberty, and the pursuit of happiness found in the Declaration of Independence. He was unalterably opposed to any new slave states, and he looked to the day when the institution would be put on the road of "ultimate extinction." But, beyond that, committed abolitionists were concerned about the railsplitter.

Indeed, despite his rhetoric, Lincoln's record on slavery was surely suspect. Although he hated slavery and like most Republicans, opposed its spread to new territories, unlike most leading Republicans Lincoln had never been terribly circumspect about the cases he took. In 1841 he successfully helped a black gain her freedom,[9] but six years later—when men such as Chase and New York's William Henry Seward were solidifying their reputations as powerful antislavery advocates—Lincoln represented a slave owner trying to regain custody of a slave he brought to Illinois.[10] As a representative to Congress, Lincoln proposed a bill allowing Washington, D.C., officials to return fugitive slaves to southern masters. As a presidential candidate he did not demand repeal of the Fugitive Slave Law. During the campaign Wendell Phillips referred to him as "the Slave Hound of Illinois."[11]

To everyone's surprise, the "slave hound" of 1860 had become, by January 1, 1863, the "Great Emancipator." Even more astounding, by this time pacifist, religious, and moral arguments ceased to be the driving force in the struggle against slavery.

began by asking a simple question about the enslavement of Africans: "Is there any that would be done or handled in this manner?" Because no one would choose to be "handled in this manner," it was obvious that slavery violated that most central of Christian injunctions to "do unto others as you would have them do unto you." The Germantown Quakers then confronted the question of race. Again, their analysis was brilliant in its simplicity, as they concluded, "Now, though they are black, we cannot conceive there is more liberty to have them slaves as it is to have other white ones." After condemning the practice of separating husbands from wives and children

"bottom rail on top dis time!"

The most compelling abolitionists were no longer Garrison, Phillips, or Douglass; they were William T. Sherman, Oliver O. Howard, and Ulysses S. Grant. Ultimately, slavery ended through the power of Lincoln's rhetoric, the strength of Lincoln's army, and the actions of hundreds of thousands of individual slaves who abandoned their owners to fall in behind the armies of freedom. Some 200,000 soldiers and sailors—10 percent of the U.S. Army and Navy—were African Americans. Many of these heroes of freedom were former slaves. In the last year of the war, a former slave, proudly wearing U.S. blue, was guarding some Confederate prisoners. He noticed that one of the captured enemies was his former owner. "Hello, massa," he called out, "bottom rail on top dis time!"[12]

Antislavery in the Morning of America

To understand how the bottom rail came to be on top, even for this brief moment in history, we must begin in the early colonial period, when a few Americans began to doubt the morality of enslaving their fellow humans.

The first American protest against slavery came in 1688 when Quakers in Germantown, Pennsylvania, issued a remonstrance against slaveholding. Motivated by their religious beliefs, these Quakers laid out a number of the basic arguments against slavery that would be repeated and refined over the next two centuries. They

from parents, the Quakers wondered whether blacks did "not have as much right to fight for their freedom" as whites had "to keep them slaves."[13]

The next attack on slavery came from a Puritan lawyer, Samuel Sewell of Boston. In 1700 Sewell published the first antislavery book in America, *The Selling of Joseph*. As with the Germantown remonstrance, Sewell's book had little immediate impact on the public mind. Both the Quaker manifesto and *The Selling of Joseph*, however, helped lay the groundwork for building greater support for an end to human bondage. Indeed, it is perhaps not surprising that from the earliest period to the Civil War two major centers of the abolitionist movement were Philadelphia and Boston—where the movement began.

Starting in the 1750s the New Jersey Quaker John Woolman began to agitate against slavery. His book, *Considerations on the Keeping of Negroes* (1754), was widely read and influenced many non-Quakers as well as members of his own faith. Also important was the work of the French-born Quaker convert, Anthony Benezet, who published *A Caution and Warning to Great Britain and Her Colonies on the Calamitous State of the Enslaved Negroes* (1761) and *Historical Account of Guinea* (1771).

A year after Benezet published his second book the tiny antislavery movement gained a momentous victory from a most unlikely source: the Chief Justice of the Court of Kings Bench in England. In 1772 Lord Chief Justice Mansfield ruled in *Somerset v. Stewart* that a slave brought to England could not be kept in bondage against his will. Charles Stewart, a minor colonial official, had brought his slave James Somerset to England. Somerset soon ran away, seeking his freedom in a land where there was no slavery. Stewart had Somerset seized and placed

WHAT MEANS THAT SAD AND DISMAL LOOK?

Words by Geo. Russell.   Arranged from "Near the Lake," by G. W. C.

1. What means that sad   and dis - mal look, And

why those fall - ing tears? No voice is heard, no

word is spoke, Yet nought but grief ap - pears.

Ah! Mother, hast thou ever known
The pain of parting ties?
Was ever infant from thee torn
And sold before thine eyes?

Say, would not grief *thy* bosom
swell?
Thy tears like rivers flow?
Should some rude ruffian seize and
sell
The child thou lovest so?

There's feeling in a *Mother's*
breast,
Though *colored* be her skin!
And though at Slavery's foul be-
hest,
She must not weep for kin.

I had a lovely, smiling child,
It sat upon my knee;
And oft a tedious hour beguiled,
With merry heart of glee.

That child was from my bosom
torn,
And sold before my eyes;
With outstretched arms, and looks
forlorn,
It uttered piteous cries.

Mother! dear Mother!—take, O
take
Thy helpless little one!
Ah! then I thought my heart
would break;
My child—my child was gone.

Long, long ago, my child they
stole,
But yet my grief remains;
These tears flow freely—and my
soul
In bitterness complains.

Then ask not why "my dismal
look,"
Nor why my "falling tears,"
Such wrongs, what human heart
can brook?
No hope for me appears.

The Slave Boy's Wish.

BY ELIZA LEE FOLLEN.

I wish I was that little bird,
Up in the bright blue sky;
That sings and flies just where he
will,
And no one asks him why.

I wish I was that little brook,
That runs so swift along;
Through pretty flowers and shin-
ing stones,
Singing a merry song.

I wish I was that butterfly,
Without a thought or care;
Sporting my pretty, brilliant wings,
Like a flower in the air.

I wish I was that wild, wild deer,
I saw the other day;
Who swifter than an arrow flew,
Through the forest far away.

I wish I was that little cloud,
By the gentle south wind driven;
Floating along, so free and bright,
Far, far up into heaven.

I'd rather be a cunning fox,
And hide me in a cave;
I'd rather be a savage wolf,
Than what I am—a slave.

My mother calls me her good boy,
My father calls me brave;
What wicked action have I done,
That I should be a slave.

I saw my little sister sold,
So will they do to me;
My Heavenly Father, let me die,
For then I shall be free.

Item 3-17
George W. Clark, *The Liberty Minstrel* (New York: Leavitt & Alden, 1844). This songster with music as well as words alludes in its title to the wandering singer and contains mostly well-known melodies for which antislavery words were provided here by Clark, a white musician.
Music Division.

in irons on a ship that was destined for the West Indies. Before the ship could sail, the great British abolitionist Granville Sharp obtained a writ of habeas corpus on Somerset's behalf. This brought the status of a slave in England before the nation's highest court.

Lord Mansfield was no abolitionist, and he hoped to avoid rendering any decision in the case. When he first heard arguments he urged the parties to settle the case. Had Stewart been paying his own legal fees, he might have obliged Mansfield. But by this time his case was being funded by absentee sugar planters and others involved in the West Indian sugar industry. The issue for them was important, and they hoped that by pushing the case they would force Mansfield to reach a decision favorable to their interests. Instead, Mansfield delivered a ringing endorsement of liberty.

Mansfield's opinion underscored the fundamental immorality of slavery. Mansfield declared, "The state of slavery is of such a nature, that it is incapable of being introduced" into England "on any reasons, moral or political." Rather, slavery was "so odious, that nothing can be suffered to support it, but positive law."[14] Because there were no statutes in England creating slavery, Mansfield ruled that Stewart could not legally hold Somerset against his will. The upshot was that any slave taken to England would immediately be entitled to his or her liberty. As Somerset's attorney argued, the "air of England was too pure for a slave to breathe."

Reports of Mansfield's opinion circulated in England and America in the years immediately preceding the Revolution. Almost immediately after Mansfield announced his decision a London publisher printed a pamphlet containing the arguments of Somerset's attorneys and the decision in the case.[15] In 1774 a Boston printer published the first American version of this pamphlet. Shortly after the decision Virginia masters reported that slaves were trying to escape to England, "where they imagine they will be free."[16] Thus, on the eve of the American Revolution the legitimacy of slavery was already on the table, being debated by men and women of faith, lawyers and judges, and intellectuals. In England organized opposition to the African slave trade was growing; in America organized opposition to slavery was about the begin.

The Slave's Opposition to Slavery

While whites debated the morality or legality of human bondage, Africans and African Americans in the colonies challenged slavery in a variety of ways. The desire of slaves to be free plagued masters throughout the history of bondage. The very act of running away was an obvious rejection of bondage by those held as slaves. It can be seen as the most basic form of antislavery activity. After nationhood the southern demand for the return of fugitive slaves gradually emerged as a major political issue dividing the nation. Many in the organized antislavery movement of the antebellum period devoted great energies to protecting and helping fugitive slaves and to defying the federal laws of 1793 and 1850, which were passed to help masters regain fugitives. Long before the Revolution and the adoption of the Constitution, however, slaves expressed their opposition to their condition by running away.

Since the early seventeenth century, slaves had run away. Early laws in Virginia and elsewhere provided special penalties to slaves who ran away and to those who aided them. For example, in 1662 Virginia required that white indentured servants who ran away with a slave had to serve the slave's master to compensate for the lost time caused by the missing slave.[17] A 1723 Virginia law allowed for harsh punishments, including "dismembering," for runaway slaves or those "notoriously guilty of going abroad in the night or running away, and lying out."[18] Such harsh punishments were necessary, so the Virginia masters believed, not only to prevent runaways, but also to prevent conspiracies and rebellions.

Even more than running away, actual revolt can be seen as the most intense form of opposition to slavery from within the slave community. Throughout the process of enslavement—from capture in Africa, on board ships in the Atlantic, and finally as chattel in America—a small number of slaves revolted. Early on American masters recognized the need to prevent such dangerous events. A Virginia law of 1669 declared that it would not be a crime if slaves accidently died from punishment when they were "resisting their master, mistris or overseer." In 1680 the Virginia lawmakers prohibited slaves from carrying guns, swords, clubs, "or any other weapon of defence or offence," provided thirty lashes for any slave who "raise up his hand in opposition of any christian [meaning a white]," and allowed authorities to kill any slaves "hiding in obscure places" who refused to return to their masters.

During the colonial period there were many small instances of resistance to slavery and one giant revolt, the Stono Rebellion of 1739, in South Carolina, where at least thirty whites and forty-four slaves died. The War for Independence allowed many slaves to escape bondage by joining an army on either side. Some slaves owned by patriot masters escaped to the

southern delegates demanded special protection for slavery. The new Constitution prohibited the free states from emancipating fugitive slaves and also provided that the national government would use its military force to suppress slave

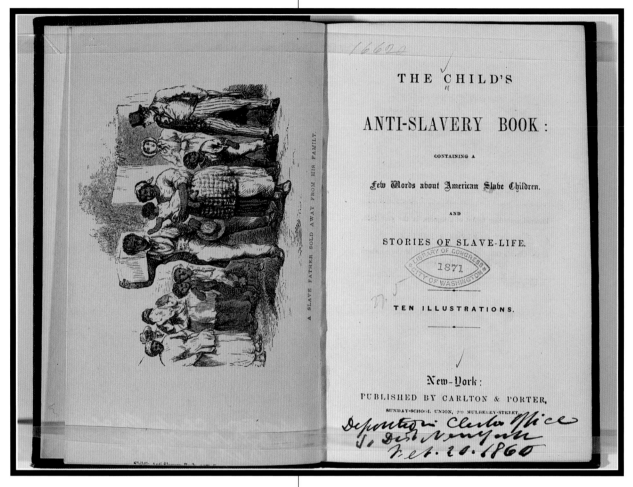

Item 3-13
The Child's Anti-slavery Book: Containing a Few Words about American Slave Children . . . (New York: Carlton Porter, 1859). This abolitionist tract distributed by the Sunday School Union recounted actual life stories of slave children separated from their parents and mistreated by their masters.
Rare Book and Special Collections Division.

British and found freedom aboard ships evacuating America at the end of the war. Other slaves took advantage of the dislocations caused by the war to find freedom in other parts of the new nation. Many slaves joined the patriot armies and earned their own freedom while fighting to make America free from England.

The experience of the war impressed the southern politicians who attended the Constitutional Convention. At the Philadelphia Convention these

rebellions. In 1793 Congress passed a law implementing the fugitive slave provision of the Constitution and on a number of occasions between 1790 and 1861 the national government used its military power to help return fugitive slaves or to suppress slave rebellions.

Despite federal and state laws, local patrols and the national army, slaves continued to escape and resist. Thus some slaves were always significant actors in the struggle against slavery, even though their activity was unorganized, unfunded, and, of course, always illegal. Moreover, the common act of running away, and the less common act of rebellion, often led nonslaves, white and black, to more organized activity such as the legal defense of fugitive slaves, helping fugitives get to Canada, and aiding them once they were there.

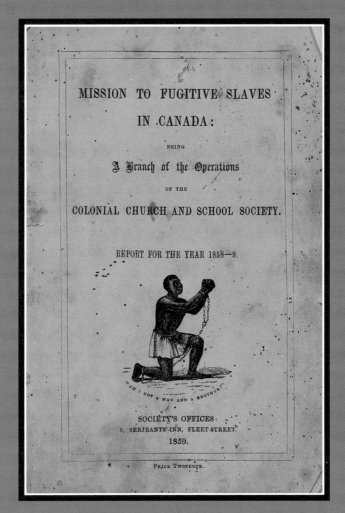

The Suppression of Southern Antislavery

Most opposition to slavery was confined to the North. But in the years after the Revolution a few southerners organized manumission societies and spoke out against slavery. Judge St. George Tucker of Virginia proposed a plan in 1796 for ending slavery, *A Dissertation on Slavery: With A Proposal for the Gradual Abolition of It, in the State of Virginia*,[19] which he later republished as part of his five-volume American edition of *Blackstone's Commentaries*.[20] Moreover, in the years following the Revolution thousands of individual slave owners voluntarily freed their slaves. Between 1782 and 1806, for example, about 25,000 slaves were manumitted in Virginia, including those of the nation's first president. Washington, like many Virginia masters, emancipated his slaves in his will. The former president provided not only for his slaves' freedom but also gave them land from which they could earn a living.

Despite the actions of Washington and many other white southerners, antislavery never took root in the South. Most white southern leaders—such as Thomas Jefferson, James Monroe, and Patrick Henry—never lifted a finger to further the cause of abolition, and often urged others not to act as well. When James Madison's former aide Edward Coles decided to free his slaves his neighbor Thomas Jefferson advised him to resist his humanitarian impulses, telling his younger neighbor that free blacks were "pests in society by their idleness, and the depredations to which this leads them." Jefferson feared their "amalgamation with the other color." Refusing to endorse manumission, Jefferson implored Coles to continue to care for his slaves. Merging his lifelong affection for states rights with his hostility to free blacks, he urged Coles to "reconcile yourself to your country and its unfortunate condition."[21]

Starting in the 1820s southern states cracked down hard on any manifestations of antislavery sentiment. With South Carolina in the lead, most slave states prohibited free blacks from coming within their borders. South Carolina provided for the arrest of any free black entering the state. In the 1830s southern states banned the mere possession of antislavery materials such as the newspapers and pamphlets being produced by the new antislavery movement in the North. Mobs in the 1830s attacked post offices, indiscriminately burning sacks of mail from the North in order to root out the pestilence of northern antislavery propaganda. From the 1830s until the beginning of the Civil War, northerners traveling in the South could face expulsion or prosecution if they were suspected of having antislavery beliefs. Those caught with antislavery pamphlets or accused of helping slaves run away faced savage penalties. Dr. Reuben Crandall, a Connecticut physician and scientist, spent eight months in jail in 1835 to 1836 while awaiting trial for having brought antislavery pamphlets to Washington, D.C., which although technically under the control of Congress borrowed its municipal laws from Maryland and Virginia. A Florida court, for example, sentenced Jonathan Walker to be branded, put in a pillory, and jailed after he was caught attempting to help slaves escape on his ship. Northerners made much of these deprivations of civil liberties, producing pamphlets, newspaper stories, and art work to illustrate the repression of the slave states.

The most famous examples of proslavery suppression of civil liberties came in the 1850s, when almost every southern state banned Harriet Beecher Stowe's best-selling novel *Uncle Tom's Cabin* and Hinton Rowan Helper's *The Impending Crisis*. Helper, a native of North Carolina, was forced to leave his home state after he argued that slavery was detrimental to the interests of non–slave-holding southern whites. Helper, although opposed to slavery, was no friend of African Americans, and was not central to the antislavery movement. Rather, he is important as an example of the limitations of southern opposition to slavery and the suppression of antislavery ideas in the South, even when articulated by white native southerners.

Northern Opposition to Slavery: The Early Years

The American Revolution proclaimed that all people had the right to "life, liberty, and the pursuit of happiness." In the South most whites simply ignored the implications for slavery of this ideology. Other southern whites just concluded that this ideology did not apply to slaves or Africans and their descendants. In the North, however, the ideology had a more universal application. In 1780 Massachusetts declared in its constitution that all people were born "free and equal" and the state's highest court interpreted this clause to have ended slavery in the state. In 1780 Pennsylvania adopted a gradual emancipation statute, which provided that the children of all slaves would be born free. This meant that within a generation or two slavery would literally die out. In a startling preamble, Pennsylvania's lawmakers explained that the statute was a direct result of the Revolution. The legislators were adopting this statute after "contemplat[ing] our abhorrence of that condition, to which the arms and tyranny of Great-Britain were exerted to reduce us" and with "a serious and grateful sense of the manifold blessings" of freedom they had received "from the hand of that Being, from whom every good and

accomplished in 1808. The Pennsylvania Abolition Society continued to bring legal cases but shifted much of its energies toward social issues, working for better employment and educational opportunities for African Americans. Starting in 1794 members of these societies often met at national meetings, called the American Convention for Promoting the Abolition of Slavery and Improving the Condition of the African Race. The American Convention remained in existence until 1837,

"life, liberty, and the pursuit of happiness."

perfect gift cometh." They "rejoice[d]" at the opportunity "to extend a portion of that freedom to others, which hath been extended to us, and release from that state of thraldom, to which we ourselves were tyrannically doomed." Rhode Island (1784), Connecticut (1784), New York (1799), and New Jersey (1804) followed Pennsylvania's lead in passing gradual emancipation statutes, while New Hampshire (1784) and Vermont took the route of Massachusetts, using a constitutional provision to end bondage.

The early opponents of slavery in the North formed state-based organizations, called *manumission societies,* with a local orientation and an elite membership. John Jay, the coauthor of the *Federalist Papers* and the nation's first Chief Justice, was the founding president of the New York Society for Promoting the Manumission of Slaves, founded in 1785. Another early leader was coauthor of the *Federalist Papers* Alexander Hamilton. The early presidents of the Pennsylvania Society for Promoting the Abolition of Slavery and the Relief of Free Negroes Unlawfully Held in Bondage, usually called the Pennsylvania Abolition Society, included two signers of the Declaration of Independence: Benjamin Franklin and Benjamin Rush.

These societies concentrated on ending slavery in their own states or preventing the reenslavement of blacks legally entitled to their freedom. The Pennsylvania Abolition Society was especially active in litigation to help blacks illegally held in slavery or even those legally enslaved in the state. The early societies also worked to prevent the kidnapping of free blacks and agitated for the abolition of the African Slave Trade, which was

and held a national meeting as late as 1832, but following the War of 1812 the movement ceased to focus on the abolition of slavery. In 1825, for example, the New York Society declared that its chief function was to support schools for blacks, which in the absence of sufficient state funds relied on private money. Thus, by 1815 there were no institutional vehicles for those Americans who wanted to make the words of the Declaration of Independence apply to everyone in the country.

Colonization and the Emergence of Antislavery

The early manumission societies were stunningly successful in accomplishing their initial goals: to end slavery in their own states. They also were active in promoting black institutions, such as schools, churches, and orphanages, and in providing legal aid for kidnapped blacks or blacks illegally held in bondage. But the societies failed to work with African Americans on an integrated basis. More important, the manumission societies never challenged the existence of slavery in the South. After the War of 1812 the old manumission societies rapidly diminished in importance.

A new organization, the American Colonization Society, stepped into this vacuum. Founded in 1816 by moderate slave owners, including Representative Henry Clay of Kentucky and Supreme Court Justice Bushrod Washington (a nephew of the late president), the goal of the society was to encourage the resettlement of free blacks in Africa. Eventually the society was instrumental in establishing the nation of Liberia as a homeland for former slaves from the United States.

Some members of the society genuinely believed it would provide an opportunity for masters to free their slaves and send them to Africa. From its founding until the Civil War thousands of emancipated slaves did in fact go to Africa under the auspices of the society. A few northern blacks supported colonization, including John B. Russwurm, a graduate of Bowdin College. But most free blacks saw the Colonization Society as a threat to their well-being. They believed the society was designed not to stimulate manumission but to encourage free blacks to leave the nation. For free blacks and their white allies, the society was a racist organization of slave owners who wanted to remove from the nation the free blacks whose very presence challenged slavery. In 1817 some 3,000 blacks in Philadelphia attended a meeting to condemn colonization. Among the speakers were James Forten, perhaps the richest black in the nation, Bishop Richard Allen of the African Methodist Episcopal Church, and Reverend Absalom Jones. In Boston, New York, and other northern cities similar meetings gathered large numbers of free blacks to protest the idea that they should leave their homeland.

By the 1820s a few whites joined northern blacks in challenging the whole concept of colonization. In 1829 David Walker, a free black from North Carolina who had moved to Boston, published his *Appeal . . . to the Colored Citizens of the World,* asserting that colonization was a plan devised by slaveholding whites "to select the free people of colour from among the slaves" in order to remove them to Africa. Walker argued that "This country"—the United States—"is as much ours as it is the whites, whether they will admit it or not, they will see and believe it by and by."[22] Colonization, Walker complained, served the slave owners by removing from America the example —so dangerous to slavery—of blacks surviving and even prospering as free people. In the end, Walker urged blacks to revolt if the Christian masters of the nation would not free them.

Walker had little immediate impact on the nation, but he frightened southern leaders who encountered his pamphlet. The mayor of Savannah, Georgia, and the governor of Virginia both contacted Mayor Harrison Gray Otis of Boston, demanding that he arrest Walker. Citing the right to a free press, Otis refused to take any action against this obscure black pamphleteer. Shortly after this correspondence, however, Walker was found dead on the street near his home, apparently poisoned. It seems likely he was murdered

at the behest of southern politicians, who could not tolerate such outspoken opposition to slavery, especially by a black.

Organized Antislavery

In the wake of Walker's death, two events occurred that shaped the evolution of antislavery: the Nat Turner rebellion and the publication of William Lloyd Garrison's newspaper, the *Liberator*. In August 1831 Nat Turner, a Southampton County, Virginia, bondsman led more than a hundred slaves in a brief rebellion that thoroughly frightened southern whites. In the space of two days Turner's band killed more than sixty whites before the army, navy, and militias from two states suppressed the rebellion, killing more than one hundred slaves. In the aftermath of the rebellion the Virginia legislature actually debated a proposal to gradually end slavery in that state, but the measure failed. The rest of the South responded with new laws restricting slaves and free blacks, stepped up patrols, and sporadic panics in response to real or imagined slave conspiracies. For the next thirty years southern whites would always wonder who the next Nat Turner might be and where he might strike.

Turner's rebellion was a short-lived affair that only marginally affected the power of the master class and slavery itself. Of greater long-term consequence was the emergence in 1831 of the abolitionist movement.

Since 1829 William Lloyd Garrison had been denouncing slavery and colonization throughout the Northeast. He had a large following among northern free blacks and those whites who were looking for a vehicle to express their disgust and hatred of slavery. On January 1, 1831, Garrison published the first issue of his newspaper, the *Liberator*. He dedicated the paper to unabashed, uncompromising antislavery efforts. In his first issue he wrote, "I will be harsh as truth, and as uncompromising as justice. On this subject, I do not wish to think, or speak, or write, with moderation." For the next three-and-a-half decades he remained true to his word. Garrison, a brilliant propagandist, sent free copies of his paper to southern newspapers. Shocked by his harsh denunciations of slavery and slaveholders, these editors often reprinted Garrison's editorials, only to attack them. Thus, even though his paper could not legally be sold in the South, Garrison and the *Liberator* became infamous. Throughout the region masters read his editorials, or read about them, in their own proslavery southern newspaper. Meanwhile, Garrison found ample opportunity to attack slavery by simply reprinting stories about the peculiar institution that he found in southern papers. Garrison was particularly fond of printing reports of legal cases that involved the mistreatment of slaves. Ironically, in the North Garrison was initially less well known, because his paper had a small circulation; most of his early subscribers were blacks, and few whites cared what he had to say.

In 1833 Garrison helped organize the American Anti-Slavery Society. Most of the delegates to the first meeting were white Protestant or Quaker men, committed to religious principles that led them to oppose slavery. This is not surprising for an age when public life was largely segregated by race and gender. Nevertheless, the society's first convention, and all subsequent ones, also had both black and female delegates. The members of the society resolved at their first meeting to "spare no exertions nor means to bring the whole nation to speedy repentance"—a repentance that would require the end of slavery.

Garrison spent the next three decades working with the American Anti-Slavery Society and with his own Massachusetts Anti-Slavery Society, as well as publishing the *Liberator*. In the early years he was mobbed in Boston and shunned by many whites with whom he had once socialized. He argued for an end to slavery and for racial equality. He supported integrated schools, equality for women, and even legalizing interracial marriages. Most radical of all, by 1840 Garrison advocated that the North leave the Union to separate itself from a government dominated by slave owners protected by a proslavery Constitution. Garrison referred to the national compact as "A Covenant with Death, and an Agreement in Hell."

Garrison's radical tactics and views—especially his disunionism—alienated many northerners. But, in the end, he served vital functions in shaping the movement against slavery. Many southerners viewed all northerners as abolitionists, and eventually all Republicans as Garrisonians. This prevented any serious dialogue on slavery in the antebellum years, but it also helped lay the groundwork for the southern miscalculation that led to Civil War and emancipation. Even as Garrison's radicalism annoyed many northerners it also encouraged them to think about the ways in which slavery affected the nation. Moreover, Garrison was so radical, on so many issues, that others who also wanted to end slavery could seem moderate by comparison. Those who opposed his radical

constitutionalism were forced to develop competing theories. In the end the antislavery constitutionalism of Salmon P. Chase, John Bingham, and Abraham Lincoln would lead the nation to end slavery. But their theories of law and constitutionalism were in part developed in response to Garrison.

In two ways, however, Garrison was central to the antislavery movement and the ending of slavery. Garrison and his followers, especially the brilliant Wendell Phillips, kept the issue alive, never allowing northerners to forget the fundamental immorality of human bondage. No church leader or politician who aided slavery was safe from the editorials of Garrison or the eloquent defamation of Wendell Phillips. Garrison, Phillips, and their colleagues were the greatest, and in the end, the most successful, agitators in American history.

The second great contribution of Garrison and Phillips was their racial egalitarianism. The antebellum period was an age when most whites assumed the natural superiority of their own race and the inferiority of blacks. Not so the Garrisonians. Surely some of Garrison's followers were uncomfortable with blacks, and some were perhaps even racists. But unlike any other group in the nation, the Garrisonians were integrated and egalitarian. Garrison worked side-by-side with blacks on his paper and in the lecture halls.[23] Garrison "discovered" and promoted the young fugitive slave Frederick Douglass. He worked with black ministers in Boston, black civil rights advocates, and black abolitionists. Wendell Phillips, the most talented Garrisonian, and perhaps the best speaker in the entire nation, made it a point to sit in the "Negro car" when riding on a train that had segregated facilities. Garrison usually stayed at the homes of African Americans when traveling. Phillips and other Garrisonians also protested segregation in the courts and the legislatures. It is no accident that the black Garrisonian William C. Nell was the organizer of the first school desegregation case in America, *Roberts v. Boston* (Mass. 1850).

Garrison helped create state and local organizations that supported his views on slavery, race, and women's rights. In 1833 women followers of Garrison organized the Boston Female Anti-Slavery Society and a similar one in Philadelphia. Like the larger American Anti-Slavery Society, the women's organizations were racially integrated. Indeed, from the beginning and throughout their existence, the Garrisonian organizations were, at least for the era, remarkably egalitarian on issues of race and gender.

Not all abolitionists followed Garrison. Reverend Theodore Dwight Weld and scores of ministers and lay preachers who worked with him, abolitionized Ohio, Indiana, Illinois, and upstate New York through meetings in churches, lecture halls, or even tents. Often chased out of town by mobs, Weld and his disciples returned again and again to towns and villages until they were able to present their message of Christian antislavery. By the mid-1840s they had "converted" hundreds of thousands to the cause. Weld organized massive petition campaigns to Congress, protesting every aspect of the national government's connection to slavery.

Unlike the Garrisonians, many of Weld's associates moved into the Liberty Party in 1840, backing James G. Birney, a former slaveowner turned abolitionist. The Liberty Party continued

former slaves could offer the most damning critiques of the peculiar institution; third, when black abolitionists worked with whites they threatened the central argument of slavery—that whites could never accept black freedom and equality and in turn blacks could never survive unless as subordinates to whites. In essence, black abolitionists threatened and undermined the white supremacy that made American slavery possible.

Slavery in the United States was indeed predicated on white supremacy and the certainty of whites that blacks were inferior. As public speakers, authors, editors, and historians, black abolitionists such as William C. Nell, Frederick Douglass, Sojourner Truth, David Ruggles,

"Am I not a Woman and a Sister"

to run candidates until 1860, but was always a minor party with a small following. In 1848 the more politically active abolitionists supported Martin Van Buren, the candidate of the Free Soil Party. That party was not strictly antislavery, because it was only dedicated to stopping the spread of slavery in the territories. It was also the most plausible vehicle for opponents of slavery to express their hostility to the institution at the ballot box. By 1856 the Free Soilers had shifted into the Republican Party, which was also dedicated to ending the spread of slavery, but specifically rejected any notion of ending slavery. Thus, neither the Free Soil nor the Republican parties were either antislavery or abolitionist, and many party members were unconcerned about slavery, as long as it was confined to the states where it already existed. Southerners, however, saw little merit in such distinctions. They lumped all opponents of slavery into one pile, hating and fearing them all.

Black Abolitionists

At one level the greatest threat to slavery came from black abolitionists. This fear was not based on the political power of black abolitionists, because in reality they had little power. The threat from black abolitionists stemmed from three facts: first, they were living proof of the equality of blacks and thus undermined the racial basis of slavery; second, black abolitionists who were

Sarah P. Remond, Henry Highland Garnet, and William Wells Brown proved the absurdity of white supremacy. As speakers, authors, editors, and organizers, these and hundreds of less famous black abolitionists were living proof of the equality of blacks. Fugitive slaves, such as Douglass, William Wells Brown, Reverend Jermain Loguen,[24] Reverend James W. C. Pennington, or Henry "Box" Brown,[25] were able to offer firsthand accounts of the horrors of slavery. As speakers and authors of numerous slave narratives, fugitive slaves were able to make slavery come alive for northern audiences. The symbol for the English abolitionists was a kneeling slave in chains, with the caption, "Am I not a Woman and a Sister," or "Am I not a Man and a Brother." This famous icon, originally produced as a medallion by Wedgewood, was a powerful appeal for sympathy for the slave. But another weapon of American antislavery was even more powerful: the ex-slave on the pulpit or at the lectern, describing the horrors of servitude in the land of liberty. Black abolitionists elevated the slave beyond the role of victim to one of actor in the war against bondage. Fugitive slaves worked to end bondage for their sisters and brothers in the South, urging a variety of tactics. Henry Highland Garnet, for example, believed in the ballot box early in his career, but by 1848 urged a more violent response, arguing in one famous speech, "If you must bleed, let it all come at once—rather *die freemen than live to be slaves.* . . . In the name of the merciful God, and by all that life is worth, let it no longer be a debatable question, whether it is better to choose *liberty or death.*"[26] Later Garnet would urge blacks to leave the United States for a more hospitable land.

I Sell the Shadow to Support the Substance.

SOJOURNER TRUTH.

Item 3-11 A

Sojourner Truth. 1864. Cartes de visite reached the United States soon after their invention in Paris in the 1850s and Sojourner Truth "found a new means of reaching supporters and raising money in the 'cartomania' of the 1860s. As in the 1840s, when the demand for slave narratives enhanced her venture into that profitable line, Truth seized upon new technology for her work of self-representation," writes Nell Irvin Painter in *Sojourner Truth: A Life, a Symbol* (New York: W.W. Norton & Company, 1996) (p. 185).

Carte de visite. Gladstone Collection, Prints and Photographs Division.

Black abolitionists worked with their white counterparts in numerous ways. Nell worked with Garrison to publish the *Liberator*. Douglass shared the platform with whites throughout the North, often spending the night at the home of a white family while on the road. So too did other

George Housman Thomas's sheet of sketches for an illustrated edition of *Uncle Tom's Cabin*. London, 1852. Preparatory sketches for an 1852 edition of Harriet Beecher Stowe's antislavery novel illustrated by George Thomas and published by N. Cooke in London show that the English artist who had seen the slave trade firsthand nevertheless depicts Simon Legree and some of the book's other central characters not as caricatures but as complex human beings.
Pencil, pen, and ink. Prints and Photographs Division. (LC-USZC4–4574)

black speakers. Similarly, black families often hosted white abolitionist speakers. Thus the black abolitionists, whether as speakers or as hosts of speakers, did not merely advocate an end to the color line: They put their theory into practice.

Blacks worked with each other, and with whites, to help fugitive slaves. A few blacks, such as Harriet Tubman, actually went South to lead slaves out of bondage. More important, blacks throughout the North helped runaway slaves who made it North. In addition to the actions of individual blacks in such cities as Boston, Philadelphia,

and New York and in smaller places such as Chicago, Rochester, and Syracuse, blacks and whites worked together to protect fugitive slaves, to intimidate slave catchers, and where necessary, to rescue those captured under the laws of 1793 and 1850.

Antislavery in the Decade of Crisis

In the 1850s numerous strains of antislavery activity interacted and intersected. Garrison and his followers still rejected the Constitution and voting; purist political abolitionists remained wedded to the tiny and ineffective Liberty Party; antislavery politicians and more realistic political abolitionists gravitated to the new Republican Party; black abolitionists continued to struggle for liberty and equality; and in Kansas and later at Harpers Ferry, Virginia, John Brown led armed men in an abortive attack on slavery.

Slavery dominated the politics of the 1850s. The decade began with the adoption of a new fugitive slave law and ended with John Brown's raid at Harpers Ferry. The most important literary event of the decade, if not the century, was the publication of *Uncle Tom's Cabin*, an antislavery novel. The central political event was the emergence of the Republican Party as a broad-based political movement dedicated to ending the spread of slavery in the United States. During the decade the Supreme Court issued its most infamous decision, *Dred Scott v. Sandford* (1857), a case about the rights of free blacks and the power of Congress to prohibit slavery in the territories.

The Constitution of 1787 prohibited the free states from emancipating fugitive slaves. In 1793 Congress enforced this provision with a statute providing mechanisms for the return of runaway slaves. The law was always the bane of abolitionists, but, despite some surrendering of fugitive slaves, it was generally unenforced. By the 1840s at least 1,000 slaves a year were escaping to the North, often aided by black abolitionists such as William Still, David Ruggles, and Lewis Hayden. Henry Highland Garnet claimed at least 150 fugitives stayed in his New York City home in just one year. Harriet Tubman went into the South at least fifteen times, helping more than 200 slaves escape. In Newport, Indiana, the white Quaker Levi Coffin aided more than 2,000 fugitives from 1830 until the end of the Civil War, and Thomas Garrett aided runaways from his home in Delaware, a slave state. Another white, the Canadian-born physician Alexander M. Ross, traveled in the South, helping slaves who wanted to escape. Other whites, including Delia Webster, Daniel Drayton, and William Chapin, spent time in southern

UNCLE TOM'S CABIN

A.S. SEERS PRINT. (COPYRIGHTED)

Alfred S. Seer, *Uncle Tom's Cabin,* 1882. Advertising poster with woodcut
illustration for the play based on Harriet Beecher Stowe's novel.
Prints and Photographs Division. (LC-USZC2–1461)

prisons for helping, or trying to help, blacks escape their bondage.

Resistance to the return of fugitive slaves bedeviled slave owners. In 1837 Pennsylvania prosecuted a Maryland farmer, Edward Prigg, for helping his neighbor capture an alleged slave, Margaret Morgan. In *Prigg v. Pennsylvania* (1842) the Supreme Court reversed Prigg's conviction, but also indicated that state officials could not be forced to implement the federal law, although Justice Joseph Story, writing for the Court, declared that states had a moral obligation to do so. On the heels of *Prigg*, citizens in Boston forced the county sheriff to release George Latimer, a fugitive slave in his custody. This made it impossible for James Gray of Norfolk, Virginia, to hold Latimer long enough to bring his claim into court. Latimer went free when Bostonians paid Gray a token amount. A master passing through South Bend in 1849 did not even get a token amount, because almost the entire town of South Bend, Indiana, turned out to prevent the return of his fugitive slaves. The master later successfully sued many South Bend residents for the value of his slaves, but it would be more than half a decade before he saw any money. Meanwhile, northern judges often refused to hear cases involving fugitive slaves, and state legislatures passed "Latimer Laws" that prohibited state officials from aiding in the return of fugitives.

In this atmosphere, in 1850 Congress adopted a new fugitive slave law. This law placed responsibility for enforcement in the hands of the executive branch, and thus made fugitive slave rendition an aspect of presidential politics. President Millard Fillmore, who signed the 1850 law, went to great lengths to enforce it, although his efforts often backfired. In 1851 Fillmore participated in the decision to bring treason charges against thirty-eight blacks and five whites in Christiana, Pennsylvania, after a fugitive slave killed a Maryland slave owner trying to recapture his runaway slaves. The U.S. attorney was forced to drop all prosecutions after Supreme Court Justice Robert Grier, while riding circuit, ruled in *United States v. Hanway* (1851) that opposition to the Fugitive Slave Law did not constitute treason. Similarly, the Fillmore administration arranged for the arrest of a slave named Jerry in Syracuse, New York, to prove the law could be enforced in abolitionist centers such as upstate New York.

This plan backfired when a mob led by the black minister and fugitive slave Jermain Loguen and the white abolitionists Reverend Samuel May and Gerrit Smith rescued Jerry. Subsequent prosecutions of the rescuers went nowhere.

The Jerry Rescue followed a similar event in Boston, as a mob of blacks rescued the fugitive slave Shadrach while he was in a courtroom; later in 1851 a mob failed in its attempt to rescue Thomas Sims, who was one of only two slaves successfully removed from Boston. Among those aiding both Shadrach and Sims was the black lawyer Robert Morris.

The second fugitive slave removal from Boston, that of Anthony Burns, brought national attention to abolitionist opposition to the return of fugitive slaves. After his master had Burns seized, the antislavery lawyer Richard Henry Dana, Jr., managed to delay the proceedings for a week, forcing a full-scale trial on the status of Burns. A rescue attempt led by Reverend Thomas Wentworth Higginson failed. Eventually Burns went back to Virginia, but only after the administration of President Franklin Pierce used the army, the marines, the coast guard, and numerous federal deputies to remove him from Boston. Estimates of the cost of this removal ran as high as $100,000. Although proving he could have the law enforced, even in Boston, Pierce also proved that it was in the end counterproductive and enormously expensive to do so.

Black and white abolitionists worked together in Boston, Christiana, and Syracuse to protect fugitive slaves. Integrated "vigilance committees" in these cities and elsewhere made slave catching difficult and often dangerous. In Wellington, Ohio, an integrated mob from nearby Oberlin College rescued from the custody of his master a fugitive slave in 1858, and in Milwaukee, Wisconsin, a white abolitionist, Sherman Booth, led a rescue.

Peaceful enforcement of the 1850 law was more common than violent opposition. Claimants recovered more than 300 fugitives under the 1850 Act. Southerners, however, estimated that as many as 10,000 slaves escaped during that period. The resistance to the law was integrated and often organized. It profoundly affected the politics of the era. By 1860 fugitive slave rendition was a key aspect of the sectional conflict. Lincoln believed he had a constitutional obligation to enforce the federal law, but in his inaugural address he tiptoed around the question, asking rhetorically, "Shall fugitives from labor be surrendered by national or by State authority? The Constitution does not expressly say." He used the issue to try to persuade the South not to secede by noting that if the Union collapsed "fugitive slaves, now only partially surrendered, would not be surrendered at all."

Tied to the problem of fugitive slaves was the appearance in 1852 of Harriet Beecher Stowe's *Uncle Tom's Cabin*, arguably the most important novel ever published in the United States. The novel became an instant best seller in the North, selling more than 300,000 copies in its first year. By 1860 readers in Great Britain had purchased more than a million copies of the book. In the South this book was banned and thus unread. Northerners meanwhile thrilled to the struggle of the fugitive slave Eliza Harris to reach freedom and be reunited with her husband, George, who had also escaped bondage. Similarly, Northerners saw in Uncle Tom a Christ-like nobility of a man who went to his death rather than reveal the whereabouts of two slave women who were hiding from the evil Simon Legree, who had been sexually abusing them.[27]

Uncle Tom's Cabin brought the abstraction of slavery into the sitting rooms of the northern middle-class. Stowe was enormously successful in humanizing slavery through the adventures, loves, and tragedies of her fictional characters. Her book struck home because her characters were complex and believable on many levels. With the exception of the evil Legree, most of the southern whites were realistic, and, except for the fact that they owned slaves, reasonable, decent, and moral people. The message of the book was clear: Slavery, not southerners or slave owners, was the problem.

Two years after Stowe published her book Congress repealed part of the Missouri Compromise by allowing slavery in the Nebraska territory (which included present-day Kansas, Nebraska, and the Dakotas). In 1820 Congress had prohibited all slavery in the territories west of Missouri as part of the Compromise of 1820 (the Missouri Compromise). In 1854 Congress reversed this policy with the Kansas–Nebraska Act. The 1854 act provided that the settlers of the new territories would decide for themselves whether or not to have slavery. This was known as *popular sovereignty*. One response to the Kansas–Nebraska Act was the formation of the Republican Party, which was dedicated to the prevention of any more slave states.

In Kansas itself, however, violence broke out as proslavery and antislavery forces battled over the fate of the western prairies. In hindsight we see that "bleeding Kansas" was really a prelude to the Civil War of 1861 to 1865. For abolitionists it marked a turning point. In the 1830s opponents of slavery had hoped to end the institution through moral suasion and appeals to the Bible. In 1854 and 1855 abolitionists in New England began shipping "Beecher's Bibles" to opponents of slavery in Kansas. Named for the Reverend Henry Ward Beecher (the brother of Harriet Beecher Stowe), these "Bibles"—rifles—were manufactured at the Springfield armory and were designed to send slave owners to eternity rather than to provide them with guidance for eternity. Many men on both sides of the slavery issue participated in the violence in Kansas. John Brown, a uncompromising foe of slavery, emerged as a new abolitionist hero for his use of weapons in fighting slavery and because he helped nearly a score of slaves escape from Missouri to Canada. In 1859 Brown led an integrated band of men who seized a federal armory at Harpers Ferry, Virginia (today in West Virginia), in a futile attempt to start a slave rebellion in the South. Virginia authorities hanged Brown less than two months after the raid, thereby creating a martyr to the cause of freedom.

By the end of the decade the Republican Party had emerged as the most powerful political force in the North. Lincoln, the party's candidate, was no abolitionist. But he was the most forthright major-party opponent of slavery to run for the presidency since John Quincy Adams had lost to the slaveholding Andrew Jackson in 1828. Lincoln's victory set the stage for secession, Civil War, and emancipation.

The war in turn created new opportunities for black and white abolitionists. Lifelong social pariahs, such as Garrison and Wendell Phillips, were suddenly seen as prophets of a new era. Political abolitionists such as Chase, Seward, and Hannibal Hamlin found themselves in high office.[28] Frederick Douglass became the first black invited to the White House. His sons became sergeants in the U.S. Army, a fighting force that only a few years earlier had been used to return fugitive slaves to their masters and stood ready to suppress slave insurrections. And, in the end, it was this Army that brought liberty to millions of slaves, under the direction of a president who had once defended the rights of a slave owner but by 1865 had become the most effective abolitionist in the nation.

"MAKE WAY FOR LIBERTY!"

Henry L. Stephens, "Make Way for Liberty!" Collector's card from
"Stephen's Album Varieties: The Slave in 1863," copyright 1864.
Prints and Photographs Division. (LC-USZC4-2521; LC-USZ62-41836)

Liberty won by white men would lack half its lustre.
Who would be free themselves must strike the blow . . . .
This is our golden opportunity.

FREDERICK DOUGLASS
March 1863

❸ Battlefield and Home Front: African Americans and the Civil War, 1860 to 1865

ERVIN L. JORDAN, JR.

National tensions were exacerbated by several factors during the 1850s: slave unrest and free black anti-slavery agitation, the Underground Railroad—a secret network that smuggled runaway slaves to freedom in the North or Canada—John Brown's 1859 Harpers Ferry raid, and five years of warfare in Kansas between antislavery and proslavery forces that foreshadowed civil war. In a nation founded on the principles of democracy and liberty, slavery was an ominous political balancing act ostensibly maintaining America's unity at African Americans' expense.

Under the Constitution slaves and blacks could not be citizens, but the law counted slaves as three-fifths of a person, giving the South more congressional representatives—and more political power—than it would have had otherwise. In the North, antislavery activists (abolitionists) waged verbal and sometimes physically violent warfare against proslavery advocates. The South's internal repressions infringed on constitutional freedoms in its suppression of antislavery mail, organizations, and advocates. Slavery's defenders also engaged in tactics of rhetorical filibustering and threats of disunion.

1860: Between a Rock and a Hard Place

The 1860 federal census enumerated 4.4 million African Americans (3,953,760 slaves and 488,070 free blacks) as 14 percent of a total population of 31 million people. Slave states having the most slaves were Virginia (490,865), Georgia (462,198), Mississippi (436,631), and Alabama (435,080). Free and border states with the most free blacks were Pennsylvania (56,949), New York (49,005),

stereotyping in literature, laws, and entertainment, especially minstrel shows. Northern free blacks endured these and other adversities, however, and developed a collective community consciousness. Proud of their free status, they carefully signed their letters and legal documents with identifying abbreviations such as "f. c. p." (free colored person) or "f. n." (free Negro).

As has been the case of oppressed peoples throughout history, African Americans employed survival techniques appropriate to their circumstances. Free blacks established

"the law counted slaves as three-fifths of a person"

New Jersey (25,336), and Delaware (21,627). Of America's 488,070 free blacks, more than half (258,346) lived in the South, mostly in Maryland (83,942) and Virginia (58,042). More African Americans (548,907) lived in Virginia than anywhere else in North America.[1]

On the eve of the Civil War, most African Americans were slaves, and slavery was the key to the South's identity, culture, and political power. The greatest strength of white supremacy was its overwhelming white population and sanctioning of slavery and racism by law and custom. Economics, politics, and social dominance motivated racism, the belief in inherent Negroid inferiority and Caucasian superiority. Slaves and free blacks, disenfranchised, exploited, ostracized, or suppressed, had little apparent choice except to concede white supremacy. Whites dominated the bodies and labors of African Americans held in hereditary servitude from cradle to grave. Slaves could not vote, marry, or become citizens, attend school, learn to read or write, or own firearms or other property. They could be borrowed, leased, mortgaged, raffled, sold or traded, inherited, or waged in games of chance.[2]

The free black situation was hardly better. Forced to use segregated seating in theaters, denied access to most public schools, discriminated against in housing and employment, free blacks in Northern states were nevertheless required to pay taxes and obey discriminatory laws. Their freedom and civil rights were severely limited. They did not have the right to vote, hold public office, or serve on juries or in militias. They were the frequent victims of mob violence and of racist

churches and fraternal organizations for the care and protection of their widows, orphans, and destitute. African American newspapers kept blacks and whites informed of black progress, and black national conventions enabled black community leaders to articulate the aspirations of their race. In the years before the Civil War, northern blacks became an increasingly vocal, visible, and politicized minority.[3]

1861 : Now Is the Hour

Abraham Lincoln's election as sixteenth president of the United States in November 1860 was the catalyst for Southern secession. He and the Republican Party were not abolitionists but willing to accept slavery where it already existed. Republicans favored the exclusion of slavery from the territories (to protect free white labor) and opposed any future expansion of the peculiar institution. President-elect Lincoln offered the South a compromise: to leave slavery alone in states where it already existed and to vigorously enforce—at the federal level—the Fugitive Slave Act of 1850, which required citizens to assist in the return of escaped slaves to their owners. The South rejected this offer, and by the time of Lincoln's March 1861 inaugural seven slave states, led by South Carolina, had seceded and formed the Confederate States of America, with Jefferson Davis as president and a constitution that permitted and protected slavery.

Three and a half million African Americans were now part of a nation devoted to the perpetuation of hereditary slavery as articulated by Confederate Vice President Alexander Stephens in March 1861: "Our new government is founded upon the great truth that the Negro is not equal to the white man; that slavery-subordination to the superior race is his natural and normal condition." After a thirty-four-hour bombardment, the federal garrison at Fort Sumter, South Carolina, surrendered on April 13, 1861. Lincoln issued a call for federal troops to put down the rebellion while four more states joined the Confederacy. For him and the North the purpose of the war was the preservation of the United States of America, not slavery's abolishment.

Frederick Douglass, realizing blacks could not help win a war against the South unless the government destroyed the institution of slavery, declared that slavery and secession must be crushed by military force. He called on "all the righteous forces of the nation to deal a death-blow to the monster evil of the nineteenth century. Now is the day, and now is the hour!" An escaped Maryland slave who became a noted abolitionist speaker, writer, and newspaper editor, Douglass, black America's spokesperson and leader during most of his adult life, was renowned throughout the North and Great Britain as an uncompromising opponent of slavery and racism. He was also the first notable male American public figure to speak out in support of equal rights for women.[4]

Three Virginia slaves—Shepard Mallory, Frank Baker, and James Townshend—fled in May 1861 to Fort Monroe, Virginia, where they received sanctuary and became the first of thousands of "contrabands of war"—as runaway slaves were called—employed by the Union army as laborers. This, and the Confiscation Act of August 1861, which declared free any Confederate slave used as military labor to wage war against the Union, severely hampered the Confederate war effort and contributed to the fatal weakening of slavery. African Americans fought on the battlefield and the home front against racism in the North and black slavery in the South. Yet some Northern whites, fearing postwar labor competition, advocated African American emigration to Haiti or South America. Nevertheless, blacks reaffirmed their citizenship and intention to stay. "We are to have a word to say and a blow to strike," Boston, Massachusetts, blacks defiantly resolved in November and April 1862. "We don't want to go [and] if anybody wants us to go, they must compel us." They vowed to reject any consideration of emigration until every slave was freed.[5]

It could be said that Lincoln's maturation as an interracial leader began the day after his inauguration when Elizabeth Keckley, a Virginia slave who had purchased her freedom before the war, began working as a dressmaker for his wife Mary after having

Item 4-9
"Camp Brightwood, D.C. Contrabands in 2nd R. I. camp." Washington, D.C., 1863. Carte de visite. Gladstone Collection, Prints and Photographs Division.

worked for Varina Davis, wife of Confederate President Jefferson Davis. During the war Keckley became a trusted confidante of the Lincolns and in her own quiet way proved the capability of blacks for self-development.[6]

Southern ex-slaves took their first steps toward freedom by aiding in the establishment of schools. Black schools founded in South Carolina and Virginia reinforced the development of the African American community and provided

Item 4-1
Alfred Waud, *Contrabands Coming into Camp,* 1863. In the *Harper's Weekly* of January 31, 1863, that carried this illustration, Alfred Waud wrote: "There is something very touching in seeing these poor people coming into camp—giving up all the little ties that cluster about home, such as it is in slavery, and trustfully throwing themselves on the mercy of the Yankees, in the hope of getting permission to own themselves and keep their children from the auction-block."
Prints and Photographs Division.

models for other Southern states as Union forces advanced into the Confederacy. The first black public school was opened in September 1861 at Hampton, Virginia, by Mary Peake, a free black woman. Within two weeks of its opening she was teaching spelling, reading, writing, singing, arithmetic, and Bible studies to forty-five students. She also taught night school for adults until her death from tuberculosis in February 1862. It is an irony of American history that her school was founded near the site where enslaved Africans first arrived in America in the year 1619.

In November 1861, at Port Royal, South Carolina, Northern abolitionists undertook what they perceived to be a social experiment to determine whether newly freed slaves could become educated, moral, self-sufficient, free laborers. Whites overlooked the fact that Northern free blacks had established their own communities, schools, and benevolent societies without white assistance decades before the war. Susie King Taylor, a fourteen-year-old escaped South Carolina slave, became a teacher and one of the war's first black nurses. In April 1862 King, the wife of a sergeant in the 1st South Carolina Volunteers (later the 33rd United States Colored Troops) began teaching black soldiers. She also worked in the regiment's camp as a laundress and after the war opened a school in Savannah, Georgia.[7]

1862: This Is Our Country

As the year 1862 began, the Lincoln administration's reluctant steps toward black emancipation continued. In April, Congress abolished slavery in the District of Columbia, compensating owners $300 for each slave. For the first time in its history the self-proclaimed capital of the world's greatest democracy truly represented human liberty. This was the first time the federal government had taken a strong stand to abolish slavery on American soil.

Lincoln, concerned by adverse Northern opinion and the possible loss of loyal slave owners' allegiance in border states, was at the moment unwilling to fully employ emancipation as a weapon in the war against the Confederacy. He rebuked Union generals who prematurely attempted to liberate slaves. General John C. Fremont invoked martial law and issued a pro-

clamation freeing Missouri slaves in August 1862, and General David Hunter attempted the same for Florida, Georgia, and South Carolina slaves in May. Lincoln, however, revoked Fremont's and Hunter's freedom manifestos. Hunter also organized a black regiment of ex-slaves at Hilton Head, South Carolina. This unit, issued arms and

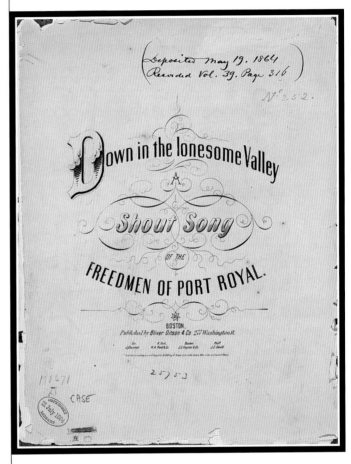

Item 4-18
"Down in the Lonesome Valley: A Shout Song of the Freedmen of Port Royal." Boston: Oliver Ditson, 1864. The African American spiritual, which emerged during slavery, first saw its way into print during the Civil War, when contrabands sang their songs to Northern musicians who transcribed and harmonized the melodies. Music Division.

uniforms consisting of baggy red Zouave trousers and braided jackets, was disbanded in August after failing to obtain federal authorization.[8]

Although rejected as soldiers, blacks did display military aptitudes. The war's first black hero, Robert Smalls, an experienced slave-pilot, daringly led a group of fellow slaves to seize the *Planter,* an armed Confederate steamer, and sailed it out of Charleston, South Carolina, under the guns of Fort Sumter to the Union navy. On the evening of May 12, 1862, after the ship's officers went ashore to attend a party, the black crew summoned their families aboard and at 3:00 in the morning quietly steamed toward the Union fleet blockading the harbor. Smalls disguised himself by putting on the clothes of the white captain and gave the correct passwords and signals as the *Planter* sailed unmolested past Confederate vessels and forts.

Sixteen blacks escaped because of Smalls's courage and planning, and he proudly delivered the vessel to astonished Union officers saying, "I thought the *Planter* might be of some use to Uncle Abe." By an act of Congress he and his comrades shared ten thousand dollars in prize money. In November 1863, while serving as the *Planter's* pilot, he took command of the vessel during a failed night attack against Fort Sumter and refused to surrender it despite heavy damage. In recognition of his gallantry he was promoted to captain and commanded the ship for the duration of the war. After the war Robert Smalls served five terms as an elected representative—first as a South Carolina state legislator and later as a member of the U.S. House of Representatives.[9]

By June 1862 the United States, free from obstructions posed by Southern congressmen, extended diplomatic recognition to Haiti, which in 1804 had become the world's first independent black republic, and Liberia, independent since 1848. Many free black Northerners worried that this was setting the stage for their forced emigration to those countries. Congress banned slavery in all U.S. territories without compensation to slaveholders, and in July Lincoln signed the Second Confiscation Act, which declared the freedom of Confederate slaves who reached Union lines and authorized the employment of blacks to suppress the rebellion. It also called for emigration of African Americans to establish foreign colonies.

After secession of the South, four slave states—Delaware, Kentucky, Maryland, and Missouri—remained in the Union. Delaware and Maryland were of vital concern. If they seceded, Lincoln's capital, Washington, D.C., would be surrounded by Confederate territory. Concerned about antagonizing loyal Union slaveholders in these states, Lincoln urged the four states to consider gradual, compensated emancipation of their slaves with federal funds, but slaveholders rejected Lincoln's offer. He also decided to convince Northern free blacks to leave in hopes their doing so would influence freed Southern slaves to follow them.

Lincoln met with a group of District of Columbia free blacks who hoped to persuade him to abolish slavery. Instead, he urged voluntary emigration of blacks to Liberia or the colonization of suitable locations in Central America and added a promise of federal assistance. The delegation and other blacks quickly voiced strong opposition. "Sir, we were born here, and here we choose to remain," thundered Robert Purvis of Philadelphia, a longtime abolitionist and member of the American Anti-Slavery Society. "In the matter of rights, there is but one race, and that is the *human race*. This is our country as much as it is yours, and we will not leave it."[10]

Black churches and benevolent societies in the North organized relief efforts for their Southern brethren, but black Southerners also took it upon themselves to establish their own settlements and schools for the great work of uplifting their race from the shadows of slavery. Freedman's Village was founded in the summer of 1863 at Confederate General Robert E. Lee's confiscated estate in Arlington, Virginia, as a place of self-sufficient refuge for runaway Maryland and Virginia slaves. This community of tidy streets and neat houses surrounded by black-owned farms included a church, a hospital, a school, a home for the elderly, and establishments for a blacksmith, a wheelwright, a carpenter, a tailor, a shoemaker, and similar trades. Freedman's villagers, who produced hay and corn netting profits of $60,000 by the end of 1863, frugally deposited their earnings in their own savings bank. This prosperous black-run community lasted until its forced closure by the federal government in 1900.

As defeats and stalemates increased, Northern free blacks, abolitionists, and their congressional allies pressured Lincoln to fight Southern treason and slavery by liberating Dixie's slaves. *New York Daily Tribune* editor Horace Greeley's "Prayer of Twenty Millions," an open letter to the president in August 1862, called for the immediate and complete emancipation of slaves. Lincoln replied, "My paramount object in this struggle is to save the Union and is not either to destroy or save slavery. If I could save the Union without freeing any slave I would do it; if I could save it by freeing all the slaves, I would do it; if I could do it by freeing some and leaving others alone, I would also do that." He also stated his "oft-expressed personal wish that all men, everywhere, could be free."[11]

Other whites, convinced of the necessity of enlisting black troops in light of mounting Union casualties, took matters into their own hands. Senator Jim Lane of Kansas opened a recruitment office in Leavenworth in August 1862 and organized a regiment, comprising mostly ex-slaves from Arkansas and Missouri, as the 1st Kansas Colored

Volunteers. At the same time, Lincoln told a delegation of senators that he opposed the military employment of blacks. Regardless of governmental foot-dragging, three regiments in Cincinnati, Ohio, were organized by free blacks to construct fortifications in a response to a proposed Confederate invasion of Kentucky. Some historians consider the Ohio brigade to be the North's first black military unit, and its flag bore the inscription

federal service during October and November 1863. The 1st South Carolina Colored Volunteers, organized at St. Simon's Island, South Carolina, in October 1862, was formally mustered into service on January 31, 1863. Many of its enlistees had already acquired training during their brief experience as part of General David Hunter's regiment—now disbanded—two months before.

The first battle involving an African American regiment occurred at Island Mound, Missouri, where the 1st

Ent'd according to Act of Congress, A. D. 1863, by W. T. Carlton, in the Clerk's Office of the District Court of the District of Mass.

Item 4-21 A
W. T. Carlton, "Waiting for the Hour [Emancipation] . . . Dec. 31, 1862."
Carte de visite. Washington, 1863. Prints and Photographs Division.

"The Black Brigade of Cincinnati." Disbanded after three weeks when the threat of Confederate attack had passed, the brigade received neither uniforms nor weapons. Many of its 700 members later served in other Union regiments.[12]

After the battle of Antietam, Lincoln announced in September 1862 a preliminary emancipation of slaves in the seceded states to take effect in 1863. The time had finally arrived to employ black warriors to crush slavery and treason, and more black regiments were enrolled. The 1st Regiment of the Louisiana Native Guards, "Chasseurs d'Africa/Corps d'Afrique," was organized for federal service in New Orleans. Officially, it was America's first all-black regiment. The 2nd and 3rd Native Guards regiments enrolled in

Kansas Colored Volunteers (later designated the 79th United States Colored Volunteers), drove off a Confederate guerilla force in October 1862. "They fought like tigers," conceded a surprised white reporter. This regiment was formally mustered into federal service as the government's fourth black regiment on January 13, 1863—three months after its first battle.[13]

Provisions for slaves who were liberated by Union forces were sometimes inadequate and often uncoordinated. Many private organizations and individuals provided relief in the form of teachers, schools, food, clothing, and housing. Some ex-slaves were given abandoned Confederate land and became self-sufficient farmers. African Americans, not always passive recipients of assistance, undertook efforts to help each other. Ex-slave Elizabeth Keckley, Mary Lincoln's dressmaker and confidant, founded the Contraband Relief Association in Washington in August 1862 and raised funds throughout the North and in Great Britain. As its president, Keckley managed the distribution of food, clothing, cash, and housing and gave moral and spiritual guidance. Her organization eventually expanded its efforts and renamed itself "The Freedmen and Soldiers' Relief Association of Washington," extending support to black Union soldiers and their families. Meanwhile, Charlotte L. Forten, a free black Philadelphian abolitionist whose diary contained revealing insights on nineteenth-century African American life, arrived in November 1862 to teach South Carolina freedmen at Hilton Head and the Sea Islands. She wholeheartedly praised her students: "I never saw children so eager to learn, although I had had several years' experience in New England schools."[14]

In December 1864 the National Freedman's Relief Association hired ex-slave Sojourner Truth, one of the nation's most prominent antebellum abolitionist orators, as a charity worker for freed slaves in Arlington. As nurse, advocate, teacher of morality, and religious leader of her people, Sojourner stressed strong moral values, personal hygiene, and hard work and urged her listeners to prepare for full citizenship. When Maryland slaveholders crossed into Virginia to seize black children as slaves, Sojourner's protests to federal officials helped end the kidnappings.[15]

1863: To Save the Country from Ruin

At noon on the first day of 1863, Abraham Lincoln became the Great Emancipator when he signed the Emancipation Proclamation declaring free all slaves held in the rebellious states except-ing those in the seven Virginia counties, thirteen Louisiana parishes, and forty-eight West Virginia counties that were under Union occupation. These were exempted because Lincoln still hoped to convince Southern Union loyalists he would pro-tect their right to hold slaves as property if they remained loyal. He extended a similar promise to Confederates if they ended their rebellion. The proclama-tion recognized the ex-slaves' right of reasonable self-defense should anyone attempt to re-enslave them, ordered Union armed forces to acknowledge and main-tain their freedom, and authorized black troop enlist-ments. Across the North African Americans celebrated the Emancipation Proclamation as a black "grapevine telegraph" spread the news of the dawn of freedom across much of the Confederacy, despite efforts made to suppress it.

The only slaves publicly able to celebrate the procla-mation in the Confederacy were in the very areas exempted from its provisions, areas occupied by Union troops. In cities such as New Orleans, Louisiana, Port Royal, South Carolina, and Norfolk, Virginia, however, black celebra-tions including the burning of Confederate flags and effi-gies of Confederate President Jefferson Davis took place. The proclamation changed the course of the war for sev-eral reasons. Although Lincoln and most Northerners had rejected slavery as a reason for the conflict, the realiza-tion of the Emancipation Proclamation's military and political advantages temporarily converted them into quasi-antislavery crusaders. It renewed slaves' hopes for freedom, and thousands deserted their Confederate own-ers, causing internal stresses on the South's war effort. Northern blacks intensified their efforts to recruit African American regiments and otherwise contributed to the growing Union war effort. In many Northern states and Europe the proclamation recast the war as a battle for human freedom and deterred Great Britain and France from any formal recognition of the Confederacy. Mean-while, slaves in border states and areas occupied by Union troops remained in bondage until the adoption of the Thirteenth Amendment in December 1865.

Confederate President Davis blasted the Emancipation Proclamation as a license for slaves to murder whites and issued a counterproclamation, "An Address to the People of the Free States by the President of the Southern Confederacy," blaming abolitionists for the Union's enlist-ment of black soldiers. Davis ordered that as of February 22, 1863, all free blacks in the Confederacy and in terri-tories captured by Confederate forces were to be enslaved. He also threatened to try Union officers as criminals for inciting slave insurrections. Although the Confederacy never completely implemented the Davis proclamation, it provided additional proof that black slavery was the

Item 4-16
C. W. Foster, U.S. War Department, to Frederick Douglass, August 13, 1863.
A request for Douglass to recruit black soldiers for the Union troops.
Frederick Douglass Papers, Manuscript Division.

War Department,
Adjutant General's Office,
Washington D.C. Augt. 13, 1863

Fredrick Douglass Esqr.
Rochester, N.Y.

Sir,

I am instructed by the Secretary of War to direct you to proceed to Vicksburg, Mississippi and on your arrival there to report in person to Brig'r General L. Thomas Adjutant General, U.S. Army, to assist in recruiting colored troops.

Enclosed please find copy of order for your transportation at public expense.

(Over)

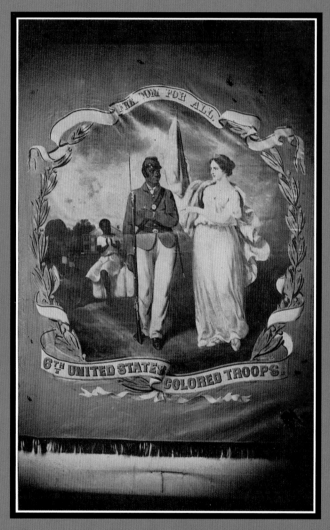

Item 4-7
"Regimental Flags of the 6th United States Colored Troops."
Carte de visite. Gladstone Collection, Prints and Photographs Division.

Confederacy's predominant goal and that South-erners would not have abolished it had they won the war.[16]

The second military engagement involving black Union soldiers occurred during a raiding and recruitment mission by the First South Carolina Colored Volunteers (later the 33rd United States Colored Infantry) along the St. Mary's River to Georgia and Florida in late January. The regiment, attacked by Confederate guerrillas near Township, Florida, successfully repelled their attackers. In the North, the 54th Massachusetts Volunteer

assigned unit numbers in the order they were raised, making them truly federalized African American regiments. The 1st U.S. Colored Troops, mustered in Washington, D.C., in June 1863, became the first black federal regiment enrolled by the Bureau for the Union government. It subsequently fought gallantly for two years in North Carolina and Virginia.[18]

From December 1863 to September 1864 Camp William Penn, Philadelphia, was a major training site of black Union troops and headquarters for a specialized facility, the "Free Military School for Applicants for Command of Colored Troops" for the instruction of

"To save the country from ruin."

Infantry (Colored) began recruiting in Boston. It became the North's first and the Union's most famous black regiment for its courageous but failed 1863 attack at Fort Wagner, South Carolina. Frederick Douglass issued "Men of Color, To Arms," a March 1863 declaration to blacks to enlist in the Union army: "Liberty won by white men would lack half its lustre. Who would be free themselves must strike the blow. Better even to die free than to live slaves. This is our golden opportunity." After a personal meeting with Lincoln in August, Douglass suspended publication of his newspaper *Douglass' Monthly* to become a full-time recruiter of black soldiers.[17]

Slowly Northern attitudes toward African American soldiers continued to change to a positive one. "So much ignorant prejudice is still entertained in many parts of the North to the employment of colored troops that it is due to the country that the capacity of the Negro to drill and fight can not be too strongly insisted upon," declared one New York newspaper in March 1863. "With proper drill and training the Negroes will be the steadiest rank and file in the world." The War Department created the Bureau of Colored Troops, headquartered in Washington, in May 1863 to coordinate the enrollment and deployment of black troops and commissioning of white officers to command them. Known by a variety of designations as Corps d'Afrique, United States Colored Infantry (USCI), United States Colored Troops (USCT), or United States Colored Volunteers, these black regiments were

white Union officers designated to command black troops. A special manual, *U.S. Infantry Tactics, for the Instruction, Exercise, and Manoeuvers of the Soldier, a Company, Line of Skirmishers, for the Use of the Colored Troops of the United States Infantry, Prepared under the Direction of the War Department* (1863), was devised for white officers complete with tactics and drills, bugle and drum beats, salutes, and marching instructions.

The manual's lack of apparent discrimination—it assumed black recruits could count and were in good physical condition to carry out drills—betokened the Union's growing confidence in black soldiers. Lieutenant F. W. Browne, a white officer in the 1st U.S. Colored Cavalry, was impressed by the quality of his black troopers and described them as "a better class of men" and as good soldiers as whites. Black Northerners joined the Union Army in such numbers that some regiments were organized overnight. When asked why he enlisted, Christian Fleetwood, later a sergeant major in the 4th U.S. Colored Troops and recipient of the Medal of Honor, patriotically replied, "To save the country from ruin."[19]

A few blacks served as commissioned officers. Among the highest ranking black field officers were Major Martin Delany of the 104th U. S. Colored Troops, Major Francis E. Dumas of the 74th USCT, and Lieutenant Colonel Alexander T. Augusta, the 7th USCT's regimental surgeon. In early 1865 Delany received permission to recruit an all-black army commanded by black officers, perhaps to be headed by himself with the rank of general, but the war ended before he could fully carry out this plan. Nevertheless, black officers often encountered racial prejudice from white officers and civilians, discriminatory pay, and the hatred of Confederate soldiers who preferred to kill them rather than treat them as prisoners of war.[20]

African American soldiers eagerly sought the forefront of the fighting. In May, two black Union regiments (the 1st and 3rd Louisiana Native Guards) three times unsuccessfully assaulted Confederate positions at Port Hudson, Louisiana. Before the battle Flag Sergeant Anselmas Planciancois of the 1st Regiment proudly accepted the honor of carrying the regiment's flag and told his commanding officer, "Colonel, I will bring these colors to you in honor or report to God the reason why!" He was killed when a cannonball decapitated him as he led a desperate charge; and six of his comrades lost their lives carrying the flag. News accounts of the battle paid tribute to the courage and valor of black soldiers. "This settles the question that the negro race can fight with great prowess," wrote a *New York Times* reporter. "It is no longer possible to doubt the bravery and steadiness of the colored race." At the battle of Milliken's Bend, Louisiana, in June 1863, an "African Brigade" comprising three black regiments—the 9th and 11th Regiments of Louisiana Volunteers of African Descent and the 1st Mississippi Regiment (later the 51st United States Colored Troops)—and one all-white regiment, the 23rd Iowa Infantry, were initially pushed out of their camps by Confederate forces but rallied and drove their foes back. A remarkable aspect of this battle was that the black soldiers who fought had been in uniform for less than a month.[21]

African American women, too, joined the fight against slavery, and sometimes on the battlefield. Harriet Tubman, nurse, spy, and scout, served unofficially as chief of military intelligence in the Department of the South and became the only American woman to lead troops in battle during the war. One of history's most fearless women, Tubman escaped Maryland slavery in 1849 and became the Underground Railroad's preeminent conductor. She led more than 300 slaves, including her elderly parents, to freedom and never lost any of her passengers to slave-catchers. The South offered rewards totaling $40,000 for her capture, dead or alive. In June 1863, Union raids under the command of abolitionist Colonel James Montgomery and led by Tubman destroyed or confiscated millions of dollars of Confederate property and freed nearly nine hundred South Carolina slaves.[22]

Although black soldiers risked their lives for liberty and equal rights, the federal government discriminated against them. In June 1863 the War Department announced that under the provisions of the Militia Act of July 1862 it would pay black soldiers $10 a month (with $3 deducted for clothing) while paying white soldiers $13 a month. Thomas Wentworth Higginson, the first colonel to lead a black regiment (the 1st South Carolina Infantry), other white USCT officers, and Northern political leaders such as Massachusetts Governor John A. Andrew denounced this as an injustice to black soldiers. Many black soldiers, concerned about the hardships a pay reduction would cause their families, refused to accept the discriminatory pay and sent letters of protest to newspapers and government officials.

Writing from Morris Island, South Carolina, where his regiment suffered heavy casualties two months earlier at the battle of Fort Wagner, Corporal James Henry Gooding of the 54th Massachusetts Volunteer Infantry, in September 1863, appealed to President Lincoln for justice: "The patient, trusting Descendants of Afric's Clime have dyed the ground with blood, in defense of the Union, and Democracy. We have done a Soldier's Duty. Why Can't we have a Soldier's pay?" Massachusetts Governor John A. Andrew wrote numerous letters on behalf of black soldiers and declared, "I will never give up the rights of these men while I live, whether in this world, or the next." After the attorney general's opinion that blacks were entitled to equal pay, Congress passed legislation in June 1864 ordering retroactive pay to black soldiers who were free as of April 19, 1861. This measure unfairly penalized African American soldiers because most had escaped from slavery after that date. Not until March 3, 1865, did Congress finally authorize equal pay for black soldiers, some of whom for as long as two years had refused to accept unequal pay.[23]

Black soldiers with family members held in bondage especially yearned to strike a blow against slavery. Samuel Cabble, who joined Company G of the 55th Massachusetts Volunteer Infantry in June 1863, wrote his enslaved wife: "Great is the outpouring of the colored people that is now rallying with the hearts of lions against that very curse that has separated you and me. I am a soldier now, and I shall use my utmost endeavor to strike at the rebellion and the heart of this system that so long has kept us in chains."[24]

Racism continued throughout the North during the war and ignored blacks' battlefield and civilian sacrifices. The New York City draft riot of July 13 to 17, 1863, was one of the worst antiblack riots of the nineteenth century. Irish immigrant laborers and other whites, enraged by a federal law exempting men from the military draft if they

Item 4-2
William R. Pywell, "Slave Pen in Alexandria, Va."
Photograph, [1862]. Prints and Photographs Division.

Item 4-8
"Wounded Colored Troops at Aikens Landing."
Stereograph. Gladstone Collection, Prints and Photographs Division.

paid a $300 fee for hire of a military substitute, believed they were being forced to fight for slaves while blacks took white men's jobs. During a savage three-day riot they killed or assaulted every black person they encountered on sight. Black homes, black businesses, and an orphanage housing 230 black children were attacked, looted, and burned to the ground. State militia and federal regiments eventually restored order after a week of lawlessness but many blacks fled the city, never to return. Approximately twelve hundred people were killed or injured and $2 million worth of property was damaged or destroyed. Ashamed New Yorkers raised $41,000 and organized relief efforts for black victims.

As the riots subsided the 54th Massachusetts Infantry, led by Colonel Robert Gould Shaw, spearheaded an evening assault against Fort Wagner, a Confederate stronghold in Morris Island, South Carolina. On July 18, 1863, the 630-man regiment braved a wave of rifle and cannon fire as it dashed two hundred yards across the beach and scrambled up the fort's walls. Shaw urged his men forward until he was shot through the heart and fell face forward into the fort. His troops, howling for revenge, charged up and into the fort but were eventually driven back after suffering nearly 45 percent in casualties (34 killed, 93 captured, 146 wounded).

Sergeant William H. Carney of the 54th Massachusetts became the first African American to receive the Congressional Medal of Honor. During the attack, the flag bearer fell, but before the national flag touched the ground Carney caught and advanced it to the head of the regiment. After crossing a ditch of waist-deep water, Carney reached the fort's ramparts and, though three bullets hit him, fought off Confederates who tried to take his flag. When ordered to the rear, he insisted on holding on to the flag. On Carney's return to camp, he was bleeding but defiant, and his comrades cheered when he declared, "The old flag never touched the ground!" Confederate officers refused truce requests for the retrieval of Shaw's body and contemptuously buried him in a trench with his dead soldiers. In spite of this attempt to shame him, Shaw in death became a martyr to the cause of freedom and his men were hailed as heroes in the finest tradition of military service.

This was neither the first nor the bloodiest battle in which black Union troops participated,

but the bravery of the 54th against almost impossible odds greatly contributed to the acceptance of blacks as citizen–soldiers. "The men of the 54th behaved gallantly on the occasion—so the Generals say," wrote black Corporal James Henry Gooding shortly after the battle. "It is not for us to blow our own horn; but when a regiment of white men gave us three cheers as we were passing them, it shows that we did our duty as men should." In September Union forces occupied the fort after Confederates abandoned it. The story of the 54th Massachusetts and its most famous battle became the subject of the 1989 Academy Award-winning movie *Glory*.[25]

By the end of July, thirty black regiments were in federal service. In response to Confederate atrocities and enslavement of black Union prisoners of war and in recognition of black soldiers' bravery, Lincoln issued a retaliation order:

> It is the duty of every Government to give protection to its citizens, of whatever class, color or condition, and especially to those who are duly organized as soldiers in the public service. If the enemy shall sell or enslave anyone because of his color, the offense shall be punished by retaliation upon the enemy's prisoners in our possession. It is therefore ordered that for every soldier of the United States killed in violation of the laws of war, a rebel soldier shall be executed; and for every one enslaved by the enemy or sold into slavery, a rebel soldier shall be placed at hard labor on the public works until the other shall be released and receive the treatment due to a prisoner of war. [26]

The federal government had finally deemed black American citizens entitled to its protection and appreciation.

Racial Renegades: Afro-Confederates in the South: 1861 to 1865

The war not only divided whites of the South and North but also pitted slaves and free blacks against each other. One remarkable manifestation of this was the Afro-Confederates, black Southerners apparently loyal to the Confederacy. These were slaves who refused to betray their owners, free blacks who donated money and labor to the Confederacy, slaves who faithfully supervised the plantations of absentee owners, blacks who joined the Confederate army as body servants or offered their services as soldiers.

The support of free blacks, who rightly feared reprisals such as being reduced to slaves, was counterfeit, because they believed the South was winning the war. Such behavior was not, how-ever, confined to the South. Standing on a flour barrel, John Jones, a black New York City resident, publicly announced his support of secession and the Confederacy in an impromptu speech before a large crowd in October 1861. He was arrested and confined in a lunatic asylum.[27]

In January 1861, Charleston, South Carolina, blacks volunteered their services to the state even before the formal creation of the Confederate States of America. A black military company in Nashville, Tennessee, offered its services to the Confederacy in April; the next month Tennessee became the first state on either side of the conflict to enact a law for the recruitment of black soldiers (free blacks) between the ages of fifteen and fifty. However, it employed blacks recruited under this law as manual and camp laborers, not as soldiers. In September two Afro-Confederate regiments publicly drilled in Memphis but the Confederate government refused to accept them.

Louisiana's governor accepted the Louisiana Native Guard of New Orleans as a state militia regiment in May, and commissioned black officers for this volunteer Afro-Confederate unit. Its 1,400 free black members held a grand review in November, but their patriotism proved problematic when Union forces captured the city in April 1862. The Native Guards refused to evacuate with white Confederate troops and instead joined the Union army in September 1862 as the 1st Regiment of the Louisiana Native Guards (73rd United States Colored Troops).[28]

A member of the Virginia legislature proposed the enrollment of free blacks as soldiers in February 1862, but Confederate victories during the spring and summer campaigns thwarted further discussion of this radical idea. Nevertheless, Afro-Confederates participated in an attack on Union gunboats near Franklin, North Carolina, in October 1862, and fully armed and uniformed Afro-Confederate military sentries were seen patrolling Confederate camps near Fredericksburg, Virginia, in December 1862. Between December 1862 and February 1863 a Savannah, Georgia, slave named Davy worked as a Confederate spy in Beaufort, South Carolina.[29] African American community leaders in the North feared the enrollment of black Confederate regiments. In March 1863 Reverend James W. C. Pennington, an escaped Maryland slave who became an author, minister, teacher, and antislavery crusader, stated, "It would be an awful state of things, to see the 200,000 Union colored troops confronted by

200,000 of our own race, under the rebel banner!" Pennington's fears were valid; Afro-Confederates killed Union soldiers at First Bull Run (1861), the Peninsula Campaign (1862), the Seven Days (1862), Fredericksburg (1862), and Gettysburg (1863). Members of the 54th Massachusetts Volunteer Infantry reported the presence of Afro-Confederate sharpshooters in South Carolina during August 1863.[30]

Confederate General Patrick Cleburne (killed at the battle of Franklin, Tennessee, in November 1864) submitted a detailed proposal to his superiors in January 1864 calling for the recruitment of Afro-Confederate regiments, but President Jefferson Davis ordered its suppression. More than a year later, on March 13, 1865, the Confederate Congress finally authorized the enlistment of 300,000 slave and free black troops between ages eighteen and forty-five into black Confederate regiments. Slaveholders' permission was required before any of their slaves could enroll. To prevent the possibility of armed black rebellion this law permitted only one fourth of all the male slaves in a given state to enlist. Afro-Confederate soldiers were to be freed after the war as reward for faithful service but were promised nothing about their families' postwar freedom. This measure arrived too late to prevent Confederate defeat. Incredibly, when Lee surrendered the Army of Northern Virginia in April 1865 thirty Afro-Confederates, half of whom were slaves, insisted on being paroled with white Confederate soldiers—preferring to be treated as prisoners of war. And as late as May 2, 1865, Confederate army officers were planning to recruit black soldiers in Mississippi.[31]

Afro-Confederates were a minority within a minority (i.e., blacks in the South) within a minority of blacks in the Confederate South. Their enrollment as Confederate soldiers might have changed the war's outcome and perpetuated slavery well into the twentieth century.

1864: Slavery's Death Throes

Black Union soldiers experienced triumphs and defeats throughout 1864. At the February battle of Olustee, Florida, three black regiments (including the 54th Massachusetts) and six white regiments engaged in a fighting retreat after their repulse by Confederate forces. Upset because they were paid half of what whites soldiers earned, the 54th

Item 4-17
Charles Douglass to his father, Frederick Douglass, July 6, 1863, concerning the son's Civil War service.
Autograph letter. Frederick Douglass Papers, Manuscript Division.

Readville Camp Meigs July 6th 1863

Dear Father

I have just returned to camp
from Boston where I spent the fourth
and fifth, Yesterday I went to Mr Grimes
Church and Dr. Rock read a letter that he
had recd from his wife who is in Philadelphia
and that the rebels were sending the negroes
south as fast as they advanced upon
our lines and that the colored people
were rushing into Philadelphia
and that yourself and Stephen Smith
and others were doing all you could
for them I was glad to hear that only
keep out of the hands of the rebels.
This morning as I was about to take
the train for camp I saw some
returned soldiers from Newbern N. C.
we had just got the news that Meade
had whipped the rebels and behind
me stood a Irishman

went into battle shouting as their battle cry, "Three cheers for Massachusetts and seven dollars a month."[32]

In April, 1,500 Confederate soldiers at Fort Pillow, Tennessee, massacred black soldiers and

Item 4-10
Unidentified sailor.
Carte de visite. Gladstone Collection, Prints and Photographs Division.

their white officers who had surrendered to Confederate General Nathan Bedford Forrest. According to survivors' testimony, 90 percent of the black soldiers were shot, bayoneted, burned, or buried alive. Only 80 of the 290 white Union soldiers present were killed. The Confederate government denied that a massacre had occurred, but black survivors such as Private Ransome Anderson testified before a congressional com-

mittee: "Most all the men that were killed on our side were killed after the fight was over. They called them out and shot them down. Then they put some in the houses and shut them up, and then burned the houses." For his part, Forrest reported the capture of 164 white soldiers, 73 black soldiers, and 40 black women and children and the burial of 238 black soldiers. "Remember Fort Pillow!" became a rallying cry of black Union soldiers.[33]

During the siege of Petersburg (June 15, 1862 to April 2, 1865) twenty-five black regiments participated in military actions against the Confederacy's Army of Northern Virginia. During the siege federal engineers tunneled beneath Confederate lines and packed the tunnel with explosives. The plan called for a specially trained black division to take advantage of the explosion and attack the Confederates. Last-minute accusations of blacks being deliberately placed in the front to exterminate them led to their replacement with untrained white troops. When the tremendous explosion occurred, on the morning of July 30, 1864, the Union attack failed because of the cowardice and incompetence of some white officers and the confused white troops who milled around the 150-foot-long, 25-foot-deep crater, blocking the black division's advance. Confederates and black Union troops clashed in a frenzy of bloodshed that sickened both sides as the blacks were killed, captured, or driven back. In some cases, white Union soldiers deliberately shot black Union soldiers to avoid Confederates' racial wrath. An investigative committee later concluded black soldiers might have achieved victory had they spearheaded the attack as planned.[34]

Black sailors too demonstrated fearlessness. In December 1863 Robert Blake, a Virginia ex-slave, became the first African American in the Union Navy to receive the Congressional Medal of Honor after his gallant service during a battle on the Stono River, South Carolina. John Lawson of Pennsylvania received the Congressional Medal of Honor for conspicuous bravery during the battle of Mobile Bay in August 1864 when he refused to leave his post aboard the USS *Hartford* despite being badly wounded in the leg. Black regiments contributed to the defeat of Confederate forces in September at the battle of Chaffin's Farm, Virginia. Thirteen African Americans were awarded the Congressional Medal of Honor for bravery during this battle, among them Christian Fleetwood.

Black soldiers in the Army of the Cumberland contributed to General George Thomas's decisive victory over the Confederacy's Army of Tennessee during a two-day battle at Nashville, Tennessee, in December 1864. Eight black regiments successfully achieved their assigned task of launching a diversionary assault on the Confederate right flank distracting rebel attention from the main Union

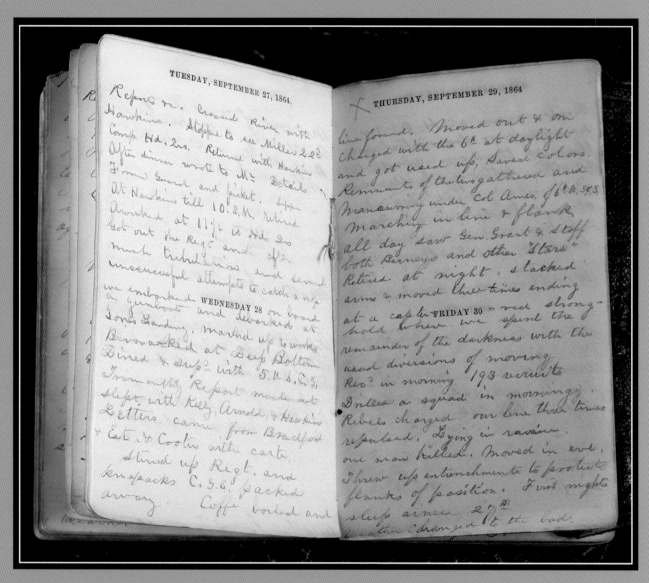

Item 4-14

Christian A. Fleetwood, diary, September 27, 1864, to Thursday, September 29, 1864. In his small leather diary, Christian Fleetwood recorded having seen General Ulysses S. Grant and "other stars" and having "saved the colors," during the Battle of Chaffin's Farm, Virginia, on September 29, 1864, for which he was awarded the Congressional Medal of Honor.

Christian A. Fleetwood Papers, Manuscript Division.

assault. Afterward, as Thomas and his staff rode over the battlefield and saw numerous black bodies at the front lines, he paid African American soldiers the ultimate compliment: "Gentlemen, the question is settled. Negroes will fight."

By year's end the 25th Army Corps, made up of fourteen thousand troops (the Army of the James and the Army of the Potomac), was created as the war's largest single black military organization.[35]

African Americans increasingly displayed a sense of citizenship and political activism. Although

President Andrew Johnson. "Forty acres and a mule" became yet another in a cycle of broken promises to African Americans.[36]

1865: Our Peace Will Flow Like a River

"Some say there's no God in this war," one Union soldier remarked in early 1865, "but the hand of the Lord *is* in this war." Congress submitted the Thirteenth Amendment to the states for ratification in January 1865. Illinois was the first to ratify it (February 1, 1865), and Oregon, the

"◆ ◆ ◆ the hand of the Lord is in this war"

declared eligible for the draft in February 1864, most black soldiers voluntarily enlisted. A National Convention of Colored Men (144 delegates from eighteen states) met in September at Syracuse, New York, to demand slavery's abolishment and black voting rights. Lincoln, reelected in November for a second term and by then a staunch champion of black civil rights, supported a constitutional amendment abolishing slavery. The Senate approved the Thirteenth Amendment on April 8, 1864; the House of Representatives followed on January 31, 1865.

Freed slaves anticipated that their lack of property would be a major impediment to their postwar economic survival. Union General William T. Sherman's November—December "March to the Sea" campaign from Atlanta to Savannah, Georgia, designed to destroy the Confederacy's supplies, had the added outcome of freeing thousands of Georgia slaves, some of whom enlisted in the Union Army. Sherman, no friend of blacks or slaves, viewed his campaign strictly as a military means to quell Confederate resistance in Georgia. He issued Special Field Order No. 15 on January 16, 1865, chiefly to rid himself of the 20,000 black refugees following his army. This order reserved almost forty square miles of coastal Georgia and its Sea Islands for black settlement. Forty thousand black families each received forty acres as homesteads, but the land that they farmed and worked so hard was forcibly taken in March 1866 and returned to its original owners, who had been pardoned by

last (December 11, 1865). By February 1865 the state constitutions of Arkansas, Louisiana, Maryland, Missouri, and Tennessee abolished slavery. Significantly, three of these were ex-Confederate states that had agreed to do so under Lincoln's reconstruction plan, and the other two—Maryland and Missouri—were Union slave states. Practically everyone realized American slavery was in its final days.

Fulfillment of freed slaves' hopes that the federal government would distribute among them captured property that had formerly belonged to Confederate slaveholder— the forty acres and a mule—seemed possible under the Freedmen's Bureau. The bureau (formally, the Bureau of Refugees, Freedmen, and Abandoned Lands), established by Congress on March 3, 1865, had the responsibility of managing and protecting the civil rights of the freed persons, restoring civil law, organizing black labor, and distributing vacant property in the defeated South. It also helped and fed refugees of both races and provided health care and schools.[37]

As one of its last, desperate acts the Confederate Congress in late March approved the recruitment of black soldiers, but the measure was too little, too late, too implausible. Petersburg, Virginia, a major Confederate communications and railroad transportation link to Richmond, besieged by the Union Army for nine months, was evacuated on April 2, and among the first federal regiments to take possession of the city was the 116th U.S. Colored Troops. Union troops occupied Richmond the next day; the 36th USCT was the first regiment to enter the fallen Confederate capital. Thomas Morris Chester of the *Philadelphia Press,* one of the war's few accredited black journalists, described the reaction of Richmond slaves: "Nothing can exceed the rejoicing of the

Camp Lincoln
-1897-

Item 6-23
"Camp Lincoln, 1897."
Cabinet card. Gladstone Collection, Prints and Photographs Division.

Item 5-1
Alfred A. Waud, *Mustered Out*, 1865. Little Rock, Arkansas.
Prints and Photographs Division.

Negroes since the occupation of this city. The highest degree of happiness attainable upon earth is now being enjoyed by the colored people of this city. They all declare that they are abundantly able to take care of themselves."[38]

Lincoln visited Richmond and Petersburg and praised black soldiers. He promised them that their race would be "forever free," and slaves regarded his appearance as proof of their freedom. "I know that I am free," exclaimed one, "for I have seen Father Abraham and felt him." Lee's surrender of the Army of Northern Virginia at Appomattox on April 9 for all practical purposes ended armed Confederate resistance—and slavery. Despite this, 250 soldiers of the 62nd USCT participated in the war's last battle at Palmetto (Palmito) Ranch near Brownsville, Texas. Ironically, this battle, fought five weeks after Lee's surrender, was a Confederate victory.

In all, more than 185,000 African American soldiers (92,000 from the South), 30,000 sailors, and 400,000 free black and slave civilians risked their lives or freedom or both in the war. African Americans made up 10 percent of all Union armed forces. Officially, 166 black regiments (145 infantry, 13 heavy and light artillery, 7 cavalry, 1 engineer) served with the Union Army. Of 37,000 black casualties, 291 died as prisoners of war and another 3,000 fell in battle. The other 33,700 succumbed to sickness and disease.

The quiet courage and perseverance of black troops impressed their white commanding officers and Confederate foes alike.[39]

In this, the hour of their greatest triumph, blacks lost their most powerful defender. Lincoln's assassination on April 14, 1865, horrified and stunned African Americans, particularly slaves, for he, more than any other white man in America, was the basis of their future hopes and guarantor of their freedom. "We mourn the loss of our Noble Chief Executive," grieved army chaplain Leonard Chauncey. "We have looked to him as our earthly Pilot to guide us through this National Storm, and Plant us Securely on the Platform of Liberty, and Equal Political right . . . . Brave men weep for him, for he is no more." Another black soldier sorrowfully added, "Humanity has lost a firm advocate, our race its Patron Saint. Abraham Lincoln will ever be cherished in our hearts." Led by ex-Virginia slave Charlotte Scott, African Americans raised $20,000 for a national

"Emancipation" monument to Lincoln. Dedicated in 1876 in Lincoln Park in Washington, D.C., it depicted Lincoln and a rising slave together breaking the chains of bondage.[40]

The news of freedom took a long time reaching some areas of the former Confederacy. Slaves in Galveston, Texas, were officially informed of their freedom when Union General Gordon Granger publicly read the Emancipation Proclamation on June 19, 1865. They had been free in principle since January 1863, and in fact since the defeat of the Confederacy two months previously. "Juneteenth" became a regularly celebrated black event well into the twentieth century. When the Thirteenth Amendment was declared ratified on December 18, 1865, 250 years of black slavery finally ended in America. Poet Frances Ellen Watkins Harper celebrated by articulating her race's aspirations:

> God bless our native land,
> Land of the newly free,
> Oh may she ever stand,
> For truth and liberty.
> ◆◆◆◆◆◆◆◆◆◆◆◆◆
> God bless our native land,
> Her homes and children bless,
> Oh may she ever stand
> For truth and righteousness.[41]

African Americans had had more at stake in the war's outcome than any other ethnic group. Freedom and liberty were more than mere words to them, for in the conflict they risked losing both forever. Had the Confederacy prevailed, blacks—at least those in the South—would have had little hope for either, let alone for attaining civil rights.

The humanity, achievement, ability, and determination of African Americans proved the falseness of racism. Among the Union's most loyal and patriotic citizens, they participated actively in winning the victory. Frederick Douglass eloquently envisioned their next struggle in the construction of a new America: "I end where I began—no war but an Abolition war; no peace but an Abolition peace; liberty for all, chains for none; the black man a soldier in war, a laborer in peace; a voter at the South as well as the North; America his permanent home, and all Americans his fellow-countrymen, Such, fellow-citizens, is my idea of the mission of the war. If accomplished, our glory as a nation will be complete, our peace will flow like a river, and our foundations will be like the everlasting rocks."[42] African Americans embarked on a new future.

Item 5-22

Elizabeth White, *All God's Chillun's Got Wings!*

Soft-ground etching and aquatint, ca. 1933. Ben and Beatrice Goldstein Foundation
Collection, Prints and Photographs Division.

A man's position in life is not measured
by the heights which he has attained,
but by the depths from which he has come.

BOOKER T. WASHINGTON

4 Forty Acres and a Mule: Reconstruction and the Booker T. Washington Era

KENNETH MARVIN HAMILTON

We cannot fully appreciate the intellectual and material accomplishments of African Americans during the years between emancipation and World War I until we understand the adversities encountered by the vast majority of blacks during this era. Because our insight into these challenges is continuing to evolve as historians uncover more about the life experiences of African Americans, we can possess no more than an incomplete acknowledgment of the accomplishments of black people. The available information highlights many of the mammoth obstacles faced by African Americans in their struggle to enjoy a lifestyle parallel to that of most other American citizens. We therefore must judge the lives of blacks living in pre–World War I post-emancipation years in the manner advocated by Booker T. Washington, who asserted that "success is to be measured not so much by the position that one has reached in life, as by the obstacles which he has overcome while trying to succeed."[1] Given the historical reality, it is remarkable that so many African Americans achieved such extraordinary accomplishments.

These successes occurred even though the struggle for economic mobility and security, more than anything else, defined and constrained the life of African Americans during the "Era of Booker T. Washington." Much of America's white society, including the federal government, politically and socially repressed black people. Economic constraints created by the nation's white population, however, produced the most devastating effect on the lives of black people. Throughout the pre-World War I years of freedom, blacks simultaneously suffered from many forms of oppression, but none of them made life for blacks as difficult as their inability to secure an above-poverty-level income and accumulate a measurable amount of wealth.

During the years of enslavement, whites controlled and predetermined the amount of prosperity for the vast majority of blacks. After the Civil War several federal laws altered the economic relationship between blacks and whites. On December 18, 1865, the nation abolished slavery with the ratification of the Thirteenth Amendment to the Constitution. More than a year later, March 2, 1867, the U.S. Congress enacted the first of four reconstruction acts. These statutes allowed black men living in southern states to vote and exercise rights as U.S. citizens.

The laws did not provide African Americans with a means to improve their economic conditions, however. Blacks throughout the slaveholding states (the political South) still suffered considerable deprivation. Although emancipation allowed the ex-slaves (freedmen) the ability to enjoy a greater portion of the profits made by their labor, legal, social, and institutional restrictions minimized their potential rewards. African Americans suffered during the first few months of freedom from the constraints produced by the U.S. Supreme Court's 1857 *Dred Scott v. Sanford* decree, in which the Court declared that African Americans possessed no U.S. citizenship rights. The ruling allowed state governments to restrict money-making opportunities for the freedmen. South Carolina, for example, enacted laws that prohibited freedpeople from certain occupations, and Mississippi denied them the right to purchase land.

The *Dred Scott* decree remained the law of the land until the April 9, 1866, enactment of the nation's first civil rights law. Two years later, the nation made the citizenship of black people a constitutional provision with the July 1868 ratification of the Fourteenth Amendment. This addition to the Constitution ensured that blacks would enjoy, with European Americans, equal

legal recognition. None of the federal laws, though, provided blacks with anything other than personal freedom and statutory equality. They failed to furnish the freedpeople with any money, land, or means to make a living in postslavery America.

Some southern blacks began the fight for economic autonomy as early as November 1861, on the islands off the coast of South Carolina and Georgia. When the U.S. armed forces liberated the area's islands, they found a community of black people living in a well-ordered society.

State of South Carolina certificate of appointment of Francis L. Cardoza as state treasurer, December 12, 1868.
Manuscript Division.

In fleeing the onslaught of the federal government, their former masters deserted the old, sick, and very young bondsmen. The abandoned African Americans, who maintained stable cooperative communities, rationed dwindling food supplies and continued to cultivate an impressive cotton crop. The federal government ended the black islanders' dream of economic freedom, however, and took control of both the labor of the ex-slaves and their cotton crop.

In addition to inhibiting the economic activities of the black islanders, the federal government, before the cessation of the fighting, regulated the labor of thousands of blacks living in territories liberated from rebellious forces. For much of the Civil War, the federal government labeled and treated those blacks freed during the years preceding the surrender of the Confederacy as contraband of war.

As such, they became wards of the government. During the hostilities, the Union government, like that of its southern counterpart, used blacks as both warriors and laborers. Although no more than a few thousands blacks served in the Confederacy home-guard militias and armed forces, tens of thousands of African Americans fought in the federal army and navy for less pay than that received by their white counterparts. The U.S. government also employed large numbers of freedmen who did not serve in the military as noncombat laborers. These workers too received lower pay than their white counterparts.

The vast majority of blacks, even after the issuing of the Emancipation Proclamation on January 1, 1863, remained enslaved and under the domination of their masters until the end of the war. Whereas bondsmen held by former Confederates received the possession of themselves on or before June 19, 1865 (the day that the federal government declared slaves in Texas free), many did not secure legal freedom until the December 1865 enactment of the Thirteenth Amendment to the Constitution.

The new law did not provide the freed African Americans with opportunities to pursue economic self-determination. The nation still had not settled the question of what kinds of liberties the United States would extend to the freedmen. The April 14, 1865, assassination of President Abraham Lincoln increased the uncertainty concerning the status of freedmen. Before the war, Lincoln did not adhere to abolitionism (a belief in the eradication of slavery in all areas of the nation); he instead advocated the principles of free-soil (a belief in using nonslave laborers and containing the territorial growth of slavery). During his years as president, he considered relocating the freedmen outside of the United States. After he realized the impracticality of this idea, he attempted to persuade pro-Union governments in the several ex-Confederate states to grant blacks improved economic opportunities by providing them equal citizenship rights—an effort that met with little success. His successor, Andrew Johnson, a pro-Unionist former slaveholder from Tennessee, made no serious attempt to improve the financial lot of southern African Americans.

The U.S. Congress made the first comprehensive attempt to establish a policy that would address the issue of the economic freedom of the ex-slaves by enacting the Bureau of Refugees, Freedmen, and Abandoned Lands (Freedmen's Bureau) on March 3, 1865. This law provided the Freedmen's Bureau with the authority to control every aspect of the civic lives of four million ex-slaves. The agency legally married freedmen, secured and supervised wage work for them, established schools for freed children, dispensed justice in legal cases concerning freedmen, and regulated the commercial life of freedmen.

Because Congress gave Bureau officials the power to frame labor agreements and compel the respective parties to honor them, Freedmen's agents occupied most of their time overseeing labor contracts and disagreements between former slaves and landowners. An agent in Texas, for example, proclaimed that his work included mainly "settling difficulties between the freedpeople and their employers, explaining away doubtful points in contracts, and giving instruction and advice to freed people."

Top management of the Bureau restricted money-making opportunities of the freedpeople by strongly encouraging them to commit to year-long contracts, reflecting the prevailing skepticism among whites concerning the dependability of free blacks as laborers. Until the time limits of these contracts expired, blacks could not legally move from one employer to another in their search for better working conditions or higher pay. Most supporters of slavery and many champions of free labor doubted that blacks would work without compulsion. Throughout the early months of Reconstruction, employers in the South, as well as federal authorities, often complained about ex-slaves leaving their employers before the completion of the harvest. In addition, white farmers and plantation owners grumbled about the quality of work produced by the freedpeople. Most often employers protested the freedpeople's refusal to labor at one or more parenthetically agricultural chores (such as repairing fences or other like tasks) for no additional compensation.

In theory, the contractual labor agreements should have helped lessen freedpeople's anxieties about pay and the employers' concern with the freedpeople's work discipline. These documents stipulated what employers expected from the laborers and the type and amount of wages to be given to the worker. In effect, however, these agreements guaranteed that landholders would enjoy long-term dependable labor and ensured the laborers fair wages. Often, however, the employers cheated their workers.

Enslavement had taught blacks not to trust southern landowners, and most of their post-emancipation experiences reinforced that lesson. Freedpeople primarily wanted cash for their contract labor. Throughout the pre-World War I post-Civil War era, however, most southern land-

Item 5-5
James E. Taylor, "Glimpses of the Freedmen—The Freedmen's Union Industrial School, Richmond, Va.,"
from Frank *Leslie's Illustrated Newspaper,* September 22, 1866.
Wood engraving. Prints and Photographs Division.

holders had little currency to pay out. The consequences of the war, including limited access to northern and foreign capital markets, destruction of manufactories and staple crops, and the freeing of slaves, along with white racist practices and unfair social and financial institutions, caused many of the cash flow problems.

Realizing that most southern employers suffered a real cash shortage, the federal government strongly encouraged the freedpersons to work for a share of the crop instead. Evidence of this practice occurred even before the end of the war. On May 15, 1865, the commander of the Army of Ohio, stationed in Raleigh, North Carolina, declared that if employers could not pay cash wages, black employees "ought to be contented with a fair share in the crops to be raised."[2]

Throughout the Booker T. Washington era the federal government, especially during the first few years after emancipation, maintained two pressing reasons for wanting year-long contracts between landowners and black workers. First, it wanted to minimize the number of African Americans on the dole, and second—and more significant—it desired the production of a large cotton crop. In an effort to pay off some of its war debt, the federal government placed a 2.5- to 3-cent tax on each pound of cotton sold during the first three years following the close of the Civil War. The drive to keep African Americans in the fields partly mirrored the federal authorities' desire to quickly pay back loans made during the war. Afterward, the nation's balance of trade substantially benefited from the international sale of the crop. Throughout the pre-1920, post-Civil War years, the value of cotton that Americans sold on the international market exceeded that of all other exports.

The producers of this important American crop, including both large and small cotton farmers, liked the idea of paying their hired laborers with shares of the harvest. During the first few years after slavery, employers continued, as they had during the years of slavery, to work the freedmen in groups. By the early 1870s, employers found it more profitable and satisfying to divide their holdings into plots of 20 to 100 acres and hire complete family groups to cultivate each subdivision. The landowners and the workers called this arrangement *sharecropping,* and labeled the smaller tracts of land worked by the cropper as

one-mule parcels and the larger tracks as two-mule plots. In 1900, the vast majority of blacks working other people's land received some or all of their wages in "shares." This form of deferred compensation constituted a no-interest loan to the employer, which is nothing less than worker exploitation. Year long contracts, moreover, denied farm laborers the right to relocate to a better paying job, and far too often landowners cheated workers out of their fair share. Regardless of the disadvantage to laborers, sharecropping arrangements between employee and employer remained common until the mid-1950s. From that time onward, mechanization, which became the principal means of cultivating cotton and other sable crops, greatly lessened the demand for African American farm labor.

Financial, social, and political forces combined to restrict the majority of African Americans to cotton farming. The South possessed few jobs apart from farming, and white racial-based discrimination, in general, did not allow blacks to compete for them. At the same time, northern industrialists preferred European immigrant laborers. Thus blacks possessed little financial motivation to move out of the South. In 1900, 80 to 90 percent of African Americans continued to live in the area.

Two-thirds of all southerners depended on farming for their livelihood. That population included four-fifths of the area's black residents. For a multiplicity of reasons, including the high cost of credit in the region and the populace's inefficient and backward agricultural practices, the South suffered slow economic growth. Responding to institutional pressures, primarily local country merchants, southerners depressed the world market for staple crops that they produced, especially cotton.

The people of the South used antiquated and unenlightened farming methods, for the most part. Having even less access to capital, credit, and new farming methods than their white counterparts, blacks engaged in the most backward farming techniques. Not until the late 1800s did southern farmers use a system of crop rotation to restore the nutrients in their lands. Because few of them placed their farm animals in stalls, southern farmers did not collect and spread manure. They instead used commercial fertilizers to maintain the productivity of their farms, which increased the farmers' expenses and reduced net income.

More blacks worked in the nation's cotton fields than at any other occupation. Although the evidence indicated that more whites than blacks grew the crop, most Americans, throughout the life of Booker T. Washington, associated black labor with agricultural work, especially cotton production. This relationship inspired William H. Baldwin, Jr., the Long Island Railroad president in the late

Clarence Cameron White, "From the Cotton Fields, for Violin, with Pianoforte Accompaniment"
(New York, Boston, Chicago: Carl Fischer, ca. 1920).
Sheet music, dedicated to Fritz Kreisler. Music Division.

1890s, to make the exaggerated statement that only blacks and mules produced cotton in America.[3]

Black farmers, like most southern agrarians, owned few tools and implements. They possessed primarily out-of-date simple equipment. Most blacks owned one or more hoes. Some, but not all, possessed one-mule plows. Only the exceptional black farmers owned a mechanized implement such as a cotton gin, reaper, or mower.

Although 90 percent of black farm operators owned some kind of animal, many of them did not own any draft stock. About 80 percent of black farm households possessed poultry. Two-thirds owned one or more swine, which accounted for more than 66 percent of all domestic animals owned by black southern farmers. Fewer than 50 percent of African American agrarians possessed one or more cows. The same percentage held true for those who owned mules and horses. White landholders claimed most of the draft stock used by blacks.

Whites also owned most of the land farmed by African Americans, and many of them, throughout the pre-World War I post-emancipation era, refused to sell property to blacks. Many whites wanted the African American population to remain a dependable and inexpensive source of labor. A large number of whites alleged that black land ownership would increase the cost of labor and undermine white supremacy. Therefore, when those few whites who wanted to sell land to blacks revealed their intentions, they risked the wrath of their white neighbors. In numerous cases, whites who sold land to blacks suffered community sanctions that ranged from ostracism to violence. Resistance to blacks buying land lessened, however, after lower staple crop prices, especially for cotton, significantly decreased land values.

As agrarians, blacks understood the independence and financial rewards that owners of farmlands enjoyed. Over time, a growing number of blacks did purchase land, mostly small plots that were marginally fertile. A few freedmen had earned and saved enough money while in bondage to purchase real estate after slavery ended. A much larger group, but still an insignificant number of ex-slaves, secured land grants from the U.S. government. Other blacks bought property with money that the federal government paid to former soldiers or the relatives of deceased service-men for joining the Union army during the Civil War. The largest

group of African American landowners procured land with credit extended to them by white landholders. By 1880, African Americans owned almost 10 percent of all the cultivated land in the South. More than 190,000 blacks, or 25 percent of all African American southern farmers owned their land in 1900. In total they held 15,976,098 acres, or 24,963 square miles.

On the other hand, 75 percent of black farm operators did not own the land that they cultivated. White people living in the South controlled unenlightened economic institutions that, more so than their individual racist practices, created a financial reality that prevented most black farm operators from purchasing land. The crop-line system and the small country store are cases in point. After the Civil War, local merchants replaced the large cotton brokers. Being small and undercapitalized, northern lenders and wholesalers assessed the retailers a high interest rate for materials that they purchased on credit. They in turn charged the farmers, who rarely had money for most of the year, let alone an additional twenty to sixty cents in interest for every dollar's worth of goods bought on credit.

To help ensure that the merchant received remuneration, southern states enacted crop-line laws. In most instances, these laws gave the merchant first claim to the farmer's crop. At the end of the harvest, before the farmer could sell any of his crop, the store owner took a portion of the harvest equivalent in value to the debt owed. Many times the merchant overcharged the farmers.

Making matters worst, during most of the pre-1915 era, cotton prices remained low. Too many people harvested too much cotton. Thus cultivation of staple crops, particularly cotton, limited the amount of money that black farmers could hope to make. As a consequence, the region suffered the highest poverty rate in the nation.

People living in the South made far less money than those living outside of the region. Although southerners produced an excess of 10 million bales of cotton in 1900, more than twice the size of the largest pre-Civil War harvest, per capita income remained almost flat. Residents of the major cotton-producing states in 1900, for example, made just 50 percent of the per capita income earned by non-southerners. People living in the states of Louisiana, Arkansas, Mississippi, and Georgia, made no more money per person in 1900 then they had in 1840.[4]

Although southerners, both black and white, suffered a stagnant economy, northerners, primarily whites, experienced unprecedented prosperity. At no time in the history of the nation did so many Americans gain so much wealth. In 1892, for example, John D. Rockefeller had a net worth of more than $800 million. Nine years later, the investment group headed by J. P. Morgan paid Andrew

Carnegie a quarter of a billion dollars for his share of Carnegie Steel.

Although few Americans secured wealth that approximated that of Rockefeller, Morgan, or Carnegie, countless other non-southerners enjoyed very prosperous lives. The increases in the urban middle-class (clerical workers, salespeople, government employees, technicians, and salaried professionals) both produced and mirrored an unprecedented rise of income for ordinary Americans. This group experienced unparalleled growth in its membership. Most of the wealth came from America's growing industrialization and for the most part occurred in the North. This area led the nation in the number and size of manufactories and in trading enterprises and financial institutions.

Virtually every nationally renown industrialist, merchandiser, manager, and capitalist resided in the North. Such noted manufactures as Carnegie, Cyrus McCormick, and Rockefeller lived there. Leading merchants, including, John Wanamaker, Henry Spiegel, and Marshall Field lived north of the Ohio River. J. Pierpont Morgan, Levi Parsons Morton, George Bliss, and all other major financiers called the North home. Moreover, the top managers of almost all national corporations inhabited one of the northern states. In addition, in 1890, the residents of the North produced more than 85 percent of the goods manufactured in the nation. Twenty years later, they accounted for 75 percent of all agricultural wage earners in America.

The South possessed only a fraction of the nation's economic infrastructure. Railroad companies, in 1880, had located fewer than 16 percent of their total track mileage in the South. Ten years later, the area had only 39,000 of the nation's 166,000 miles of tracks. In 1890, the area's residents produced only one fifth of the pig iron in the nation. People in the region made a better showing in the production of cigarettes and cotton cloth—the most important refined product in the South. In 1900, textile industries in southern states led the nation in the manufacturing of cloth. Using only a few African American workers, they produced 60 percent of America's cotton cloth. Because the firms located in the area rarely fabricated finished nonagricultural goods, southerners possessed only 10 percent of the total value of America's industrial base, and southerners owned a mere 11 percent of the country's capital.

Blacks, the poorest of the poor, suffered considerably under the burden of the South's restricted economy. Although African American farmers increased their standard of living in freedom from what they had during slavery, most of them lived in abject poverty. For the entire period, African American farm workers made from eight to twelve dollars a week. Their meager incomes inspired them to retain a basic diet similar to the one most slaves ate, consisting primarily of corn and fat meat. For a few months a year, those lucky enough to have a garden supplemented their meals with vegetables and fruits.

African Americans' limited income did not allow them to buy adequate clothing or secure good housing. To save money, parents often allowed children to go without shoes for much of the year. Many in the deep South permitted their offspring as old as young teenagers to wear only a long shirt-like garment or nothing at all during the summer months. These youngsters and their parents lived in housing just a little better than the shelter they endured during enslavement. Most African Americans did not own the housing that they inhabited. Their employers or landlords held ownership, and they either did not care about the conditions or they could not afford to make the needed repairs. During the early postslavery years, a typical house was nothing more than a poorly built fourteen-by-sixteen-foot one-room, dirt-floor log cabin. Later, many landowners either improved the dwellings or allowed the farm workers to do so. Most often someone added a plank floor and an additional room.

Poor diets, inadequate clothing, and squalid housing increased the rate of bad health among southern African Americans. More often than their white counterparts, blacks suffered typhoid, malaria, smallpox, scarlet fever, diphtheria, yellow fever, measles, tuberculosis, and pneumonia. These diseases were contracted most often by persons living in crowded filthy conditions associated with poverty.

Severe ill-health contributed substantially to the relatively high mortality rates of southern African Americans. So many black men had died prematurely by 1890 that 25 percent of all African American women over the age of fifteen lived as widows. These early deaths further hampered the chances of a sizable number of black people improving their material status. Because most black families consisted of six or more children, widowed mothers had extraordinary burdens in caring for their large families as single parents.

Poverty, along with hostility and indifference by the government of several southern states, restricted the educational opportunities of blacks. During 1900, more than 32 percent of African American children between the ages of ten and fourteen years of age did not attend school.

Item 6-18
Photographer unknown. "24th Infantry Leaving Salt Lake City, Utah, for Chattanooga, Tennessee," April 24, 1898.
Gladstone Collection, Prints and Photographs Division.

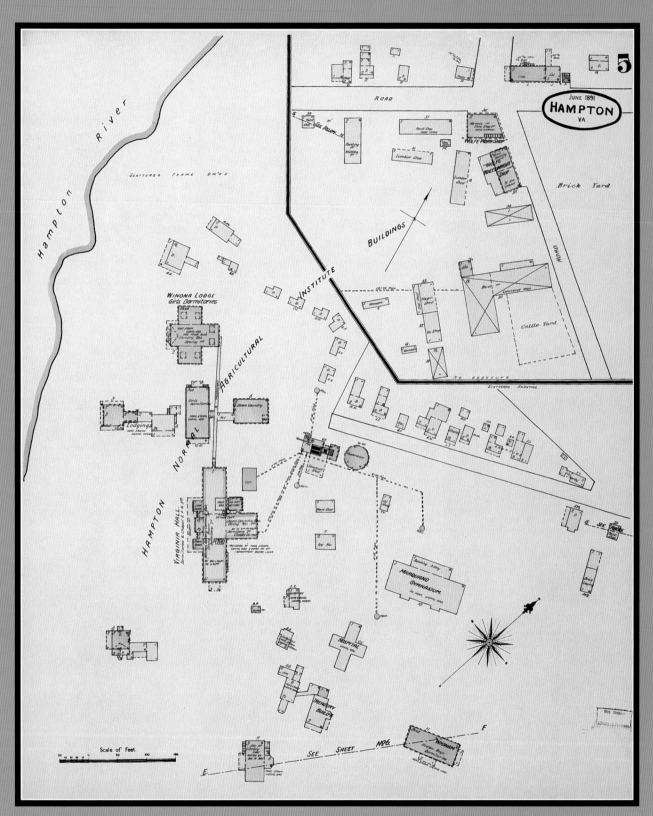

Item 6-4, sheet 5 (above)
Hampton Normal and Agricultural Institute, Elizabeth City
County, Virginia. New York: Sanborn Perris Map Co., 1891.
Hand-colored lithograph. Geography and Map Division.

Item 6-8 (right)
National Negro Committee platform, adopted 1909.
National Association for the Advancement of Colored People (NAACP) Collection,
Manuscript Division.

NATIONAL NEGRO COMMITTEE

500 FIFTH AVENUE

NEW YORK

Platform Adopted by the National Negro Committee, 1909

We denounce the ever-growing oppression of our 10,000,000 colored fellow citizens as the greatest menace that threatens the country. Often plundered of their just share of the public funds, robbed of nearly all part in the government, segregated by common carriers, some murdered with impunity, and all treated with open contempt by officials, they are held in some States in practical slavery to the white community. The systematic persecution of law-abiding citizens and their disfranchisement on account of their race alone is a crime that will ultimately drag down to an infamous end any nation that allows it to be practiced, and it bears most heavily on those poor white farmers and laborers whose economic position is most similar to that of the persecuted race.

The nearest hope lies in the immediate and patiently continued enlightenment of the people who have been inveigled into a campaign of oppression. The spoils of persecution should not go to enrich any class or classes of the population. Indeed persecution of organized workers, peonage, enslavement of prisoners, and even disfranchisement already threaten large bodies of whites in many Southern States.

We agree fully with the prevailing opinion that the transformation of the unskilled colored laborers in industry and agriculture into skilled workers is of vital importance to that race and to the ration, but we demand for the Negroes, as for all others, a free and complete education, whether by city, State or nation, a grammar school and industrial training for all and technical, professional, and academic education for the most gifted.

But the public schools assigned to the Negro of whatever kind or grade will never receive a fair and equal treatment until he is given equal treatment in the Legislature and before the law. Nor will the practically educated Negro, no matter how valuable to the community he may prove, be given a fair return for his labor or encouraged to put forth his best efforts or given the chance to develop that efficiency that comes only outside the school until he is respected in his legal rights as a man and a citizen.

We regard with grave concern the attempt manifest South and North to deny black men the right to work and to enforce this demand by violence and bloodshed. Such a question is too fundamental and clear even to be submitted to arbitration. The late strike in Georgia is not simply a demand that Negroes be displaced, but that proven and efficient men be made to surrender their long-followed means of livelihood to white competitors.

As first and immediate steps toward remedying these national wrongs, so full of peril for the whites as well as the blacks of all sections, we demand of Congress and the Executive:

(1). That the Constitution be strictly enforced and the civil rights guaranteed under the Fourteenth Amendment be secured impartially to all.

(2). That there be equal educational opportunities for all and in all the States, and that public school expenditure be the same for the Negro and white child:

(3). That in accordance with the Fifteenth Amendment the right of the Negro to the ballot on the same terms as other citizens be recognized in every part of the country.

I herewith subscribe $_____ to the National Negro Committee, and desire to become a

member of the permanent organization growing out of the present Conference.

(Make checks payable to Oswald G. Villard, Treasurer).

Of those who did, they most often studied in a rundown log cabin. Even blacks who attended class in a well-built structure received instruction for only four or fewer months per year.

Many times during the era of Booker T. Washington, black farmers took a major risk if they outwardly improved their material lot. It was

Item 5-16

"I Am the Door." From *Songs of the Jubilee Singers from Fisk University* (Cincinnati: John Church & Co., 1881). A series of tours, beginning in 1871 to raise money for the university chartered in 1867, by the Fisk Jubilee Singers was instrumental in the spread of spirituals throughout the United States, to Great Britain in 1873–74, to Europe in 1875–78, and around the world, with a world tour in 1884. Publications spread the spirituals in print. On the cover of this sheet music is Jubilee Hall, the first permanent new building of Fisk University, which was built with money raised by the Jubilee Singers.

Sheet music cover. Music Division.

not unusual for southern white people to take hostile action against prosperous African Americans. This occurred in 1904 in the southern Mississippi county of Lincoln. White terrorists, using the threat of bodily harm, forced a black man who owned 1,500 acres to sell his land and relocate his family. A large number of murders, or lynchings, resulted from the efforts of whites to appropriate the

wealth of African Americans. Hard financial times inspired whites to increase the lynching of blacks. During the economic depression of the 1890s, on average white southerners lynched one African American every two and a half days.

Although these realities disheartened thousands of black people, countless others prospered. Many of the individuals who markedly improved their quality of life found guidance and inspiration from the proclamations of Booker T. Washington and other black spokespersons. Washington and others attempted to teach black people a lifestyle that they believed would produce a more comfortable existence. With the assistance of white philanthropists and missionaries, late nineteenth- and early twentieth-century black social activists encouraged and enabled thousands of African Americans to achieve both material and intellectual advancement.

Perhaps no person spent more time and energy in this noble effort than Booker T. Washington. Even his most renown adversary William E. B. DuBois credited Washington for his success at inspiring blacks to improve and increase their "economic development" and "technical education."[5] Washington's philosophy partly reflected a rational interpretation of the economic events of his era. He asserted that, more so than anything else, hard intelligent work, coupled with thrift and moral living, would provide African Americans with substantial increased prosperity and status.

Although he gave as many as two thousand speeches in his lifetime, Washington was a builder of institutions and organizations and not just a social preacher. He and his subordinates built the world-famous Tuskegee Institute, which provided teacher education and trade training to hundreds of young blacks. He assisted with or directly inspired the establishment of dozens of primary schools and several institutes for the teaching of teachers (normal institutes) and dozens of primary schools. In 1892, Washington organized the annual Tuskegee Negro Conference and commissioned the creation of similar gatherings in several other southern states. These two-day meetings allowed delegates to discuss the nature of life conditions of African Americans living in their respective locales while learning of simple realistic ways of improving their lives. Eight years after the first Negro Conference, Washington established the National Negro Business League. The League inspired the creation of the National Negro Bankers Association, National Negro Insurance Association, National Negro Funeral Directors, National Negro Press Association, and National Negro Bar Association. In addition, he published twelve books, countless articles, and two Tuskegee Institute newspapers.

Item 6-10B
Photographer unknown, "A Man Was Lynched Yesterday," flag flying from NAACP Headquarters, 69 Fifth Avenue in New York City, to report lynchings, until, in 1938, the threat of losing its lease forced the association to discontinue the practice.
Gelatin silver print. NAACP Collection, Prints and Photographs Division.

Item 6-24

A horse-drawn carriage pulls up in front of Dr. MacDougald's Drug Store. Georgia, ca. 1900.

W. E. B. DuBois Collection, Prints and Photographs Division.

He supplemented these efforts by distributing an untold number of press releases.

These endeavors promoted and assisted blacks in their efforts to attain a better material life. In addition to securing 10 percent of the land in the southern states, African Americans made other noted achievements. By 1915, blacks and their white supporters had established six high schools, fifty colleges, twenty-six schools of theology, three schools of law, four schools of medicine, two schools of dentistry, three schools of pharmacy, and hundreds of normal and industrial schools for African American students. These academies were responsible in great part for the marked increase in black literacy, which increased from 25 percent in the 1870s to 60 percent in 1890. Blacks made similar gains in their business pursuits. By 1915, African Americans owned 51 banks, 695 pharmacies, approximately 1,000 mortuaries, 240 wholesalers, and 25,000 retailers.

Although thousands of blacks internalized the concept of self-help and entrepreneurship and met with varied degrees of success, the mass of blacks remained destitute. Only the mass relocation of blacks to the political North enabled a large number of southern African Americans to improve their material lives. Approximately 1.5 million left the South for the industrial Midwest and Northeast during the years of World War I. Northern manufactures needed manual workers. They had met their labor needs previously by employing millions of European immigrants, but the war had all but stopped their migration. Black southerners replaced them, and blacks continued to move North in large numbers until the 1980s. Within a sixty-five-year time span more than 5.5 million would move from the ex-slave states to the political North.

This massive migration of African Americans to the North reduced the pool of cheap laborers available in the South. Fearing a serious labor shortage, white landowners and politicians temporarily lessened their social repression of blacks. They also increased wages for those African Americans who remained in the South. Only in the North, however, did southern African Americans enjoy a significant improvement of their long-term material well-being.

Item 8-1 3

William H. Johnson, *Training for War,* ca. 1941. Painter and printmaker William H. Johnson executed a series on African American soldiers during World War II, showing daily life in camp and activities of Red Cross nurses and doctors.

Screen print. Harmon Foundation Collection, Prints and Photographs Division.

They felt dying stateside was just as good, if not preferable, to dying on foreign soil. Moreover, they didn't give a damn about military careers. It boiled down to this: All they had to lose was their lives.

COLONEL HOWARD DONOVAN QUEEN

5 " If We Must Die": African Americans in the World Wars

CHARLES JOHNSON, JR.

Congressional legislation passed in 1866 reorganized the military and permitted the first enlistment of African Americans into the Regular Army. Serving in units that became the 9th Cavalry, the 10th Cavalry, and the 24th Infantry and 25th Infantry Regiments, together with the Seminole-Negro Indian Scout Detachment, African Americans served with distinction on the western frontier where they protected settlers, guarded stagecoach and freight transportation, fought outlaws, and joined campaigns against Native Americans. The cavalry and infantry units rendered valuable service in Cuba during the Spanish-American War, and the cavalry units participated in the Philippine Insurrection. Their participation in the world wars continued the military legacy of African Americans.[1]

The assassination of the heir to the Austro-Hungarian throne in June 1914 at Sarajevo, Serbia, unleashed the confrontations between the Triple Alliance—Germany, Austria, and Italy—and the Triple Entente—Great Britain, France, and Russia—that started World War I. As expansion of hostilities brought other European nations into the conflict, Italy defected to the Triple Entente, which became the Allied Powers, and the Triple Alliance became the Central Powers. Declaring neutrality, the United States attempted to maintain cordial diplomatic relations with all belligerent nations, and President Woodrow Wilson tried to persuade them to terminate their activities and negotiate for peace. Modern technology—use of poison gas, the introduction of tank and air warfare, the expanded use of submarine warfare—was causing tremendous loss of life. Submarine warfare affected American shipping and on May 1, 1915, the American merchant ship *Gulflight* was destroyed, followed a week later by the loss of the British liner *Lusitania,* where 128 Americans were among the 1,198 passengers who lost their lives.[2] With the passage of the National Defense Act of 1916, the United States authorized the expansion of peacetime Regular Army strength to 175,000 over a period of five years and a wartime army strength of nearly 300,000. The National Guard responded to the president's call and strengthened its numbers to 400,000. The legislation also established an Officers Reserve Corps, an Enlisted Reserve Corps, and a Volunteer Army to be raised during wartime. Colleges and universities were to provide military instruction through the Reserve Officer Corps Training program.

Implementation of this legislation affected African Americans serving in the several segregated units—the 9th Cavalry Regiment assigned to Camp Stotsenburg in Luzon, Philippine Islands; the 10th Cavalry Regiment at Fort Huachuca, Arizona; the 25th Infantry Regiment stationed at Scholfield Barracks in Hawaii (later transferred to Camp Stephen Little in Arizona to patrol the Mexican border with the 10th Cavalry); and the 24th Infantry Regiment. The 24th Infantry was located at Fort Furlong near Columbus, New Mexico, but its 1st Battalion was stationed at Waco, Texas, the 2nd Battalion at Dennin, New Mexico, and the 3rd Battalion at Logan Camp near Houston, Texas. These four regiments had been organized under military legislation enacted by Congress in 1866 and were usually referred to as the Buffalo Soldiers.

African Americans recruited to serve in segregated National Guard infantry units also felt the effects of the National Defense Act. Assigned to units usually designated as separate organizations, they served in the 1st Separate Companies of Connecticut, Maryland, Massachusetts, and Tennessee, 1st Separate District of Columbia Battalion, the 9th Ohio Battalion, the 8th Illinois Regiment, and the 15th New York Regiment. For

African American commissioned officers in companies, the highest possible rank was captain, in battalions, major, and in regiments, colonel.[3]

Many African Americans who were interested in the mobilization of the armed forces were eager to receive military training. The fourteen Plattsburg camps, for instance, offered training to white businessmen and students seeking commissions, but denied admission to African Americans. In response, African American recruits formed the Central Committee of Negro College Men, consisting of students and graduates from Howard University, Lincoln University in Pennsylvania, Atlanta University, Morehouse College, Morgan College, Virginia Union University, and Fisk University, as well as Brown, Columbia, Harvard, and Yale Universities. The Central Committee, with the assistance of Joel E. Spingarn of the National Association for the Advancement of Colored People (NAACP), petitioned the War Department for equal officer training for African Americans. General Leonard Wood supported Spingarn's effort, and on April 19, 1917, a separate Reserve Officer's Training Camp was authorized for applicants from the ages of twenty-four to forty. Under a plan approved by Major General Tasker H. Bliss, assistant to the chief of staff, the War Department planned to train 1,250 black men, recruiting 1,000 from civilian volunteers and mobilized National Guard units. The remaining 250 came from four Regular Army units—the 9th and 10th Cavalry Regiments and the 24th and 25th Infantry Regiments. On June 15, 1917, the first candidates began their training at Fort Des Moines in Iowa. The program commissioned 639 officers who were assigned to training camps. College students were unhappy that the Iowa location prevented their participation in the officers' training program, but many joined the Student Army Training Corps (SATC). An instructional summer camp was organized at Howard University on July 16, 1917, for students and college officials, who then returned to their institutions to form SATC units.[4]

After the United States declared war on Germany on April 6, 1917, many African Americans were eager to enlist, but the War Department issued an order terminating their recruitment after 4,000 volunteers had filled vacancies in the Regular Army's African American units. When the Selective Service Act of May 1917 required the registration of all men between the ages of twenty-one and thirty, local draft boards registered 2,291,000 African American men. Of these, the army drafted 346,410 into the armed forces by the end of the war, which represented 13 percent of all draftees. In southern states, local draft boards refused to grant deferments to African Americans and administered selection systems that tended to draft a higher percentage

Item 6-17
Charles Barthelmess, "Buffalo Soldiers," 25th Infantry, Fort Keogh, Missouri. Thirty-eight soldiers were photographed here, some wearing the buffalo robes for which the soldiers in the 25th Infantry were named.
Cabinet card. Gladstone Collection, Prints and Photographs Division.

of African Americans. African American draftees represented 34.1 percent of the total induced, compared with 24.04 percent of all white men who were registered for the draft. Major General Bliss on August 1, 1917, planned the use of 45,000 African American recruits in sixteen new infantry regiments and assigned the remainder of the initial draftees to special units to serve as support personnel, working as bakers, drivers, and laborers. In many instances, assigned duties did not correspond to the civilian professions or skilled occupations of the African American soldiers.[5]

The sixteen new regiments were never formed, however, because of the difficulty of locating southern camps where combat units could be deployed. White residents who feared the presence of armed African American soldiers opposed the camps. War Department officials had experienced similar problems in locating camps for African American National Guard units. An incident that illustrates negative attitudes occurred in Houston, Texas, on August 23, 1917, and involved Private Alonso Edwards and Corporal Charles Baltimore, both African Americans. Private Edwards, assigned to the Third Battalion of the 24th Infantry Regiment stationed at Camp Logan near Houston, intervened to prevent local police officers from assaulting an African American woman, and Corporal Baltimore in his capacity as a noncommissioned military police officer approached the local officers to inquire about the incident. Both Edwards and Baltimore were assaulted. When information of the attacks reached Camp Logan, several soldiers with rifles marched to the city seeking revenge, and after a brief confrontation sixteen whites, including four police officers and four soldiers, were killed. The Army held three courts-martial between November 1917 and March 1918. In *U.S. v. Sgt. William C. Nesbit et al.*, sixty-three defendants were charged with mutiny, murder, and felonious assault, and when *U.S. v. Cpl. Robert Tillman et al.* was conducted, forty additional soldiers were incriminated. *U.S. v. Cpl. John Washington* was convened to judge fifteen members of the Camp Logan guard who abandoned their posts, acts that ultimately resulted in the death of a bus driver. The courts-martial of Nesbit and Tillman convicted ninety-five defendants, imposing twenty-four death sentences, fifty-three life sentences, and eighteen prison sentences ranging from two to fifteen years. Seven

defendants were acquitted on insufficient evidence and one was released from arraignment because of insanity. The *Washington* trial convicted all fifteen defendants, sentencing five to death and ten to sentences ranging from seven to ten years. Details of the *Nesbit* court martial were not made public until after the secret executions on December 13, 1917. Neither President Woodrow Wilson nor Secretary of War Newton D. Baker were given the opportunity to review the sentences, because military law authorized the corps area commander to act as the final authority in time of war. The battalion was disarmed and transferred to Camp Furlong, New Mexico.[6]

The records of the courts-martial did not reach the Judge Advocate General's Office for legal review until three months after the initial thirteen executions. Provost Marshal General (PMG) Enoch Crowder issued General Order Number Seven, which prohibited the execution of death sentences until they were reviewed and upheld by the president. PMG Crowder may have been motivated by the fear of a congressional investigation that would have resulted in the creation of a civilian court of appeals concerning court-martial decisions. After the submission of a petition by the NAACP to President Wilson in February 1918 for clemency and acting on the recommendation of Secretary of War Baker who believed the real source of trouble in Houston was the enforcement of Jim Crow laws, President Wilson commuted ten sentences to life imprisonment but six others were executed. Another petition for clemency in 1921 influenced President Warren Harding to reduce the sentences of those still imprisoned. The Majority of the former soliders were released by 1924 but the last convicted soldier was not released until 1938. The injustice of the courts-martial prompted Congress to provide for appellate review at the departmental level before extreme sentences such as death could be executed.[7]

Although African Americans were depressed by the treatment of personnel in the 24th Infantry Regiment, most envisioned a wartime promotion for Colonel Charles Young, the third African American to graduate from the Military Academy at West Point. If he attained the rank of brigadier general, they expected that he would be able to command a regiment. After considering a transfer from Wilberforce University in Ohio, where he gave military instruction to African American students, to Fort Des Moines, where he would have had an opportunity to command officer candidates, Colonel Young was ordered on May 23, 1917, to proceed to Letterman General Hospital for observation and treatment after surgeons reported that he was unfit for duty because of hypertension. His physical examination also revealed that he was suffering from an advanced case of Bright's disease. He was

Item 7-5
"803rd Pioneer Infantry Band, No. 16," on board the troop ship U.S.S. *Philippines* that sailed from Brest, France, on July 18, 1919.
Silver gelatin print. Prints and Photographs Division.

assigned to the adjutant general of Ohio for duty until he retired from active service with the rank of colonel. This action pleased many military commanders who did not want senior African American officers commanding combat units, because Colonel Young was a senior Regular Army Officer he had seniority over most Regular Army and National Guard officers. On June 6, 1918, in an attempt to prove his physical fitness for active service, he began a 497-mile trip from Wilberforce, Ohio, to Washington, riding on horseback all of the distance except for a quarter of the way which he walked. Young arrived in Washington on June 22, 1918, having rested only one day during the sixteen-day march. Nevertheless, he remained on the retirement list until five days before the hostilities were terminated, when he was assigned to Camp Grant, Illinois, then reassigned to Monrovia, Liberia, as military attaché in 1919. On December 25, 1921, he was admitted to Gray's Hospital in Lagos, Nigeria, suffering from nephritis (in fact, Bright's disease). Colonel Young died on January 8, 1922, and was buried in an English cemetery; later his body was reinterred with full honors in Arlington National Cemetery.[8]

War Department officials did not consider a transfer of African American Regular Army regiments to France for participation in the war. The 9th Cavalry remained in the Philippine Islands, but the 25th Infantry Regiment, which was assigned to Schofield Barracks in Hawaii, was transferred to assist the 10th Cavalry and 24th Infantry in providing security along the southwestern border, because intelligence indicated that Germany was interested in assisting Mexico in an invasion to reclaim territory lost during the Mexican War. The so-called Zimmerman message raising this possibility and a perceived German threat in the Caribbean influenced the United States to purchase the Danish Islands. The War Department, concerned with sabotage and the security of vital installations within the United States, studied the ethnic composition of available units for this mission. Cognizant that many units were composed of individuals who were descendants of immigrants from Europe with some association with the Central Powers, President Wilson directed Secretary of War Baker to deploy the 1st District of Columbia Separate Battalion to vital facilities and structures within the national capital area.

Other African American National Guard units performed similar duties until transferred to southern camps where training was usually conducted with black guardsmen from the respective states.

In the National Guard as in Regular Army units, racial integration of personnel was not considered to be an option, and the War Department consolidated African American guardsmen into brigades. The separate units from Connecticut, Maryland, Massachusetts, Ohio, Tennessee, and the District of Columbia were organized as the 372nd Infantry Regiment and joined the 371st Infantry Regiment, composed of draftees at Camp Jackson, South Carolina, to form the 185th Brigade. The 8th Illinois Regiment and the 15th New York Regiment formed the 186th Brigade. The brigades were combined in December 1917 to form the 93rd (Provisional) Infantry Division (other elements such as artillery, engineer, ordnance, quartermaster, and transportation were never organized).[9] Because elements of the division did not train as a unit, it lacked the cohesion and experience gained from divisional-size combat operations. With the formation of the 92nd Division, which included all of the required elements, the service of some of the assigned personnel should have been extended to aviation. Aviators assigned to the divisions, however, were required to serve as airborne artillery spotters, but most of the African Americans who attended the Aerial Observers School at Fort Sill, Oklahoma, were not permitted to complete the aerial course requirements, and those who entered the program withdrew in frustration.

Lieutenant Charles A. Tribbitt did not have the opportunity to enter the program because while en route to the school he was removed from a Pullman car by local police officers who were enforcing segregation policies in Oklahoma. This delay caused the War Department to amend his orders and eliminate Tribbett from the aerial course. The only African American to serve in aviation was Eugene Jacques Bullard, who joined the French Lafayette Flying Corps, and destroyed at least one German aircraft in aerial combat. There were 42,000 African Americans assigned to combat, but this represented 11 percent of the total 380,000 African Americans serving in the wartime Army. The African American combat soliders comprised 20 percent of the 200,000 African Americans who served in France.[10]

Racial prejudice and segregation influenced the transfer of the first combat soldiers to France. African American soldiers were denied service in American towns, forced to ride in Jim Crow sections of transportation carriers when they were provided, and assigned to quarters in isolated areas of the camps. The transfer of the first combat unit, the 15th New York Regiment, which was redesignated as the 369th Infantry Regiment, was prompted, however, by the assault on Sergeant Noble Sissle—who later gained fame for the musical *Shuffle Along*—while he attempted to purchase a newspaper in Spartansburg, South Carolina. Jazz musician Lieutenant James Europe, who later commanded the regiment's band, prevented others from seeking revenge and some were reminded of the courts-martial of personnel in the 24th Infantry Regiment.

Colonel William Hayward, who commanded the regiment and who had already been denied permission to join the New York 42nd Division, known as the Rainbow Division, visited the War Department to request a change of assignment for the 369th Regiment (known to all personnel in the unit at the 15th Infantry Regiment). The War Department could either condemn racial prejudice in South Carolina, relocate the unit to another area where racism was not as prevalent, or reassign the unit to France.

The French government had requested American personnel to fill vacancies in their front line, but General John J. Pershing, commander of the American Expeditionary Forces (AEF), refused to relinquish command of American units to the French. Racial disorder in the South and the potential for violence caused him to acquiesce and offer the operational control of the 92nd and 93rd Infantry Divisions to Marshal Ferdinand Foch. By allowing this transfer, General Pershing could avoid confronting the issue of white American soldiers not wanting to serve with African Americans.[11]

African Americans serving in France were affected by racial policies implemented by AEF personnel. A circular titled "Secret Information Concerning Black American Troops" was distributed to urge French civilians to avoid all social contacts and all attempts to integrate black soldiers into activities beyond military operations. The French Chamber of Deputies, however, denounced the persistent effort to discredit African Americans soldiers and ordered the collection and destruction of the inflammatory circular. Ralph Tyler, the only African American war correspondent during the First World War, and William E. B. DuBois both visited France and confirmed the existence of the negative racial campaign conducted by white Americans.

Fear of possible mutiny prompted AEF intelligence officials to try to identify incipient insubordination and to keep an eye on officers who expressed interest in promoting social equality in the United States after the war. Intelligence officers were pleased with the tour of France by Robert R. Moton, president of Tuskegee Institute, who urged African American soldiers to prepare for their readjustment to the racial segregation and discrimination they would encounter on their return to the United States. Moton recommended that black soldiers marry and pursue agricultural endeavors after the war.

Commanders of the 92nd and 93rd Division alleged that African American officers were deficient and formed efficiency boards that examined the officers. By the Armistice, all of the officers in the 372nd Infantry Regiment except Captain West A. Hamilton had been replaced by white officers. The policy also affected some of the officers in the 369th Infantry Regiment and 370th Infantry Regiment, where Colonel Franklin A. Denison, senior African American officer in the American Expeditionary Forces, was relieved of duty, together with others in the command. Because African Americans made up less than 3 percent of the AEF combat strength, the War Department, which expected little achievement from the two combat divisions, did not intervene in the activities pertaining to the units. African American officers, who were removed from their assignments, resented the action because most were not transferred to another combat organization but were placed with labor units. The enlisted personnel similarly rejected the command and unit changes, because most of the officers had been assigned to the units from the formation of the divisions. They were angry about the replacement of Colonel Denison, and many refused to respect orders issued by the new commander. When white commanders threatened to replace senior noncommissioned officers with white personnel, the soliders performed their respective duties but met secretly to discuss their grievances.[12]

Despite the racism displayed by AEF personnel, the combat divisions performed their missions effectively while assigned to Meuse-Argonne sectors under the French. Casualties sustained by the 92nd Infantry Division totaled 2,100, with 176 killed in action. Casualties for the 93rd Infantry Division were 3,166, with 584 killed in action. In four years of combat, the 369th Infantry Regiment, which built an outstanding record, served 191 continuous days on the front line, never retreated in battle, and was the first Allied unit to reach the west bank of the Rhine. Sergeant Henry Johnson and Private Needham Roberts received the French Croix de Guerre and units of the two divisions received similar honors. The United States, however, though it awarded the Distinguished Service Cross to African Americans, refused to award the Medal of Honor to African American soldiers who served in

World War I. This policy was not altered until April 24, 1991, when Freddie Stowers, who served in the 371st Infantry Regiment, posthumously received the Medal of Honor.[13]

Although the Marine Corps did not accept African Americans into its ranks during World War I, the Navy continued its policy of recruiting, but only for the stewards branch, except for the enlistment of approximately thirty African American women as yeomanettes, serving in

Veterans realized while en route to the United States that their service and the casualties sustained by their units did not change the attitudes of white soldiers and that they were returning to a nation that remained essentially unchanged. Forced to stay behind in France while white soldiers were assigned the best departing vessels, African Americans were segregated on vessels and forced to take quarters in the lower sections of the ships when finally permitted to leave. Many were stationed at Camp Upton, New York, and immediately placed in segregated

"We Return. We Return from Fighting. We Return Fighting."

the office of the Navy Department. By June 30, 1918, only 4,328 African Americans served in a naval force composed of 435,398 personnel.[14]

Morale among black soldiers was partially sustained by the attitude of African Americans on the home front who were impressed by wartime slogans calling for self-determination for all people in a world made safe for democracy. They believed, like their ancestors before them, that military service during wartime would improve their peacetime prospects for better treatment. They deferred their special grievances and concurred with William E. B. DuBois who urged that they close ranks and join shoulder to shoulder with their white fellow citizens. When an incident like the violence against African Americans in East St. Louis in July 1917 provided a grim reminder of the racial hatred that existed, five thousand marched in silent protest down Fifth Avenue in New York City. African Americans supported the war effort by forming circles for the relief of soldiers and their families, and many contributed to Liberty Loan campaigns and War Saving Stamp drives. Alice Dunbar Nelson became a field representative of the Women's Committee of the Council of National Defense. William S. Scarborough, president of Wilberforce University, served on the Ohio Council of National Defense, and Emmett J. Scott served as special assistant to the secretary of war. Women participated in the Red Cross, served as nurses in several base hospitals, and were active in the Young Women's Christian Association. This enthusiasm extended to educational institutions, where students, faculty, and administrators were actively involved with the war campaigns.[15]

facilities until returned to local camps to be demobilized. Isolated instances of violence included white mobs attacking black veterans who were going home. William E. B. DuBois captured the sentiments of many veterans when he stated, "We Return. We Return from Fighting. We Return Fighting." In his poem "If We Must Die," Claude McKay, who recognized the increase in racial violence, especially the lynching by mobs influenced by the Ku Klux Klan, stressed that African Americans should aggressively defend themselves.

Major riots against African Americans began on May 10, 1919, and lasted through the following September. This postwar period was called by NAACP leader and author James W. Johnson the "Red Summer." Twenty-five major riots occurred, the most serious in Chicago; Knoxville; Omaha; Longview, Texas; and Elaine, Arkansas. Among the nearly eighty killed were ten veterans in uniform. Some of the resentment toward African Americans was attributed to their population increase in cities such as Chicago, where the black population grew from 44,000 in 1910 to 109,000 in 1920. More than 28,000 African Americans were employed in the major meatpacking houses in Chicago and East St. Louis; Kansas City, Missouri; and Indianapolis. African American employment also increased in the automobile industry, especially at Packard Motor Company and Ford Motor Company where African American workers could become apprentices in the Detroit branch. Thousands of others gained employment in the railroad, shipbuilding, shipping, and steel industries. The arrival in these cites of African Americans continued after the war primarily because of the discrimination, segregation, lack of voting rights and educational facilities, and the increase in mob violence in the South.[16]

The new aggressiveness of the returning veterans,

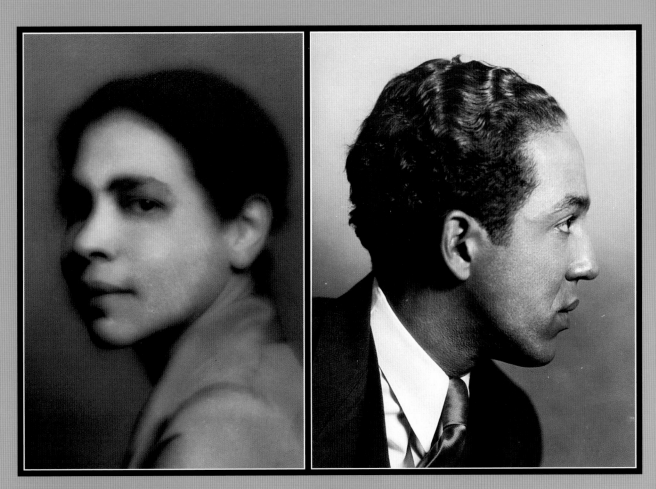

Item 7-14
Photographer unknown, Nella Larson, undated.
Silver gelatin print. Harmon Foundation Collection, Manuscript Division.

Item 7-13
Photographer unknown, Langston Hughes, undated.
Silver gelatin print. Harmon Foundation Collection, Manuscript Division.

who fought racial mobs, often armed with weapons, provoked a revision of the cultural expressions in literature, art, and music. The Harlem Renaissance, as the movement was called, sought to articulate the discontent of African Americans in literature and the arts and to project a revised consciousness of racial pride that departed from the previous image of the race. Writers and artists

Item 7-11
Photographer unknown, Claude McKay, undated.
Silver gelatin print. Harmon Foundation Collection, Manuscript Division.

produced work that was racial in theme and also universal in depth and appeal. Their work was fashioned with high technical skill and designed for any audience but did not cater to whites. The artists' rejection of dialect was also intended to discard past influences of such white writers as Joel Chandler Harris, who gave life to the fictional black character of Uncle Remus. In essence their work was part of the social protest of the postwar era. Representative writers from the Renaissance

include Claude McKay, who published "The Lynching," and Langston Hughes, whose collection of verse was published under the title *The Weary Blues*. Arguably, Jean Toomer's *Cane* is its best single literary work. Musicians embodied the themes of the period in the new creation known as *ragtime*, which was further refined as jazz. Alain Locke raised the literary movement to a higher level with his expression of the New Negro, emphasizing the major new attributes of racial pride.[17]

When, on June 4, 1920, Congress approved the National Defense Act, the War Department was required to make adjustments in the allotment of organized units. Military officials determined that a portion of the decrease of personnel should be at the expense of the four African American regiments. Fearing that the units were protected by the Army Reorganization Act of 1866, officials implemented policies to discourage enlistment into African American units. Although the Defense Act was revised to permit enlistment of men with wartime service or reenlistment in the same unit, military officials intended to eliminate the 9th Cavalry Regiment in the Philippines through attrition. Personnel scheduled to return to the United States would be absorbed by the 10th Cavalry Regiment and no replacements would join the unit. Either the 24th or the 25th Infantry Regiment would be eliminated.

Integration of remaining units with white units was unthinkable in the segregated army. In the end, the 9th Cavalry returned to the United States with both regiments gradually reduced to minimum authorized strength. The 24th and 25th Infantry Regiments were similarly diminished by the transferred allocations to the Air Corps where officials were attempting to make it a combat arm without changing the overall size of the army. The reductions and reassignment of African American cavalry to military schools essentially eliminated their combat readiness and relegated them to barracks duty because their cavalry field training was terminated. Robert R. Moton and Walter White, secretary of the NAACP, protested to President Herbert Hoover, whose chief of staff, General Douglas MacArthur, claimed the army was attempting not to disband the 10th Cavalry and 25th Infantry Regiment but to equalize the manpower burden among African American and white units. This policy assisted white organizations because allocations diverted from other units were used to maintain the manpower requirements of the Air Corps. African American units lost manpower and its discharged personnel were denied admission into Air Corps units. Major General George Van Horn, an assistant to General MacArthur, alleged that there were not enough skilled African Americans to operate a unit that normally attracted college graduates as pilots or individuals with significant mechanical aptitude or experience to maintain and service aircraft. Therefore, the War Department maintained its racial policies and continued to use Regular Army regiments as service units, disregarding significant training that supported the combat missions.[18]

The adjutants general of the District of Columbia and states where African American

Item 8-17
Arthur Herzog, Jr., and Billie Holiday, "God Bless' the Child, a swing-spiritual based on the authentic proverb, God Blessed the Child That's Got His Own.'"
New York: Edward B. Marks Music Corporation, 1941. Sheet music. Music Division.

units were organized during the war were also influenced by the policy of the War Department. Most did not immediately include African Americans in their allotments and only considered their reorganization as excess units. The 8th Illinois Regiment was organized in 1921, but in 1935 its 3rd Battalion was disbanded and the regiment was placed last on the state priority list. New York organized a unit that was designated as the 369th Infantry and had a significant cadre of white officers. Ohio reorganized its battalion and the District of Columbia, Maryland, and Massachusetts were not interested in the reorga-

nization of infantry units and formed auxiliary engineer units. These units were redesigned as infantry, however, and all were later realigned to reactivate the 372nd Infantry Regiment. Tennessee did not reorganize its company but New Jersey formed a battalion that was assigned to the 372nd Regiment because the District of Columbia unit was redesignated as the regimental headquarters company. The combined Regular Army and National Guard strength of African American units was less than 2 percent of the total army strength and it reflected the indifference of the War Department officials and the prejudice of state officials toward African Americans.[19]

There were relatively few opportunities for advancement within the military, and seldom were African Americans accepted and commissioned by the military academies. In 1936 Benjamin O. Davis, Jr., became the fourth black man to receive a commission to West Point, followed in 1941 by James D. Fowler. Both cadets were socially ostracized during their enrollment, and military officials at West Point condoned the practice. Unlike the Naval Academy at Annapolis, Maryland, the Military Academy did at least commission African American cadets. In 1936 the Naval Academy admitted James Lee Johnson but he was academically separated the next year, after which he returned to the Case School of Applied Science, which became Case Western Reserve, and completed a degree in mechanical engineering. In 1941, he was commissioned and later served with the 99th Pursuit Squadron. George J. Rivers, who in 1937 also received an appointment to the Naval Academy, was similarly dismissed on July 7, 1937.[20]

Federal denial of the significance of African American service with the AEF in France was further demonstrated by the treatment of widows and mothers invited to the graves of deceased veterans. These African American "Gold Star Mothers" were segregated during their voyage to France and escorted separately by Lieutenant Colonel Benjamin O. Davis, Sr. Among those who denounced the discriminatory policy was Emmett J. Scott, who in October 1933 expressed his disappointment that the nation had failed to deliver on promises made during the war. During the Depression, the War Department denied supervisory positions in the Civilian Conservation Corps (CCC) to African American officers, again disappointing those who had served in the war. President Franklin D. Roosevelt, however, in 1935 influenced the War Department to assign some blacks to the agency, including ten medical reserve officers and four chaplains. Authorization was granted for the establishment of two CCC camps, one in August 1936 and another in 1937, commanded entirely by African Americans.[21]

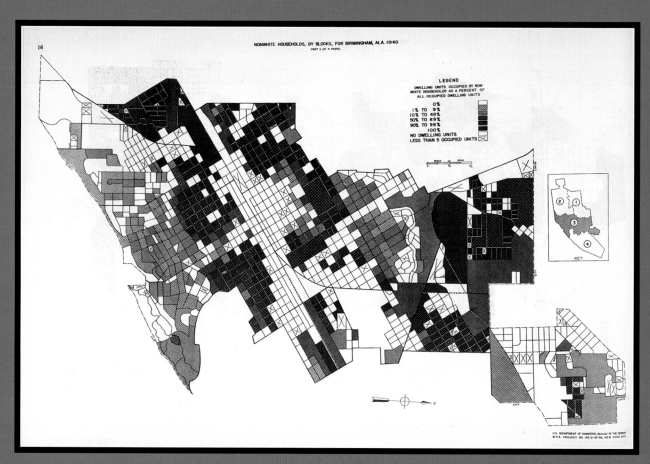

Item 8-15
U.S. Census Bureau, "Birmingham, Alabama: Block Statistics," *Sixteenth Census of the United States,* **1940 (Washington, 1943).**
Analytical map showing housing, page 16. Geography and Map Division.

"Negro Removal Act"

Other New Deal policies that were implemented during the Depression to reduce unemployment and eliminate suffering also brought disappointment to African Americans. The National Industrial Recovery Act (NIRA) was designed to increase employment by shortening the work week with a guaranteed minimum wage and approving unionization of workers. The Recovery Act provided for regional rates based on perceived standards of living and permitted employers to classify various types of work and pay based on "efficiency," a practice that eliminated many African American employees and exempted them from the minimum wage. Agricultural workers, domestic servants, cooks, and yard workers in southern textile mills were not covered by the legislation. The practice made African Americans critical of all New Deal legislation, and they began to refer to the National Recovery Act (NRA) as the "Negro Removal Act" or as "Negroes Rarely Allowed," whereas whites saw the legislation as the "Negro Relief Act" and pledged "No Roosevelt Again." African Americans claimed that the Works Progress Administration (WPA) and the Public Works Administration (PWA) lowered their occupational level because in these programs, black workers rarely found relief work commensurate with their skills. Attempts to deny federal protection to unions that barred blacks through the Wagner–Connery Relations Act of 1935 failed. Under the Agricultural Adjustment Act, southern landowners received federal payment for plowed-up cotton and pocketed the tenant's or sharecropper's share. Some African American sharecroppers, forced to work for the lowest wages, were denied access to rent-free shacks that had been previously available and to the furnishings system, whereby landowners borrowed materials from central stores that were provided to tenants and sharecroppers. Southern law further protected landowners and storekeepers by instituting crop lien legislation that gave land-owners title to the tenant's share of harvested crops until payment had been made for materials advanced them throughout the year. The number of African American sharecroppers declined from 392,897 in 1930 to 199,118 in 1940. John P. Davis, a professor at Howard University, has concluded that the status of African Americans actually deteriorated under the New Deal. African Americans receiving support from relief agencies increased from 2.1 million in October 1933 to 4 million, or 30 percent of the African American population, in January 1935.[22]

The devastating effects of the Depression dominated the economic conditions of African Americans and caused further reductions in African American units. However, the inactivity of the Regular Army regiment and National Guard units and discriminatory policies concerning enlistment prompted approximately one hundred African Americans to join the Abraham Lincoln Brigade, the three thousand volunteers who fought in the Spanish Civil War. Oliver Law, commander of a machine-gun company, became the first African American to lead an integrated force into combat. Law was mortally wounded in Spain during the Brunette campaign on July 10, 1937. The International Brigades also attracted three black pilots, James Beck, Paul Williams, and Patrick Roosevelt, although Roosevelt served as an infantryman. The only African American woman among the first nurses to arrive in Spain from the United States—she arrived as part of a group of twelve nurses and physicians—was Salaria Lee. Although the African American volunteers might have preferred to serve in Ethiopia, they would all have undoubtedly agreed with the slogan, "This Ain't Ethiopia, But It'll Do." Hubert Julian, who did go to Ethiopia, was dismissed after destroying a new Imperial aircraft during an exhibition.[23]

Increased military aggression in Ethiopia, China, and Europe caused President Roosevelt to support foreign policies protecting the nation's neutrality. After the Japanese sank an American gunboat patrolling the Yangtze River in China, an embargo was imposed on Japan, quarantining potential war materials. Charles Houston, commissioned at Fort Des Moines, was serving as special counsel for the NAACP and stressed to the president

"Negro Relief Act"

that if another war occurred the loyalty of African Americans would be indispensable to the security of the United States and they would not again silently endure the humiliation and discrimination imposed on its military and naval personnel

Item 8-8
"Why Should We March?," 1941.
Flier. A. Philip Randolph Papers, Manuscript Division.

during the last war. At issue was the extension of flight training to African American institutions under Public Law No. 18, institutions that included Hampton Institute, Howard University, North Carolina Agricultural and Technical College, Tuskegee Institute, West Virginia State College, and Wilberforce University. In 1939, the Civilian Aeronautics Authority granted West Virginia State College, Howard University, North Carolina Agricultural and Technical College, and Tuskegee the authority to offer flight training. The program at Tuskegee Institute thrived and during the Cadet Pilot Training program inspection on March 25, 1940, the average cadet's

written score for primary flight training was 88 percent correct. Flight evaluation scores were equally impressive.[24]

When ninety-one of the first hundred cadets completed flight training at Tuskegee, the next objective was to persuade the Army Air Corps to accept African Americans. Combined with other civil rights issues, this effort came to the fore in the election of 1940. On September 14, 1940, Congress passed the Burke–Wadsworth Act providing for the first peacetime draft in the history of the nation, and amendments concerning the right of individuals to volunteer for the draft and the establishment of impartial draft boards were included in the legislation. The legislation did not, however, address problems of segregation and discrimination, and African Americans therefore endeavored to make these issues prominent in the presidential election. A. Philip Randolph, head of the Brotherhood of Sleeping Car Porters and Maids, proposed a march on Washington to gain attention and redress for issues that pertained to African Americans.

The Republican nominee Wendell Willkie, who spoke against discrimination in the armed services in his campaign speeches, gained the support of the *Pittsburgh Courier* and the *Baltimore Afro-American*, neither of which had supported a Republican presidential nominee since the election of 1924. Rayford Logan, Frederick Patterson, and Howard H. Long appeared before the Senate on May 14, 1940, to deplore segregation in the military. President Roosevelt approved the promotion of 84 colonels to the rank of brigadier but denied the same recognition to Colonel Benjamin O. Davis, contributing to African American unhappiness with the incumbent presidential candidate. In response, the White House on September 5, 1940, directed the War Department to draft a statement affirming equal opportunity in the military and on September 13, 1940, to dispel the impression that African Americans would be assigned to labor battalions. Secretary Henry L. Stimson formulated a plan to accept 10 percent of the military strength from the African American population. This policy was announced on September 16, 1940.[25] Wilke lost the election to Franklin D. Roosevelt, who began an unprecedented third term as president of the United States in 1941.

Dissatisfied with military policies, Mary McLeod Bethune, founder and president of the National Council of Negro Women, and Walter White, secretary of the NAACP, urged Eleanor Roosevelt to arrange a presidential conference for a delegation that included T. Arnold Hill, adviser on Negro Affairs for the National Youth Administration, and A. Philip Randoph. At the conference held on September 27, 1940, the delegates urged the induction of qualified African Americans as commis-

Item 8-7
Photographer unknown, "Airmen with Lena Horne and Noel Parrish," 1940.
Silver gelatin print. Noel Parrish Collection, Manuscript Division.

sioned officers and enlisted men throughout the armed services, the elimination of segregation, and the assurance that African American reservists would fill the vacancies in the four Regular Army regiments and the National Guard. On October 9, 1940, the White House reaffirmed earlier policy statements promising the assignment of African Americans to each combat and noncombat branch in the army, offering qualified personnel the opportunity to attend officer training schools, allowing African American civilians to obtain employment at army arsenals and installations, and establishing African American aviation units once the necessary personnel had been trained. To appease African Americans for not endorsing integration, President Roosevelt promoted Benjamin O. Davis to brigadier general, appointed William H. Hastie special assistant to the secretary of war, and made Major Campbell C. Johnson adviser to the director of Selective Service. With the issuance of Executive Order No. 8802 on June 25, 1941, authorizing the establishment of the Fair Employment Practice Committee, A. Philip Randolph's march on Washington scheduled for July 1, 1941, was canceled.[26]

The intense debate over War Department polices did not deter the activation of African American guardsmen under the protective mobilization plan. Joint Resolution 96, approved on August 10, 1940, authorized the president to activate National Guard units for twelve consecutive months. Executive Order No. 8618, issued on December 23, 1940, federalized African American guardsmen, and the Organization and Training Division of the War Department envisioned protest from civil rights advocates seeking the formation of infantry brigades. The expected protest was averted with the conversion of the 8th Illinois Regiment into the 184th Antiaircraft Artillery and the 369th Regiment into coastal artillery. However, when War Department officials attempted to avoid agitation over the use of "Colored" in the official designation of African Americans by using an asterisk to identify the units, African Americans were once again disappointed by the discriminatory and racist nature of the policy.[27]

The War Department continued to postpone participation by African Americans in the Army Air Corps. A plan to train mechanics at the Chicago School of Aeronautics was rejected on the grounds that the school provided only pilot training and the only available quarters for students were located at the Young Men's Christian Association building where lodging was not available for African American students. Although the staff at Maxwell Field recommended Chanute Field in Illinois as the site for technical training on December 10, 1940, the Army Air Plans Division rejected the plan, and considered the assignment of Black trainees to military facilities would cause disturbances and possibly riots at Chanute Field and the nearby civilian communities. The Army Air Corps sent plans for the formation of the 99th Pursuit Squadron at Tuskegee Institute. Civilian aide William H. Hastie objected to the Tuskegee plan because it provided separate training that he felt would affect morale, fail to conform to officer training at Fort Benning, and provoke adverse African American reaction. Despite Hastie's refusal to endorse the establishment of separate training facilities, he agreed to withhold his objections, and the army implemented the plan for the 99th Pursuit Squadron, which was approved by Secretary of War Stimson on January 9, 1941.[28]

Anticipating warfare against the Axis Powers, Congress enacted the Selective Service and Training Act, the nation's first peacetime draft, in September 1940. Emergency plans indicated that if warfare involved combat operations against Germany and Japan, the armed forces would first concentrate on Germany, which was believed to pose the greatest threat to American security. To aid the British after the Germans defeated France, Congress passed the Lend-Lease Act in March 1941. The Japanese attack of Pearl Harbor in Hawaii on December 7, 1941, prompted a declaration of war by Congress the next day. Germany immediately responded with a similar declaration against the United States, which precipitated the nation's entry into World War II.[29]

In 1942 the African American army enlisted strength numbered 467,883, and by August 1, 1945, the total had increased to 1,030,255, which represented approximately 9 percent of all American draftees. The majority of the men drafted were inducted into the army and assigned noncombat duties. Other branches of the armed services imposed similar restrictions on duties assigned. Post commanders conformed to the discriminatory polices imposed by local and state laws and rarely had more than concurrent jurisdiction in matters involving soldiers and civilians. Protecting the interests of African American personnel was not a priority and in many instances when soldiers defended themselves against racist town officials and unruly civilians the military police tended to join the oppressors denying civil rights. Colonel Howard Queen, assigned to Fort Benning in Georgia before his assignment with the 366th Infantry Regiment at Fort Devens near Boston, stated that the racial policies at the installation would in no way motivate young draftees. Judging Fort Benning to be the rule rather than the exception, he was not surprised by the riotous conditions that repeatedly prevailed at many army posts and installations when large numbers of inductees arrived for basic training. African American officers were denied privileges at the Fort Benning officers' club, and throughout the post, segregation prevailed. At Fort Belvoir in northern Virginia, the fort was divided by Route 1 and all African Americans were restricted to the south post unless official activities required entrance to the northern post area adjacent to the Potomac River. In northern states, the racial incidents on army posts and in nearby towns were equally prone toward violence. Fort Dix and the white residents of New Jersey were not any more enlightened than those in the deep South, it seemed, and one of the worst racial riots occurred at Camp Shenango in Pennsylvania. Some of the Regular Army personnel of the 24th Infantry Regiment were aware of the vindictiveness displayed by local and federal authorities after the Houston incident, and they along with many draftees concluded that dying stateside was just as good, if not preferable, to dying on foreign soil. They were not concerned with military careers, and in the final analysis all they had to lose was their lives. For these soldiers, like thousands of others recruited for military service, the objectives were victory at home over racism, discrimination, segregation, and illegal mob violence and victory overseas. The double V was the motto of African Americans during the war, but to many of those in the armed services at home the immediate issue was the elimination of injustices here.[30]

Enlistment into the navy was similarly unsatisfactory because positions were available only in general service, training was provided at separate camps and schools, and assignments were primarily to shore installations and harbor crafts. Recruiting began in June 1941, but enlistment for general service did not occur until April 7, 1942, with training at the Great Lakes Naval Training Center in Illinois. Advanced training was given at Camp Robert Smalls and Hampton Institute. Graduates qualified as technical specialists, and either went on to vocational school or were assigned to sea duty, which included duty as SeaBees, doing construction, to naval ammunition depots, or to the Great Lakes Training Center. The navy in February 1943 began taking recruits through the draft instead of the volunteer system. To accommodate the increase in African American personnel, companies were created for overseas duty that essentially were groups of laborers, stevedores, ammunition handlers, construction workers, or maintenance personnel.

The explosion of ammunition at Port Chicago Naval Magazine, on Mare Island in San Francisco Bay, demonstrated the hazardous duty seamen performed both aboard ship and ashore. Two hundred fifty seamen were killed and several hundred wounded. The surviving 258 men were reluctant to continue the loading operation for fear of other explosions. Ordered to resume the loading, forty-four seamen refused to obey and later six others refused to continue. These men were court-martialed, dishonorably discharged, and sentenced to long terms of confinement. After numerous appeals and petitions for clemency, the convictions of forty-seven were set aside and the men were restored to duty on January 7, 1946. All of them became eligible for honorable discharges after the completion of their required service. The U.S. Navy, acknowledging the danger of loading ammunition and the need to more equitably assign duties, limited the number of African Americans assigned to naval ammunition depots to 30 percent of the enlisted African Americans in the navy.[31]

A program was organized on July 1, 1943, to increase the training of commissioned officers. Although Secretary of the Navy Henry Knox sought to exclude African Americans, President Roosevelt directed that they should be tested and commissioned if successful. Adlai Stevenson, assistant to Secretary Knox, urged an earlier commissioning—before the March 1944 scheduled date—of twelve enlisted men from the program. A quarter of the group was expected to fail the training program, so sixteen men were selected. In fact, all sixteen completed the program. From these, the navy commissioned twelve ensigns and one warrant officer, who became known as the Golden Thirteen. All served overseas.[32]

The navy also diverged from establishment policies by designating that one destroyer and a patrol boat have crews who were African American, with the exception of the commissioned officers. On March 20, 1944, the destroyer USS PC *Mason* was commissioned with a crew of 160 African Americans and 44 white seamen. The following year, a submarine chaser called the USS PC-*1264* was commissioned with a crew of men, and after seven months African Americans replaced the white petty officers on board. During all of World War II, one black man—Ensign Dennis Nelson—commanded an integrated

Item 8-5
Photographer unknown, "First Negro nurses land in England," 1944.
NAACP Collection, Prints and Photographs Division.

logistical support unit, one black officer reached the rank of lieutenant, and one African American gained admission to the Naval Academy.[33]

In 1942, the Marine Corps began enlisting 1,000 African Americans a month for shore and high seas service. All were trained at Montford Point, adjacent to Camp Lejeune, North Carolina. Of approximately 17,000 African American enlisted men, 12,000 served in the Pacific Theater. The Marine Corps did not commission any African American officers.[34]

African Americans also served in the Coast Guard and the Merchant Marine. Nearly 4,000 enlisted in the Coast Guard, which conducted training at Manhattan Beach in Brooklyn, at Fort Des Moines, New York. One of the unique Coast Guard stations was the Pea Island Life Saving Station, which from 1880 was manned entirely by African Americans. Ensign Joseph C. Jenkins was the Coast Guard's first African American commissioned officer, followed by September 1942 by three more black commissioned officers. Approximately 24,000 African Americans in the Merchant Marines served in every capacity aboard ship. Hugh Mulzac, the first captain, commanded the SS *Booker T. Washington,* which had an integrated crew.[35]

African American women in the armed services experienced slightly different treatment. The Women's Auxiliary Army Corps was established at Fort Des Moines and later redesignated the Women's Army Corps. Training for further classes was extended to centers at Daytona Beach, Florida, Fort Oglethorpe in Georgia, Fort Devens near Boston, Massachusetts, and a center divided between Camp Polk in Louisiana and an installation in Monticello, Arkansas. African American commissioned officers were assigned to command African American WAC personnel or to serve in administrative capacities. Two exceptions to this policy were the assignment of Major Charity Adams to supervise the Plans and Training unit at the Fort Des Moines Training Center, after which she went on to command the 6888 Central Postal Directory Battalion which served in the European Theater, and of Major Harriet West to be chief of the Planning Bureau Control Division at WAC headquarters, after which she served in the Adjutant General's Office in the War Department. African American women in the military in December 1942 numbered 220, or 1.7 percent of 12,767

women in the Army, and by April 1945 they numbered 3,900, or 3.9 percent of 99,288 women serving. By the summer of 1945, there were 120 African American WAC officers and altogether 3,961 black women in the Army.[36]

Military experiences of African American WACs and women in other service branches were similar to soldiers, because the same conditions prevailed at training and duty stations. At Fort Devens, African Americans were assigned as orderlies in the Lovell General Hospital and white WACs were assigned as technicians. When the commandant, Colonel Walter H. Crandell, observed Private Alice Young taking the temperature of another WAC, he denounced her actions and stressed that all African American WACs would perform only maintenance duties. Private Young together with Privates Anna C. Morrison, Johnnie Murphy, and Mary Green led a strike to protest Crandell's actions. All of the African American WACs were ordered to return to duty but the leaders maintained that the First Service Command should remove the commander and eliminate his discriminatory practices. As a result, the four WACs were court-martialed. Julian D. Rainey, an attorney affiliated with the Boston NAACP, defended them. Although found guilty of willfully disobeying a lawful command and sentenced to one year of hard labor, with dishonorable discharges from the service, the WACs were restored to duty in April 1945, when the War Department, during the process of review, reversed the verdict. The case, which attracted the attention of Mary McLeod Bethune and Eleanor Roosevelt during the trial, embarrassed the War Department.[37]

The navy, however, did not accept African Americans into the branch called Women Accepted for Volunteer Emergency Service (WAVES) until late in the war. Protests especially from the Alpha Kappa Alpha sorority, a black women's professional group, in October 1944, just before the presidential election, influenced an announcement concerning a change of policy. The Coast Guard on October 20, 1944, stated that African Americans would be accepted in the Coast Guard women's corps SPARS, a contraction of the service motto "Semper Paratus." The first African American WAVES reported to Smith College on November 13, 1944, for officer training. In December the first African American enlisted contingency reported to Hunter College for basic training. On July 23, 1945, there were two black commissioned officers and fifty-four black enlisted women in the WAVES, a force of 8,000 officers and 78,000 enlisted women. The SPARS in September 1946 had five African American enlisted women, but the Marine Women's Reserve, the Marinettes, had not recruited any African Americans.[38]

The National Association of Colored Graduate Nurses (NACGN) expressed interest in the Army Nurse Corps. Surgeon General James C. Magee determined that no African American personnel were required until separate wards were designated in station hospitals where African American troops were sufficient to warrant such facilities. Further, War Department plans of October 25, 1940, required a quota of 56 nurses, 120 physicians, and 44 dentists. Determined to challenge the quota, the NACGN protested, whereupon 60 black nurses were assigned to the newly opened station at Fort Huachuca, Arizona. Lieutenant Della Raney became the first chief nurse while serving at Tuskegee Air Field in 1942, and Lieutenant Sue Freeman was chief of 30 nurses assigned to the 25th Station hospital in Liberia, Africa. In December 1944, Lieutenant Agnes B. Glass served as chief nurse of the 335th Station Hospital at Tagap, Burma.

By July 1943, the army raised its quota of African American nurses to 160, with 30 of them assigned to foreign duty and 31 deployed at Fort Clark, Texas. By V-J (Victory in Japan) Day, the army total was 479, which represented 1 percent of the Army Nurse Corps. Protests continued to push the War Department to end the quota system, and finally on January 20, 1945, Surgeon General Norman T. Kirk announced that nurses would be accepted into the Army Nurse Corps without regard to race. On January 25, 1945, Rear Admiral J. W. C. Agnew announced that the Navy Nurse Corps was open to African Americans; Phyliss Mae Daley became the first ensign on March 8, 1945.[39]

The military often ignored grievances by blacks and denied recognition of their outstanding achievements. Despite numerous negative experiences, however, African Americans performed their assigned duties with confidence and in many instances exceeded the expectations of their commanders. Dorie Miller, on board the *West Virginia* on December 7, 1941, performed acts of valor and courage that included removing a wounded officer to safety and destroying several enemy aircraft by machine-gun fire. For this, he was awarded the Navy Cross, although his performance merited the Medal of Honor, which the navy refused to award to African American seamen. Marines in ammunition companies in the Pacific received the Navy Unit Commendation for action on Guam; other ammunition compa-

nies and depot companies received similar awards during the Battle of Iwo Jima.

From the British Isles in June 1944, 130,000 African American soldiers were dispersed throughout the European Theater. By V-E (Victory in Europe) Day, May 8, 1945, their strength had increased to 260,000. Assigned to more than 1,500 units that were primarily ammunition, port, quartermaster, and truck companies, they fought in twenty-two combat units (representing 9 percent of the African American soldiers in the war). The combat units were augmented by approximately 2,800 volunteer replacements organized into separate platoons that fought together with white infantry and armored units. Regardless of their unit designations, however, all of the units served in combat conditions and displays of courage were common. The "Red Ball Express," including 1,500 African Americans, supplied forward units with ammunition and materials. Another 4,500 black volunteers responded to a request by Lieutenant General Walter B. Smith to serve as infantry, even though all noncommissioned officers who volunteered were required to relinquish their ranks and serve as privates.

Personnel in the 320th Antiaircraft Barrage Balloon Battalion made significant contributions. The only unit of its type in the theater and the only African American unit engaged in combat on D Day, the battalion nevertheless received only a letter of commendation for its performance in the war. Corporal Wacerly B. Woodson, Jr., a battalion member, was awarded a Bronze Star. On Omaha Beach, First Sergeant Norman Day in the 582nd Engineer Dump Truck Company received a Silver Star, a Purple Heart, and a British Distinguished Service Medal. The 761st Tank Battalion, the 3rd Platoon of company C of the 614 Tank Destroyer Battalion, and the 969 Field Artillery Battalion received the Presidential Unit Citation. The 349th Field Artillery Group and the 777th Field Artillery Battalion were the first African American units to reach the Rhine River. Personnel in the latter unit received six Bronze Stars and eight Purple Hearts.[40]

By the fall of 1944 in the Mediterranean Theater, there were 85,000 African Americans among the 1 million American soldiers and airmen who fought from North Africa to Sicily and Italy. With approximately one quarter of the African American strength assigned to combat and combat support units, their percentage of combat strength here was higher than that in the European Theater, reflecting the combat size of the 92nd Infantry Division, the 366th Infantry Regiment, a tank battalion, several antiaircraft artillery units, a chemical company, and four squadrons of the 332nd Fighter Group. Ironically, the first Silver Stars awarded in the European Theater went to soldiers in service units and not to those in combat organizations.

The 92nd Infantry Division, activated in 1942, included nearly fifty units. British, Indian, and Italian forces attached to it made up the 366th Infantry Regiment, the 758 and 679th Tank Destroyer Battalions, and the Japanese–American 442 Regimental Combat Team, which was the most highly decorated unit in the army during the war. The 92nd Infantry Division was adversely affected by the attitude of its commander, Major General Edward M. Almond, and other white subordinate commanders who alleged the African American units failed to accomplish their combat missions. Hondon B. Hargrove, who commanded a battery of the 597th Field Artillery, stressed that most African American soldiers fought heroically in the rugged mountainous terrain where Germans defensive forces were well-prepared and attributed difficulties experienced by some units to the divisional practice of shifting personnel and parceling out of units, which weakened unit cohesion. Lieutenant Vernon Baker of the 370th Infantry Regiment was the one African American in the division to receive a Distinguished Service Cross. The division had 471 black enlisted men killed in action and 2,163 wounded in action, and 31 African American officers killed in action and 84 wounded in action. Such figures do not reflect any inactivity of assigned personnel and suggest a lack of appropriate recognition of combat service.[41]

The Tuskegee airmen accumulated a remarkable fight record, despite limited numbers of replacement pilots. They received the Distinguished Unit Citation for Action against the enemy first in Sicily, second for action at Monte Cassino in Italy, and third for a successful mission over Berlin. The 99th Pursuit Squadron flew more than 200 missions and did not lose one escort bomber. Together the 477th Bomber Group and the Tuskegee airmen were credited with destroying 111 enemy planes in the air and another 150 on the ground, while flying 15,533 sorties. They were awarded 88 Distinguished Flying Crosses and 800 Air Medals and clusters.[42]

Some 100,000 African Americans were deployed in the Pacific Theater of Operations, including those in the 93rd Infantry, the 24th and 25th Infantry Regiments, which distinguished themselves in combat at Bouganville in the Solomon Islands, and more than a dozen

antiaircraft artillery units. In the China–Burma–India Theater, an additional 21,000 soldiers worked with service units, mainly truck companies and engineer units, and served with the 484th Antiaircraft Artillery Battalion. African American units that were part of the advancing forces included the 839th Engineer Battalion and the 810th Amphibian Truck Company (DUKW), which was the first DUKW to operate in the Southwestern Pacific area, arriving from Milne Bay, New Guinea, in November 1943. Eleven other DUKW units participated in the Leyte operation. In the China–Burma–India area, 60 percent of the 15,000 soldiers who constructed the Ledo Road were African Americans. Private Mack B. Anderson of the 823rd Engineer Battalion, Private Isaac Sermon of the 25th Infantry, and Staff Sergeant Rothchild Webb of the 93rd Cavalry Reconnaissance Troop all were awarded the Silver Star.[43]

Delayed recognition of contributions to the war effort by African Americans was finally partially accorded when in February 1997, at a White House ceremony conducted by President Bill Clinton, the Medal of Honor was awarded to First Lieutenant Vernon Baker and posthumously to Staff Sergeant Edward A. Carter, Jr., First Lieutenant John R. Fox, Private First Class Willy F. James, Jr., Staff Sergeant Reuben Rivers, First Lieutenant Charles L. Thomas, and Private George Watson. This list undoubtedly could have been longer.[44]

Of course, troops with the 9th and 10th Cavalry Regiments stationed in Kansas at Fort Riley and Fort Leavenworth as part of the 3rd Cavalry Division and later transferred to Camp Funston, Kansas, Fort Clark, Texas, Camp Lockett, California, or Camp Patrick Henry in Virginia never had an opportunity to participate in combat. In March 1944, most of these units were sent to Assi-Ben-Okba, Algeria, where they were promptly disbanded. The 3rd Signal Troop, which was not transferred to Algeria, was also converted to a signal construction battalion. In this way, the Buffalo Soldiers were disbanded virtually without military honors, and their demise went unmarked, except when African American soliders and the black press complained about their conversions. Thus a portion of the heritage of African Americans in the military was effectively obscured during the war. Fortunately, however, the Buffalo Soldiers were able to be reconstituted in 1950, after the beginning of the Korean War, and their legacy continues today.[45]

Item 9-6
Max Roach, "We Insist!" Max Roach's Freedom Now Suite (New York: Columbia, 1960).
Record jacket. Motion Picture, Broadcasting, and Recorded Sound Division.

In the field of public education the doctrine of
"separate but equal" has no place.

Brown v. Board of Education of Topeka, 1954

6 The Civil Rights Era: 1946 to 1965

DAVID J. GARROW

When World War II came to an end
in 1945, most black Americans found themselves still living firmly under the yoke of racial segregation. Although
the "New Deal" years of President Franklin D. Roosevelt
saw a significant number of northern black voters convert
from Republican to Democrat, black participation in
American public life nevertheless remained limited, and
segregationist practices were widespread—not just in the
South but even in big northern cities.

The growing black presence in the northern Democratic
Party, however, helped persuade both President Roosevelt
and his successor, Harry Truman, that access for blacks
to equal employment opportunities in the government
sector deserved protection in the form of presidential
executive orders. Although these measures were generally
more symbolic than substantive, they helped send a clear
message that racial discrimination and segregation were
morally wrong. That same message was also highlighted
by the publication of Gunnar Myrdal's classic study of
race in America, *An American Dilemma* (1944).

One notable influence on the immediate postwar racial
climate was the return from military service of thousands
of black veterans who, even in segregated military units,

EXTRA — — By Executive Order

PRESIDENT TRUMAN WIPES OUT SEGREGATION IN ARMED FORCES

2nd Order Sets Up FEPC In All Government Jobs

In a dramatic and historic move, unprecedented since the time of Lincoln, President Harry Truman issued Monday afternoon two executive orders which doom forever Jim Crowism in the Armed forces of the United States and guarantee equal job opportunities in the Federal government and all of its branches.

Executive Order No. 1

Establishing President's Committee on Equality of Treatment and Opportunity in the Armed Services.

Whereas, it is essential that there be maintained in the Armed Services of the United States the highest standards of democracy, with equality of treatment and opportunity for all those who serve in our country's defense;

Now, therefore, by virtue of the authority vested in me as President of the United States, by the Constitution and the Statutes of the United States and as Commander-in-Chief of the Armed Services, it is hereby ordered as follows:

1. It is hereby declared to be the policy of the President that there shall be equality of treatment and opportunity for all persons in the armed services without regard to race, color, religion or national origin. This policy shall be put into effect as rapidly as possible, having due regard to the time required to effectuate any necessary changes without impairing efficiency or morale.

2. There shall be created in the national military establishment an Advisory Committee to be known as the "President's Committee on Equality of Treatment and Opportunity in the Armed Services," which shall be composed of 7 members to be designated by the President.

3. The Committee is authorized on behalf of the President to examine into the rules, procedures and practices of the armed services in order to determine in what respect such rules, procedures, and practices may be altered or improved with a view

(See, WIPES OUT, Page 2)

SAVE *This* PAPER *It Marks* HISTORY

NATIONAL Edition

Chicago Defender

WORLDS GREATEST WEEKLY

10¢ PAY NO MORE

Copyright 1948 By Robert S. Abbott Pub. Co., 3435 Indiana Ave., Phone: Calumet 5656

VOL. XLIV, No. 16 CHICAGO, ILL., SATURDAY, JULY 31, 1948 ★★★ THIS PAPER CONSISTS OF TWO PARTS—PART ONE

Under 'States' Rights'

Posse, Bent On Lynching, Searches Woods For Prey

Rumor Negroes Would Resist Scatters Mob

Intended Victims Escape; 2 Whites Shot As Prowlers

HAZELHURST, Miss.— A mob of 200 armed whites, including highway patrolmen lined up on the bank of Turkey Creek, at Dentville, all night Friday afraid to cross because one of their number said that some of the 75 Negroes who took refuge in a woods across the creek were armed.

The mob dispersed early in the morning, only to have two of their number shot as prowlers by a white farmer.

Armed with rifles, shotguns, pistols and rope—the mob was searching for Thurman Fulgham, 20, his father, John, 60, Luther Wiggins, and a fourth unidentified man in connection with the shooting Friday of Sheriff Julius Harper.

The sheriff was shot in the thigh when he started to strike Thurman Fulgham who was charged with slapping Mrs. Troy Templeton and drawing a knife on her husband during an argument in their store.

See, POSSE, Page 2

Come Back And Do A Job Is Truman Edict

GOP Must Decide What Comes First, Party Or Nation

WASHINGTON—The Republican dominated 80th Congress is on the spot. President Harry S. Truman put it there.

The Republican Party itself is on the spot. It is "put up or shut up" on civil rights, with the November elections at stake.

Down the line, one, two, three, four, President has demanded anti-poll tax, anti-lynch, FEPC, and anti-army Jim Crow legislation. He announced his stand to the nation in Philadelphia, three weeks ago when the New Deal Democratic Party emerged, and he put it on the line for congress this week when the special session convened.

President Truman, who has grown in stature since he told the America people the inside story of the 80th Congress on his nation-wide tour, has set an unprecedented style for campaigning.

Promises Won't Do

His dramatic call for a special session of congress means that the politicians cannot stump their districts oiling machines and making promises for "next year." They have got to return to the House and to the Senate, and "put up or shut up."

This is a crisis for the Republicans. They were not prepared to stand up and show the American people where their hearts lie. They planned to snipe at the President from long range and ride into office poking their fingers at the other man.

Two years ago, they got away

See, CONGRESS, Page 2

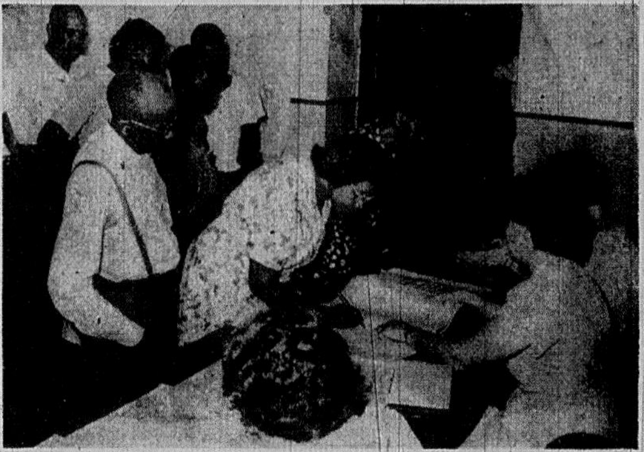

CIVIL RIGHTS IN PRACTICE is shown here as South Carolina Negroes flock to register in Charleston as Democrats after Federal Judge J. Waties Waring issued a court order forcing the state's Democratic party officials to enroll Negroes and grant them full participation in party affairs. The Dixiecrats, led by Gov. Thurmond and his lily-whites, had tried to make the Democratic party a "private club."—Keystone photo.

Aubrey Williams Bids Dixie Demos Farewell: 'Get Out And Stay Out'

By JOHN LEFLORE

MONTGOMERY, Ala.—Continuing his attack on Dixiecrats who walked out of the Democratic convention over President Truman's civil rights program, Aubrey Williams, militant southern liberal, last week let loose another blast in the form of an editorial in the Southern Farmer.

Williams, nationally-known as a liberal who headed NYA under Roosevelt, charged that the South and the nation would be better off without the leadership of "such men as Byrd of Virginia, Cox of Georgia and Rankin of Mississippi who have for years been bitterly opposed to most of the things the Democratic Party has stood for and worked for."

He charged that the revolt over civil rights was a phony cover-up for well laid plans of diabolical design. The plan, he said, was to defend powerful interests that had money at stake in any change of the status quo. To prove his point, Williams listed Gessner T. McCorvey, state Democratic chairman, and Frank Dixon, ex-governor, as leaders of the Southern revolt and at the same time big corporation lawyers in Alabama.

As for such men as these leaving the Democratic Party, Williams quipped: "It is to be devoutly hoped that they will. In all honesty they should get into a political party more in line with what they believe. It would be a God-send if they would get out and stay out."

Strongly urging the belief that many white people of the South were not in sympathy with the Dixiecrats, Williams repeatedly referred to "responsible and decent people of the South." This group, he said, was painfully aware of the shortcomings of the South as far as justice and opportunity are concerned.

"Decent and responsible people in the South know, too, that all this talk of 'State's Rights' is cover-up talk," the editorial pointed out.

The editorial—one of the strongest ever published in a Southern journal—called for an end to segregation and all other abuses listed

(See WILLIAMS, page 2)

Baltimore Sidesteps Court Order Ending Golf Link Jim Crow

BALTIMORE—A recent court order here outlawing segregation on all municipal golf courses was side stepped by means of employing separate playing time for whites and Negroes.

The Baltimore Board of Recreation and Parks recent action supercedes a July 13 ruling that called for the sale of golf tickets to all races at any time.

The court made no objection to this move.

Dustin' off the NEWS

By LUCIUS C. HARPER

South Doesn't Know About The Old Constitution

WHAT probably hasn't dawned upon most of us is that the Dixiecrats, the Rebels, led by Govs. Thurmond of South Carolina and Wright of Mississippi, are still under the belief that the Confederate Constitution, and not the U. S. Constitution, is the South's guiding star. Most of us have never read the Confederate Constitution but a glance through it plainly shows that these present day rebels feel as if it is still operative, and while the South may have lost the war, it did not, however lose Jeff Davis' Constitution.

Lucius Harper

The preamble of the U. S. Constitution reads: "We, the people of the United States, in order to form a more perfect Union, establish Justice, insure domestic Tranquility, provide for the com-

See, DUSTIN', Page 2

Wallace Says He'll Stay In Race, But Won't Predict Victory In '48

By VENICE T. SPRAGGS

PHILADELPHIA—Henry A. Wallace has no intention of abandoning his "peoples movement" whose followers approved his presidential candidacy at the founding convention of the new Progressive Party which attracted a wide- and eye-opening attendance.

"I am not going to quit the campaign," Wallace told a press conference here. He also stated: "I have never said I would win."

The former vice president of the United States and ousted secretary of commerce made these statements in reply to a direct question as to whether he, in line with the Chicago Defender demand, would quit the new party and "lead the parade of men and women who want to elect a liberal congress and a liberal president" dedicated to carry out a platform of democracy so ably set forth by the new Democratic Party born in Philadelphia at the party's national convention.

Previously Wallace had pledged to withdraw "If either the Republicans or the Democrats set forth a straightforward campaign platform and selected candidates pledged to carry out such a platform."

Wallace told reporters, "If I were president today, I would as one of my first acts put out an executive order ending all types of segregation in the armed services." He moreover stated that if

See, WALLACE, Page 2

NIGHTINGALE CLIPPED

Roy Fuller was fined $100 plus $10 costs for operating a nursing home at 4647 Calumet ave., with inadequate personnel, overcrowding of patients, and without frontage consents from neighbors.

Asks Integration Department In U. S. Department

NEW YORK—A national campaign to establish within the Federal government a "Department of Integration" to be headed by a "Secretary of Integration" has been launched by Albert F. Morris of this city.

In a circular letter to national leaders, Morris writes: "My plan is to work for a new department in the government—The Department of Integration—to be headed by the Secretary of Integration . . .whose function shall be to intergrate the interests of all citizens in the nation, individually and collectively; and without bias or favor—Moreover, this office should be filled by a black man or woman, for the time being, to form a natural balance. . ."

SHORT GARBAGE CANS

Charged with failure to provide adequate garbage cans at 4851 St. Lawrence ave., Mrs. Mae Atkins, 4812 Vincennes ave., was fined $5

Leaders To Help Raise Funds For Demo Campaign

A national committee of prominent Negroes in all fields of endeavor is being formed to raise funds for the Democratic Party as an answer to the South's refusal to help finance President Truman's campaign, it was revealed this week.

John Sengstacke, editor and publisher of the Chicago Defender, and Congressman William L. Dawson disclosed that the committee will include newspaper publishers, business and professional men and women, many of whom have never been active politically.

This will mark the first time in history that Negroes have sought to help finance a major political party in America.

The charge of some Southerners that Negroes are taking over the machinery of the Democratic Party in Dixie without assuming any of its responsibilities will be answered by Southern Negro leaders. They expect to make up the deficit in the Democratic National Committee caused by the withholding of funds on the part of some Southern Democratic Party organizations.

Demand Return To Dixie Of Coast Businessman Freed 21 Years Ago

OAKLAND, Calif.—Following unusual procedure, Gov. Earl Warren last week slated for July 27 a public hearing of the case of Wiley King, 45, well known local business and churchman, whom the state of Mississippi demands be extradited for what King supporters claim was a self-defense slaying pardoned many years ago.

The governor set the open hearing at his Sacramento office in response to petitions of more than a thousand residents from whom King's strange case received widespread sympathy.

King, whose extradition is sought under the name Jessie Stewart, was given life sentence in Tylertown, Miss., February 1926. Court records show that he stood trial for a slaying which occurred when he was attacked by five armed men who blocked the road, forced him out of his car and threatened his life. It is alleged that he was not represented by legal counsel during the trial.

Pardoned for $250

After serving 22 months, King alleges that he was told by Mississippi prison authorities that he would be pardoned and released if he paid "costs" of $250. King's family and friends raised the money and Mississippi authorities are said to have released him with what he supposed was a full pardon.

King married, went to Mem-

See, DEMAND, Page 2

Hint L. Lomax Jr. To Marry Writer Almena Davis Soon

LOS ANGELES—A current rumor here is that two of the figures in the sensational Lomax divorce case will be married when the publisher receives his final divorce decree from his wife, Carmelita.

According to a reliable source, Almena Davis, editor of the Los Angeles Tribune and third party in the divorce case, will marry Lucius Lomax Jr., publisher of the newspaper she edits.

Miss Davis will be remembered as the 1945 winner of the Wendell Willkie Award for journalism. One of her stories submitted in the contest was titled: "Negroes Are Lousy Lovers."

Snub Truman's Wife; Friends Are Too Dark

The Palmer House and the Stevens Hotel refused a fall dinner date for the first lady of the land, Mrs. Harry S. Truman, and her daughter, Margaret, because their hostesses are Negroes, it was charged Wednesday by a member of the Helping Hand Nursery banquet committee.

Mrs. Lillian L. O'Neil, a member of the committee which included Mrs. Joseph Snowden 3302 Rhodes ave., chairman, and Mrs. Mary Ward Brown, said officials of the two hotels reversed telephone promises of banquet facilities when the delegation arrived in person.

She said Mrs. Truman has accepted the invitation to be guest of honor at the banquet which will be held in the Congress Hotel, October 1.

The three women first visited the Stevens Hotel, Mrs. O'Neil reported, where the head caterer, a Mr. Mueller, said he had no dates open for dinner or luncheon until April 1, 1949. The committee then phoned the Palmer House, where a Miss Ruth Taylor promised facilities.

When they went to her office, they were met by a Mr. Belatti, who denied Miss Taylor's right to make bookings, and said there were no dates open this fall, according to Mrs. O'Neil.

Judge Moore's Reappointment Wins Bar Nod

WASHINGTON—The American Bar association has unanimously approved the reappointment of Judge Herman E. Moore to the bench of the U. S District Court of the Virgin islands.

The Bar association announced its approval in a letter to Sen. Alexander Wiley, chairman of the senate judiciary committee.

It read in part:

"The nominee is a man of notable judicial temperament, and his qualifications for the particular judgeship to which he has been appointed are oustanding. In our opinion, no further evidence of these qualifications should be necessary than the unanimous action of the members of the bar of the court of which he is judge and the strong endorsement of members of the court to which appeals from his court lie."

6 Killed, 19 Hurt As Trucks Collide On Memphis Highway

FRENCHMAN'S BAYOU, Ark.—Six workers, including two women, were killed, and nineteen others were injured, near here Wednesday morning in a collision between a truck bearing 30 colored cotton choppers and a large highway transport.

The victims were en route from Memphis to work as day laborers on the Lee Wilson Plantation at Wilson, Ark. The fatal crash occurred at 6:30 a. m., when the workers' truck, going north, sideswiped the transport and overturned twice, scattering its 30 occupants over the highway.

The dead, who were identified by a woman representative of the

See, 6 KILLED, Page 2

WRITE YOUR CONGRESSMAN—TODAY

— Urge Him To VOTE FOR —

PRESIDENT TRUMAN'S CIVIL RIGHTS LEGISLATION

Civil Rights Mean A Guarantee of Human Rights to You!

WRITE YOUR Congressman In Washington TODAY!

Klan Increases Members To Scare Negroes From Voting

STONE MOUNTAIN, Ga.—Garbed in bedsheets ranging from tattle-tale gray to sparkling white, 700 of Jim Crow's faithful were initiated into the Ku Klux Klan, festering point of native fascism, in an open air ceremony at the foot of Stone Mountain, last Saturday.

Dr. Samuel Green, who is Grand Dragon of the Association of Georgia Klans, estimated that 5,000 Ku Kluxers were present. Responsible newsmen said the number was closer to 3,000, however.

In swearing in the recruits to the night rider and terror fraternity, Green was presented as the head of the Ku Klux Klan in America. Generally, the Klan operates as a separate organization in each state, a procedure which has prevented its being cited for conspiracy to violate federal civil rights statutes.

Out of state Kluxers from Alabama, Florida and Tennessee, helped to make up the assembly of hooded figures, who danced around bonfires and whooped themselves hoarse, only taking time out to patronize the soda pop and hot

See KLAN, Page 2

had been exposed to more liberal racial climates in other countries than they had experienced in the United States. These young men often manifested an active and challenging interest in civil rights reform, and even in the South many of them set out to win an active place in local affairs for themselves and other black citizens. Although in 1940 the best surveys counted only 151,000 registered black voters in the eleven southern states of the old Confederacy, by 1947 the total had jumped to 595,000 and by 1952 it was up to 1,008,000.

housing discrimination case, *Shelley v. Kraemer,* that lower courts and government bodies could not enforce exclusionary residence agreements in place in many neighborhoods all across the country that were aimed at preventing blacks from purchasing properties. Again the importance of the case was in large part symbolic, but it provided further evidence that the Supreme Court was more responsive to demands for equal rights than other levels or branches of the government. President Truman had appointed a civil rights study commission that submitted a strong report calling for progress in civil rights

"separate" could never be "equal."

Even the last figure, however, represented only 20 percent of black southerners of voting age.

The reentry of blacks into political participation across the South had been significantly assisted by a 1944 U.S. Supreme Court decision, *Smith v. Allwright,* outlawing what was known as the "white primary"—internal Democratic Party primary elections in which only white voters could participate. Because in most southern locales the only political competition that existed occurred *within* the Democratic Party, even the minority of black voters who actually were registered were effectively disenfranchised by "white primaries." Although some southern Democrats sought to obstruct the implementation of the Court's ruling, by the early 1950s black voters had more influence in the South than they had had since the 1880s. Perhaps even more important, as more and more black Southerners migrated to the North during the 1940s and early 1950s as the increasing mechanization of southern agriculture further and further reduced the need for field workers, the northern black vote also started to become a more significant force in electoral politics, with both Democrats and Republicans striving to recruit these new arrivals.

Smith v. Allwright was not the only significant civil rights victory in the Supreme Court, however. Four years later, in 1948, the Court ruled in a

for African Americans. Truman had also ordered the U.S. military to eliminate segregationist practices, but the president had no prospects for getting civil rights legislation through the U.S. Congress, in part because so many senior congressional Democrats were southern segregationists.

Even prior to 1948, a number of civil rights lawyers had begun planning a major litigation effort premised on the assumption that the U.S. Supreme Court, when faced with persuasive evidence of the effects of segregation, would rule against segregationist practices whether or not it formally abandoned its 1896 endorsement of "separate but equal" in *Plessy v. Ferguson.* The initial area of concentration was higher education, because most major public universities in the South were completely segregated—as were virtually all public schools in the region. Although public colleges for blacks existed in each state, in most southern and "border" states black students seeking many forms of graduate education, including law school training, simply had to go to other parts of the United States in order to have access to such degree programs. Beginning with a 1938 Supreme Court decision in a case from Missouri where the only public law school was for whites only, and then in a 1948 decision concerning Oklahoma, where the only law school in the state similarly excluded blacks, lawyers for the National Association for the Advancement of Colored People—the NAACP—took their initial steps toward showing the Court that in the field of education, "separate" could *never* be "equal."

Then in two cases decided by the Supreme Court in 1950, the NAACP's attack on segregated education made significant strides. In another law school case, the state of Texas had attempted to argue that a small, newly created, and inadequately staffed law school for black students ought to obviate any constitutional requirement to admit

9-2

"President Truman Wipes Out Segregation in Armed Forces,"
Chicago Defender, July 31, 1948.
Serial and Government Publications Division.

blacks into the law school of the all-white University of Texas, far and away the leading educational institution in the state. In the second case, the state of Oklahoma had grudgingly admitted a black graduate student to the principal state university, but it had then required him to study and eat in segregated facilities and to sit in separate, fenced-off alcoves during his classroom sessions. Although the unanimous Supreme Court decisions

With particular encouragement from one of the three trial judges, the NAACP attorneys explicitly indicated that it was the very practice of racial segregation, and not simply the resulting inequalities, that ought to be expressly prohibited by the U.S. Constitution. The same frontal challenge inescapably emerged in the other cases as well, and by the fall of 1952 all four of these cases, along with a fifth from the District of Columbia, had progressed to the U.S. Supreme Court. After first hearing argument in late 1952,

"Brown v. Board of Education"

in both cases carefully avoided making any direct comments about *Plessy* or articulating any broad-gauge condemnation of segregation, they provided two additional unmistakable declarations that equal educational opportunities could not be provided within a racially segregated framework.

Initially the NAACP lawyers, captained by Thurgood Marshall, who fifteen years later would become the first black Supreme Court justice in American history, had felt that higher education, rather than elementary and secondary education, was the preferable target for their antisegregation lawsuits. But in many counties across the South, particularly in rural counties well-removed from larger cities, segregated elementary and secondary schools for African Americans were not only vastly inferior to those for whites but were often so poorly housed and staffed as to be almost unrecognizable as educational institutions. In a number of such locales, black parents and ministers began to press for increased funding and improved facilities for their children, but members of white schoolboards, believing that any improvements in black schools would have to be funded out of a diminution of the resources available to white ones, brushed the requests aside.

Out of such nascent local efforts by concerned black parents, however, a number of requests for lawsuits came to Marshall and his NAACP colleagues. One case emerged in Virginia, another in the small border state of Delaware, and another in the city of Topeka in the largely midwestern state of Kansas. Perhaps the most promising, however, emerged from an intensely segregated rural county in South Carolina, where the evidence of gross inequality under segregation was overwhelming.

the Court, uncertain of precisely how to handle such a direct challenge to so deeply ingrained a southern practice as racially segregated education, held the cases over for reargument in the fall of 1953. By that time a new Chief Justice, Earl Warren, previously the Republican governor of California, had joined the Court, and following that second argument, Warren carefully took the lead in establishing unanimous agreement among the nine justices that the only proper result was a direct and low-key opinion declaring that racial segregation in education was both immoral and unconstitutional. Seven months later, on May 17, 1954, that unanimous opinion was issued in the name of the lead case from Kansas, *Brown v. Board of Education of Topeka*.

The *Brown* decision was brief, powerful, and purposely incomplete. Holding that "in the field of public education the doctrine of 'separate but equal' has no place," the Court explicitly ruled that "Separate educational facilities are inherently unequal." But the Court frankly acknowledged that how to pursue desegregation—how to remedy the unconstitutional racial discrimination that the schools had practiced for decades—was neither simple nor immediately clear. And so it set the cases for further argument in the subsequent term of court on the question of implementation. One year and two weeks after the initial landmark decision, on May 31, 1955, Warren issued another brief and unanimous opinion for the Court stressing that the elimination of racial discrimination in public education could best be overseen by the federal district courts closest to each of the four school districts and instructing those local judges to pursue nondiscriminatory operation of the public schools "with all deliberate speed."

Without a doubt, *Brown* was a landmark decision and the most important Supreme Court ruling in almost a century—arguably the most important ruling in the Court's entire history. Immediate reaction was somewhat muted, however, for although ardent southern segregationists of course expressed displeasure and criticized the justices for pointing toward integrated schools, which many in the South declared they would never accept, no fury or angry rebellion was initially manifest. The actual decision affected immediately only the five areas that had been involved in the *Brown* cases; black plaintiffs would have to bring scores of new lawsuits if they wanted the principles of *Brown* to be applied to the hundreds of other formally segregated school systems across the South. Although black America understandably welcomed and exulted in the *Brown* ruling, again the response was modest, because most black participants in the effort that had led to *Brown* appreciated full well that a Supreme Court decree—even a unanimous one—would not bring about racial equality in education or in social relations in general.

But *Brown* undeniably marked the real beginning of America's civil rights revolution, even if the long-term importance it would have was not immediately evident in the aftermath of the decision. For black America, *Brown* was a clear and powerful signal that at least one top-ranked institution in white society had fully grasped and endorsed the moral correctness of the black litigants' assertion that racial discrimination and segregation had no place in American law or public life. That signal was as potentially empowering as it was encouraging, and it was a signal that undeniably hastened and energized the incipient activism for racial change that had been locally manifest in so many black communities in the years after World War II.

As significant as any place in which the Supreme Court's moral signal was welcomed was the black community of Montgomery, Alabama. In later years the onset of black Montgomery's boycott of segregated and abusive seating practices on the city's public buses in December 1955 would come to share equal status with the *Brown* decision, marking the beginning of the modern black freedom struggle, but the Montgomery boycott could not have occurred without earlier roots, and the intertwining of those roots with the moral power of *Brown* is an instructive and important linkage.

The actual onset of the December 5, 1955, black community boycott of Montgomery's public buses was occasioned by the arrest on December 1

of a humble and well-respected black seamstress, Rosa Parks, for refusing to surrender her seat on a crowded bus to a newly boarding white rider. The idea of a boycott by black riders to protest discriminatory treatment on the buses, however, had been discussed by middle-class women activists in black Montgomery for a number of years, and in May 1954 news of the *Brown* decision had helped stimulate the president of their group, the Women's Political Council (WPC), to write to Montgomery's mayor and politely make it clear that a boycott would occur if improvements did not take place. "Three-fourths of the riders of these public conveyances are Negroes," WPC President Jo Ann Robinson, an English professor at all-black Alabama State College, told the mayor. "If Negroes did not patronize them, they could not possibly operate."

Although discussions continued, and although several driver–passenger incidents led to a heightened desire to call such a boycott, only on December 1, 1955, as word of Parks's arrest spread through black Montgomery, did Robinson and other leading activists resolve that the time for action had indeed arrived.

Robinson and her female colleagues were largely teachers, whose jobs and incomes could be terminated by white Alabama officials if they so desired. Montgomery's other senior black activist, railroad worker E. D. Nixon, was a courageous man but with only a modest formal education. More important, for the activists to rally the support and participation of Montgomery's thousands of black citizens, the vigorous support of the city's black churches—and access to their sanctuaries for meeting space—would be necessary. Not only could the ministers of these churches help rally the support of their congregations, but they were men whose jobs and salaries were controlled wholly from within the black community, hence making them less vulnerable to white economic retaliation.

As the boycott got under way, the ministers stepped to the fore and the initial activists remained somewhat in the background. Two young pastors of highly important churches, who were also known as impressive speakers, Reverend Martin Luther King, Jr., and Reverend Ralph D. Abernathy, became the principal spokespersons for the newly formed boycott group, the Montgomery Improvement Association (MIA). White city officials and bus company executives showed no serious interest in negotiating an early end to the protest by granting the black citizens' requests for improved seating practices, which considerably surprised the black leadership. But the black community soon had an impressively well-organized car pool system up and running so that black citizens could continue to dispense with public buses with relatively little inconvenience. Black support of the boycott was virtually

The Weather

Montgomery: Cloudy to partly cloudy and continued cool. Predicted high today 54, low 38. High yesterday 57, low 43. (Details, Weather Map, Page 2A.)

The Montgomery Advertiser

127th Year—No. 291 | Full Day, Night and Sunday Service By The Associated Press | Montgomery, Ala., Tuesday Morning, December 6, 1955 | 26 Pages

5,000 At Meeting Outline Boycott; Bullet Clips Bus

By JOE AZBELL
Advertiser City Editor

An estimated 5,000 hymn-singing Negroes packed the Holt Street Baptist Church to its outer doors and spilled over into three streets blocking traffic last night as they voted to continue a racial boycott against buses of the Montgomery City Lines Inc.

Meanwhile, J. H. Bagley, manager of the Montgomery City Lines, reported that a bus driven by driver B. S. Johnson, apparently was fired on by a person with a .22 caliber rifle in the Negro Washington Park area.

Bagley said the bullet hit the rear of the bus and Johnson could not determine from where it was fired.

ENFORCE LAW

The bus company manager also reiterated a previous statement that his firm would not violate the law on segregation of bus passengers and that he would continue to require all of his drivers to enforce the law. "If they don't, the drivers can be fined or sentenced," he said.

Meanwhile, police reported an unidentified party threw a large stone and struck the front of a City Lines bus at the intersection of S. Jeff Davis and S. Holt street late yesterday. No personal injury and only slight damage to the bus resulted, officers said.

In a resolution passed at the meeting by the Negroes with a roaring applause, the emotional group voted to ask "all citizens of Montgomery" to refrain from riding buses of the Montgomery City Lines Inc. until the bus transportation situation is cleared up to the "satisfaction of citizens" who ride and patronize them.

The resolution, among other things, stated that "citizens of Montgomery" have been intimidated, embarrassed and coerced while riding the public conveyances and in view of the humiliation they have endured they agreed that they would refrain from using the buses.

It also declared that a "delegation of citizens" was prepared at all times to sit down with officials of the Montgomery City Lines and develop with them a program that the bus lines' patrons would find satisfactory and equitable.

The resolution stated that "no methods of intimidation" would be used or had been used to keep anyone from riding the buses but it asked that a person's "conscience" be his guide.

FROM PARKS CASE

The continuing boycott grew out of the arrest and conviction of Rosa Parks, 42, 634 Cleveland Ave., Negro seamstress at a department store here, on a segregation violation count.

The conviction of the Negro woman may cause a court test on segregation of Negroes and whites on Montgomery buses, The Advertiser learned yesterday.

The Parks woman and Fred Daniel, 19, 1646 Hall St., arrested yesterday for disorderly conduct, were introduced to the large audience and the audience stood, applauding loud. They each were described as churchgoers and industrious, law abiding citizens.

The Rev. M. L. King, pastor of the Dexter Avenue Baptist Church, told the crowd that the "tools of justice" must be used to attain the "day of freedom, justice and equality." He urged "unity of Negroes" for "we must stick together and work together if we are to win and we will win in standing up for our rights as Americans."

Other speakers on the program said the idea of the boycott of the buses being "anything like the "methods of the White Citizens Council" is "ridiculous" for "what we are doing is legal and constitutional."

"It is not like the Ku Klux Klan in going to our homes and taking men out and lynching them. It is not terrorism but democracy, a protest of Americans, in action," one of the speakers declared.

A collection was taken up at the meeting to finance the cam-

Regents Give Georgia Tech 'Green Light'

ATLANTA, Dec. 5 (AP)—Georgia's Board of Regents today rejected Gov. Marvin Griffin's move to have Georgia Tech's football team pulled from the Sugar Bowl on a racial issue and opened the way for nonsegregated games played outside the South.

At the same time, it closed the door on any further bowl games, played in the South, which do not follow the segregation laws and customs of the host state.

This was a direct slap at the Sugar Bowl officials who not only invited Pittsburgh, a team with a Negro player, to meet Tech, but also let Pittsburgh sell its tickets on a nonsegregated basis.

BACKED DOWN

Shortly before the regents acted, Griffin had backed down somewhat on his Friday demand for a racial policy that not only would have barred Tech from the Sugar Bowl but would have prohibited any Georgia state college teams from playing against Negroes or before unsegregated spectators.

The governor told his news conference that his request to the regents chairman, Robert O. Arnold of Covington, was aimed only at the Sugar Bowl and that he would not oppose nonsegregated games played in states where segregation is not practiced.

A storm of controversy was touched off by the governor's move, which led to a noisy, all-night demonstration Friday by Tech students who burned Griffin in effigy, smashed into the state Capitol and were restrained by a cordon of police from storming the governor's mansion.

INDIRECT VOTE

The regents did not vote directly to permit Tech to carry out its Sugar Bowl contract. They merely adopted the resolution of policy applying to any future contracts.

But to make the situation clear, Arnold commented as the meeting closed, "There should be no further doubt that Tech will play in the Sugar Bowl."

It provides that in all athletic contests played in Georgia, the state's laws which prohibit racial mixing must be observed.

And it declares that in future contests outside the state, teams of Georgia state colleges "shall respect the laws, customs and traditions of the host state." That means that in states outside the South, Georgia teams can play opponents having Negroes or before nonsegregated spectators, because laws and customs of those states do not require segregation.

But the resolution adds, "No contract or agreement shall be entered into for an athletic contest in any state where the circumstances under which it is fulfilled are repugnant to the laws, customs and traditions of the host state."

Revenue Board Adds Clerk To Office Staff

Mrs. Olive Holland has been

NEGROES TO CONTINUE BOYCOTT

An estimated crowd of 5,000 Negroes roared approval to a resolution last night at the Holt Street Baptist Church to continue a boycott against the Montgomery City Lines, Inc. until the bus situation is settled to the satisfaction of its patrons. The huge assemblage featured the appearance of Rosa Parks, 42-year-old Negro woman, who was convicted yesterday of violating segregation laws by refusing to move from the white section of a city bus to the Negro section under orders of the bus driver.—*Photo by Lesher.*

LONE NEGRO WAITS AT BUS STOP

A Negro woman waits alone at the Court Square bus stop for a city bus to take her to her Job as a domestic. She was one of the few Negroes who boarded Montgomery City Lines buses yesterday as Negroes staged a boycott against the bus lines in protest of the arrest of Rosa Parks, Negro seamstress, on a charge of violating segregation laws by sitting in the white section on a city bus. At the time this photo was taken, there usually are several hundred Negroes waiting to catch buses in the downtown area.—*Photo by Lesher*

Approval Near On 2 Matrons For City Jail

Formal approval of the hiring of two matrons for the Montgomery City Jail—the first to ever be employed at the jail—is expected at today's meeting of the city commission.

Police Commissioner Clyde Sellers recommended the hiring of the two nurse-matrons after a list of approved applicants was submitted to him by Personnel Director Wade Moss.

The women, who reported to work Dec. 1, are Mrs. Mary Alice Cannon, 40, of Speigner, and Mrs. Helen L. Kimbrough, 42, of 3 Cedar St. Their starting salary was listed at $240 per month.

ONLY PROMISE

Both women formerly held similar positions at the Julia Tutwiler Prison for Women. Mrs. Kimbrough worked fulltime at the prison for a number of years. Mrs. Cannon worked parttime at the prison. She also has worked at the Mississippi State Hospital and the Montgomery Tuberculosis Sanitorium.

Sellers said the employment of jail matrons for the city was "about the only promise I made during the elections and I tried to keep it."

WHITE HOUSE CHECKED?

Strauss Balks On Story Behind D-Y Pact Axing

WASHINGTON, Dec. 5 (AP)—A Senate search for "criminal conspiracy" in the Dixon-Yates contract today collided with a refusal by the head of the Atomic Energy Commission to say whether he had discussed repudiation of the contract with the White House.

AEC Chairman Lewis L. Strauss took his defiant stand "on penalty of whatever the penalty may be."

"Isn't it natural you would notify the White House of the possibility of fraud?" he was asked by Sen. Kefauver, chairman of a Senate Antimonopoly subcommittee which is investigating the abandoned private power contract.

"That's a natural inference," Strauss replied.

But he refused to disclose whether he had any conversations with White House officials about junking the contract "or even to imply that I had any."

"On penalty of whatever the penalty may be," Strauss said, "I'll claim the privilege under the doctrine of separation of powers."

He contended this constitutional provision, dividing the powers of the federal government among its three branches, prohibits Congress from making such inquiries. He said he was refusing to answer "even at the price of your displeasure."

Kefauver challenged Strauss position. Harking back to the Teapot Dome scandals of the 1920s, the senator said the Supreme Court held then that the doctrine of separation of powers was no defense against inquiry into "matters involving fraud or misconduct."

The Dixon-Yates contract, negotiated at the direction of President Eisenhower, provided for construction of a 107-million-dollar generating plant at West Memphis, Ark., to provide electricity

(See STRAUSS, Page 6A)

ADVERTISER TODAY

Voters To T King-Sized Over State

Education Aid Top Two Items To Face Test

By BOB INGRAM

Alabama voters make their decision today on 29 proposed amendments to the state Constitution, including two which are designed to solve the financial problems of education.

Tremendous interest has been aroused in the referendum with most of it centered on Amendments No. 1 and 2—the Goodwyn school tax and the $110 million bond issue.

But also up for consideration are four other amendments of statewide application and 23 amendments applying to various counties and cities.

ADJUSTED INCOME

The school tax proposal—named after its author, Rep. O. J. (Joe) Goodwyn of Montgomery County—would levy a tax on the adjusted gross income of individuals and corporations.

Goodwyn and officials of the State Revenue Department have estimated the tax, if ratified, will produce approximately $29 million annually, all of it earmarked exclusively for education.

Supporters of the tax, led by the Citizens Committee for Schools, have warned if the revenue sought by this measure is not provided the schools of Alabama will close in March.

This charge has been heatedly denied by opponents of the bill, and Gov. James E. Folsom on one occasion stated bluntly "the schools will not close."

BULK OF MONEY

At a later time he elaborated on that remark and said the schools would not close because he felt the voters would approve the Goodwyn tax.

The bulk of the money anticipated from the tax would be used in giving Alabama's 24,000 school teachers a pay raise averaging $600 a year, an increase which already has been granted.

Arguments in support of the amendment have stressed the point that the tax will be paid by so many people (an estimated 900,000) that no one will have to pay very much. Under the existing income tax, only 167,000 people are required to pay any tax.

Opponents of the bill have been especially critical becuase the tax is retroactive and further, because the measure does not allow any deductions for medical expenses, dependents or contributions to charity.

ONLY DEDUCTIONS

The only deductions permitted are "necessary business expenses" which would apply to corporations and businesses but would not apply to the average individual taxpayer.

Practically every major organization in the state has endorsed the amendment, including the

(See EDUCATION, Page 6A)

COUNTY EYES NO. 6 RESULT

One of the amendments on today's referendum ballot to be voted on throughout the state applies only to Montgomery county.

Sponsored by the entire Montgomery county legislative dele-

Amendm For Toda

Election officials today urged of the 30 proposed amendments to election.

It was pointed out that unless the proposals before entering the vo time might be lost and some actua

Here, on this official guide, ar

AMENDMENT NO. 1
Special income tax for educatio

AMENDMENT NO. 2
$110,000,000 bond issue for sch

AMENDMENT NO. 3
Authorizes additional property each county for public school purp voters of the district.

AMENDMENT NO. 4
Authorizes special property tax be first submitted to the voters of son, Mobile and Montgomery.

AMENDMENT NO. 5
Authorizes $2,000,000 bond issue

AMENDMENT NO. 6
Montgomery County—Special pr be first submitted to the voters of

AMENDMENT NO. 7
Re: Obligations for public imp municipalities of less than 6,000 pop

AMENDMENT NO. 8
Walker County—Each municipa all kinds of property, to promote the and the location of new industries, corporation, to lend its credit or g cial ad valorem tax, to create a

AMENDMENT NO. 9
Conecuh County—Same as No. 8 Conecuh County and must first be municipality.

AMENDMENT NO. 10
Clarke County—Compensation

AMENDMENT NO. 11
Elmore County—Legislature ma of the Judge of Probate, sheriff, ta register of Circuit Court.

AMENDMENT NO. 12
Limestone County—Special pro

AMENDMENT NO. 13
Limestone County—Special one to be used to finance a geological

AMENDMENT NO. 14
Russell County—Special prope first submitted to the voters of sai

AMENDMENT NO. 15
Coffee County—Same as No. 8 Coffee County and must first be su pality.

AMENDMENT NO. 16
Lawrence County—Special scho bonds. To be first submitted to the

AMENDMENT NO. 17
Bullock County—Legislature ma of tax collector and tax assessor.

AMENDMENT NO. 18
City of Auburn and Opelika— schools. To be first submitted to

AMENDMENT NO. 19
Lee County—Special property mitted to the voters of said coun

AMENDMENT NO. 20
Jefferson County—Method of 10th Circuit.

AMENDMENT NO. 21
Fayette County—Any municipal mitments or undertake projects. of such municipality.

AMENDMENT NO. 22
Butler County—Special proper submitted to the voters of said co

AMENDMENT NO. 23
Cullman County—Same as No. in Cullman County.

AMENDMENTS NO. 24 and NO. 25
Cullman County—Salary of C

AMENDMENT NO. 26
Tuscaloosa County—May issue To be first submitted to the vot

AMENDMENT NO. 27
Winston County—Special prope and health purposes. To be first su

AMENDMENT NO. 28
Marion County—Each municip all kinds of property, to promote t and the location of new industrie corporation, to lend its credit o special ad valorem tax, to constr poration, etc.

AMENDMENT NO. 29
Marion and Lamar Counties— bodies.

AMENDMENT NO. 30
Lamar County—Same as No. 7

total, and within several weeks the lack of patronage of public transportation made Robinson's earlier prediction come true as the bus company was forced to raise fares and cut back service.

In early 1956 the black leadership explicitly demanded fully desegregated seating on buses, and the remarkable black community unity began to draw national news attention. White Montgomery remained intransigent, however, and at the end of January, white segregationists exploded a small bomb on the front porch of the house occupied by the MIA's president, Reverend Martin Luther King, Jr. No one was injured, but the incident drew much more national press coverage to Montgomery than the boycott previously had received. In addition, some of that coverage focused on the persuasive advocacy of nonviolence, of "loving one's enemies," that King had articulated to the angry crowd that had gathered after the bombing, much as he had done in church rallies earlier in the boycott.

King's growing status both locally and outside Montgomery was given yet another boost by white Montgomery in mid-February, when local authorities indicted King and scores of other boycott participants for supposedly violating an obscure statute aimed at prohibiting boycotts in labor disputes. King's ensuing trial on that charge drew even more national and some international attention to the ongoing protest, and the car pool system remained in operation as most of white Montgomery continued to disdain any talk of compromising its tenets of segregation.

Immediately after the King bombing, the MIA filed suit in federal court, alleging that the city's maintenance of segregated bus seating practices violated the clear principle of Brown, and in June of 1956 two of three judges on the local federal court agreed, concluding that Brown's mandate necessarily applied to government-sponsored segregation in transportation as well as education. But Montgomery city officials immediately appealed the decision to the U.S. Supreme Court, and in the interim the buses remained segregated and black Montgomery remained dependent on its private, voluntary car pool system.

Five months later, in November, the Supreme Court affirmed the lower court decision, and in several weeks its formal mandate was delivered to Montgomery. Only then did city and bus company officials finally institute desegregated seating. With King and Abernathy in the lead, black Montgomery returned to the buses, as civil rights supporters across the country celebrated the achievement.

The successful Montgomery boycott, like the *Brown* case, symbolized a tremendous step forward for black Southerners. Again the importance was less in the immediate tangible changes that had occurred than in the larger political message that was conveyed. Although the NAACP's lawyers emphasized that the actual successful resolution of the boycott had, like *Brown*, depended on achieving a Supreme Court ruling, the real meaning and importance of Montgomery for almost all nonlawyers lay in the stark political message that an ordinary group of citizens, with no initial outside support and no particular organizational expertise, could through simple unity and dedication demonstrate an almost revolutionary degree of grassroots political activism—which ultimately prevailed.

King and Abernathy were not alone in appreciating that the Montgomery triumph heralded a political model that could very well prove productive in other southern cities, and with assistance from other southern black clergymen and from a small circle of northern advisers they announced the creation of a new region-wide organization, the Southern Christian Leadership Conference (SCLC). Although a number of NAACP leaders made no secret of their belief that one black civil rights organization was enough, King and his ministerial colleagues hoped to reach beyond bus desegregation campaigns to stimulate new levels of black voter registration across the South. At a Washington march called to commemorate the third anniversary of the *Brown* decision and to press Republican president Dwight D. Eisenhower to take action supportive of civil rights efforts, King delivered his first significant national address and identified the right to vote as the linchpin for freedom that black Southerners had to attain in order to get on the road to full equality.

But much of the white South, as the 1956 events in Montgomery had demonstrated, had no intention of allowing desegregation of schools, buses, and other facilities to spread quickly across the region without fierce and active opposition. Although Congress in September 1957 managed to pass a modest and limited Civil Rights Act, the first such piece of legislation in the twentieth century, arguably the most significant civil rights story of the year happened in Little Rock, Arkansas, where local segregationists, aided by Arkansas's segregationist governor Orval Faubus, obstructed the scheduled token desegregation of a city high school, one of the first such schools to actually face up to implementing the meaning of *Brown.* Eventually President Eisenhower was forced to send a detachment of federal soldiers into Little Rock in order to ensure that nine black students would be able to attend peacefully the formally all-white Central High School, but some months later the U.S. Supreme Court used a case growing out of the Little Rock turmoil as an opportunity to issue a strong and powerful reaffirmation of *Brown.* That declaration notwithstanding, however, relatively little actual school desegregation took place between the mid-1950s and the mid-1960s. In many rural locales southern blacks were simply too vulnerable to white power and pressure to want to launch battles to desegregate local schools, and even in most southern towns in which black parents did take the initiative, white school boards successfully delayed taking any meaningful action. Some local federal judges, leery of stimulating another potentially violent crisis like the one in Little Rock, also chose to tread water rather than order quick or far-reaching local school compliance with the principles of *Brown.*

By the end of the 1950s in the South, it almost appeared as if white intransigence in the face of occurrences such as *Brown,* Montgomery, and Little Rock had to some extent fought the new black activism to a draw. Martin Luther King, Jr., had certainly emerged as a new national voice for southern activists, but neither SCLC nor the NAACP had generated any notable progress across the South during 1958 and 1959, and white opposition had significantly reduced the rate of increase in black southern voter registration. King resolved that he would move from Montgomery to Atlanta and devote more of his time to civil rights work. Then, with little prior warning, the civil rights log-jam suddenly broke open in February of 1960 when a new wave of antisegregation protests sprang up among black southern college students.

The "sit-in movement," as the student protests were accurately labeled, began in Greensboro, North Carolina, when four young male undergraduates decided that something ought to be done about the whites-only lunch counters in variety and department stores that otherwise pretended to welcome black customers. Although such stores often also featured segregated restrooms and whites-only water fountains, the discrimina-

tory lunch counters could be targeted in a simple, direct, and utterly nonviolent way: Simply by sitting down in an empty seat and remaining there as waitresses ignored them or refused to serve them, the black students could both offer a quiet protest and also heavily cut into the counters' receipts.

The sit-in tactic spread first from Greensboro to other North Carolina cities with black colleges, and then moved to black college towns across the southeast with impressive speed. In many stores managers simply closed down their food service at the first sign of a sit-in, and in some cities segregationist hoodlums, with active or passive police connivance, harassed the protesters by pouring mustard, ketchup, and sugar on them, or more brutally by beating them. Despite the white response, however, the rapidly spreading sit-in campaign brought black college students into the civil rights scene to a vastly greater degree than ever had been the case before. Adult organizations such as SCLC, the NAACP, and the Congress of Racial Equality (CORE) all sought to assist and win the allegiance of the new student activists. Within just a few weeks' time, however, more than one hundred student sit-in representatives from across the South convened in Raleigh, North Carolina, for a meeting that signaled the founding of what soon came to be called the Student Nonviolent Coordinating Committee (SNCC).

The creation of SNCC represented a new stage in the black freedom struggle, much as the sit-ins themselves undeniably kicked off America's experience of the 1960s. Not only did SNCC and the sit-ins add a new generation to the civil rights effort, but they brought into the movement a cohort of nonviolent "shock-troops" whose youth afforded them more freedom to devote themselves to civil rights work than did adults with family and job responsibilities.

King and other adult activists appreciated the new energy the students brought to the movement, but the students themselves were wary of allowing the older activists—whether the NAACP or King—to call the shots. Adult–student tensions were highlighted in a fall 1960 sit-in effort in Atlanta, where those arrested included an initially reluctant King. The 1960 presidential election and the victory of John F. Kennedy meant more to the future of civil rights than those internecine differences.

Martin Luther King, Jr., was among those who hoped for a new degree of presidential support for civil rights with the advent of Kennedy. Little Rock aside, President

Item 9-18 A
Daisy Bates, State Press, Little Rock, Arkansas, to Roy Wilkins, December 17, 1957. Autograph letter. NAACP Collection, Manuscript Division. Courtesy Arkansas State Press of Kearney Publishing Group, Inc.

Mr. Roy Wilkins
20 West 40th Street
New York, N. Y.

Dear Mr. Wilkins:

Conditions are yet pretty rough in the school for the children. Last week, Minnie Jean's mother, Mrs. W. B. Brown, asked me to go over to the school with her for a conference with the principal, and the two assistant principals. Subject of conference:"Firmer disciplinary measures, and the withdrawal of Minnie Jean from the glee club's Christmas program." The principal had informed Minnie Jean in withdrawing her from the program that "When it is definitely decided that Negroes will go to school here with the whites, and the troops are removed, then you will be able to participate in all activities." We strongly challenged this statement, which he denied making in that fashion.

We also pointed out that the treatment of the children had been getting steadily worse for the last two weeks in the form of kicking, spitting, and general abuse. As a result of our visit, stronger measures are being taken against the white students who are guilty of committing these offenses. For instance, a boy who had been suspended for two weeks, flunked both six-weeks tests, and on his return to school, the first day he knocked Gloria Ray into her locker. As a result of our visit, he was given an indefinite suspension.

The superintendent of schools also requested a conference the same afternoon. Clarence and I went down and spent about two hours. Here, again we pointed out that a three-day suspension given Hugh Williams for a sneak attack perpetrated on one of the Negro boys which knocked him out, and required a doctor's attention, was not sufficient punishment. We also informed him that our investigation revealed that there were many pupils willing to help if given the opportunity, and that President Eisenhower was very much concerned about the Little Rock crisis. He has stated his willingness to come down and address the student body if invited by student leaders of the school. This information was passed on to the principals of the school, but we have not been assured that leadership would be given to children in the school who are willing to organize for law and order. However, we have not abandoned the idea. Last Friday, the 13th, I was asked to call Washington and see if we could get FBI men placed in the school December 16-18.

Item 9-9
"Lunch Counter Sit-in," Greensboro, North Carolina, 1960.
NAACP Collection, Prints and Photographs Division.

Eisenhower had said as little as he could on the subject, whereas Kennedy during his presidential campaign had given repeated signs that he intended to be a special friend to black Americans. Once in office, however, and especially in the context of being faced with a congressional situation in which southern Democratic segregationists still controlled disproportionate power in both the House of Representatives and the Senate, Kennedy adopted a decidedly low-key approach to civil rights as well. King, among others, sought to keep his hopes up, but James Farmer and his colleagues in CORE resolved to take direct action of an even more dramatic sort than the students had employed a year earlier. Identifying continued segregation in interstate transportation facilities—primarily southern bus stations serving long-distance routes—as a particularly egregious example of ongoing racism that federal government authority ought to tackle and eliminate, the CORE activists mapped out what they called a "Freedom Ride"—a two-week bus trip across the South by an integrated group of riders who would "test" or challenge any segregated facilities they encountered. Starting in Washington, D.C., they made it their goal to arrive in New Orleans, Louisiana, on May 17, 1961, the seventh anniversary of *Brown*.

The Freedom Riders encountered some segregationist obstacles and troubles in South Carolina, but only when their buses entered eastern Alabama did they experience serious terrorist violence. Outside the city of Anniston one bus was attacked and burned, and the escaping riders were beaten as they fled. Some time later, when the second bus arrived in the major city of Birmingham, a longtime Ku Klux Klan stronghold in which city police were rightfully believed to be in league with the segregationist terrorists, those riders were also attacked and assaulted. These events brought the federal Department of Justice, presided over by Attorney General Robert F. Kennedy, into the situation, and only with Justice Department prodding did Alabama and bus company officials agree to allow the bloodied but unbowed riders to head on to their next city, Montgomery.

When the riders' bus arrived in Montgomery, however, no city police were anywhere to be seen, and yet another Klan mob attacked the riders, again inflicting several serious injuries. Two days later, when the riders and the MIA attempted to hold a rally at Reverend Ralph Abernathy's downtown church, another white mob surrounded the church, bombarded it with bricks and rocks, and set fire to at least one auto. The rally participants feared for their lives as a small number of federal marshals held off the mob until a force of National Guard soldiers arrived to take charge. Two days later, under elaborate protection, one busload of riders left Montgomery headed west to Jackson, the capital of Mississippi, where they were immediately arrested and incarcerated in the state penitentiary.

The Freedom Ride was a bloody but undeniable political success for the activists, because it graphically conveyed to the American public just how great a level of violence southern segregationists were prepared to use to halt antisegregation initiatives. The lack of federal support during the Freedom Ride left many civil rights activists questioning how heart-felt a commitment to civil rights progress the Kennedy brothers actually held, but for the students who were active in SNCC the riders' experiences were yet one more sign that an intensified offensive against southern segregation could not be postponed. Several SNCC members, led by Robert Moses, had already made a commitment to pursue organizing efforts in southwestern Mississippi near the town of McComb, and by the end of the summer a second SNCC project, centered in the southwest Georgia city of Albany, was also under way.

By late 1961 Albany had become the site of the most intensive southern civil rights effort since the Montgomery boycott five years earlier. SNCC workers, in conjunction with local NAACP activists and with King's SCLC, generated a significant black community commitment to picketing and marches aimed at persuading Albany's white leadership to eliminate formal segregation from everyday public life. But white Albany did not budge. Mass arrests depleted both the emotional and the financial reserves of the black community, and King's SCLC pulled back. After several relatively quiet months in the spring of 1962, mass demonstrations and mass arrests resumed in mid-summer, but again white Albany stonewalled, even in the face of a public declaration by President Kennedy that the white officials ought to negotiate a compromise settlement. By the end of the summer the protests were moribund, and the national news media was heralding Albany as the first major defeat for civil rights proponents.

To Martin Luther King, Jr., that verdict was especially painful, and throughout the fall and winter of 1962 to 1963 King pondered how to recoup. In October, federal troops again had to be deployed after violent white rioters sought to block the admission of the University of Mississippi's first black student, James Meredith, but most signs indicated that President Kennedy, like the rest of the federal government, preferred to deal with civil

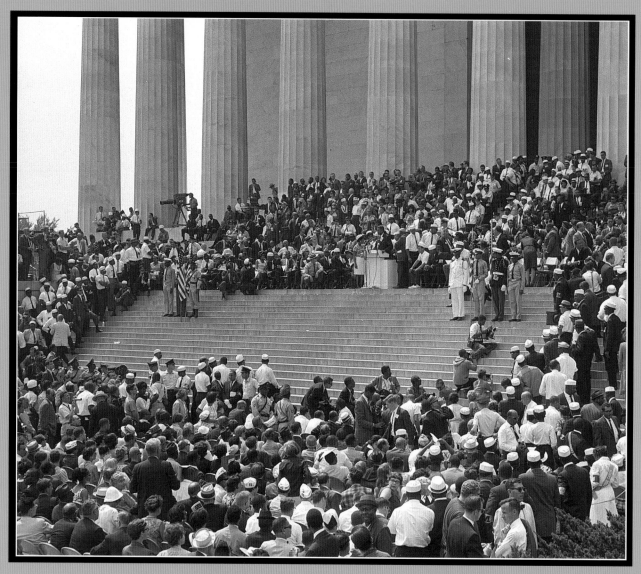

Item 9-13
"March on Washington," *U.S. News and World Report*, August 28, 1963.
Photograph. U.S. News and World Report Photograph Collection, Prints and Photographs Division.

rights issues as little as possible. In early 1963 King and his SCLC colleagues resolved that the issue had to be forced. To do so, they carefully outlined a major protest campaign for the hard-core city of Birmingham, and in April their effort was launched. It began slowly, but within several weeks, much as they had anticipated, Birmingham's hot-tempered and violently segregationist public safety commissioner, Eugene "Bull" Connor, began to live up to his reputation by turning high-pressure fire hoses and snarling police dogs loose on the protesters.

By early May, pictures of the Birmingham conflict were in newspapers and on televisions across the country and around the world. Moderate white segregationists, upset with the effects of Connor's conduct, began quiet negotiations with the civil rights forces. Kennedy administration representatives encouraged such discussions. As protest battles threatened to intensify even further, a modest agreement was reached, which mandated that downtown department stores would desegregate their facilities and that at least some black applicants would be hired for what previously had been whites-only store jobs. A Klan bombing of a civil rights gathering spot threatened to undo the accord, but pressure from the Kennedy administration helped keep it on track. Gradually the situation quieted, but the events of May 1963 had fundamentally changed the American civil rights scene.

King and other national civil rights figures had hoped for two years that the Kennedy administration would press Congress for enactment of a comprehensive and powerful civil rights bill, and a number of activists, including A. Philip Randolph, a senior civil rights figure whose political activism went back to the 1920s, revived the idea of staging a mass march in Washington to call for both presidential and congressional action. But the events of Birmingham had altered the Kennedy brothers' perceptions as well, and work on just such a bill soon got under way. In June President Kennedy gave a nationally televised, powerful speech calling for civil rights progress and declared that racial equality was first and foremost a moral issue. That very same evening, the NAACP's top activist in Mississippi, Medgar Evers, was gunned down by a racist sniper outside his home in Jackson. Within days the organized civil rights leadership—King, Randolph, the NAACP, SNCC, and CORE—announced firm plans for a

"March on Washington" on August 28, and with some apprehension the Kennedy administration decided to cooperate with the protest.

The images of Birmingham had helped stimulate new black activism in scores of towns all across the country, as northern demonstrations of support supplemented protest efforts in many previously quiet southern cities. In the summer of 1963 racial change was on the front pages of American newspapers more than ever before, and for many participants and observers, anticipation built as the date of the August 28 March on Washington neared.

Item 9-16
"Mahalia Jackson at the May 17, 1957, Prayer Pilgrimage for Freedom in Washington, D.C."
Silver gelatin print. NAACP Collection, Prints and Photographs Division.

When the day arrived, estimates of the peaceful crowd reached upwards of 200,000, with perhaps 25 percent of the participants being white. Civil rights tacticians had pulled off a superb logistical achievement in producing such a smoothly organized event. The main program was a series of songs and speeches delivered from the steps of the Lincoln Memorial, with the penultimate oration by Martin Luther King, Jr. For most people who heard it then or read it later, King's address remained the most notable of all of King's memorable speeches. "I have a dream," King repeatedly intoned in his peroration, "a dream that my four little children will one day live in a nation where they will not be judged by the color of their skin but by the content of their character." The crowd response was enthusiastic, and the media coverage a public relations coup for civil rights forces.

In retrospect, the March on Washington was as significant an emotional high point as any the civil rights struggle would experience. Barely two weeks later, however, a Klan bombing of the Birmingham church that had been one of the principal meeting spots during the May protests resulted in the deaths of four young black school-girls. Exultation over the Washington success was immediately overshadowed by fury and anger over these tragic killings. At the same time, little significant progress was being made with Kennedy's comprehensive civil rights bill. On November 22, Kennedy himself was assassinated in Dallas and Vice President Lyndon B. Johnson of Texas suc-ceeded to the presidency. Less complicit in segre-gationist policies than other southern members of Congress, Johnson had played a moderately progressive role in the passage of the very modest Civil Rights Acts of 1957 and 1960, but he sur-prised virtually everyone when, within days of taking the oath of office, Johnson firmly declared that passage of Kennedy's civil rights bill would be one of his top priorities as president.

Over the next six months congressional work on the bill was a major story. King's SCLC became involved in a protest effort in the historic Florida town of St. Augustine, and SNCC's young orga-nizers made a major commitment toward staging a sizable "Summer Project" all across the state of Mississippi. In June, just two weeks before Johnson signed the Kennedy bill into law as the Civil Rights Act of 1964, three of the Mississippi civil rights workers disappeared. Although their dead bodies were not discovered until August, hardly anyone doubted that they had been killed by Klan terrorists.

Although the Civil Rights Act, which pro-hibited racial discrimination in employment and in all forms of public accommodations across the United States, was the most significant legal achievement for civil rights forces since *Brown,* the killings and other terroristic violence in Mississippi had a far greater—and tremendously disheartening—impact on younger civil rights activists. The Mississippi summer project sent an integrated delegation to the 1964 Democratic National Convention to challenge the seating of the traditionally all-white "regular" Mississippi delegation. The integrated "Freedom" Democrats

anticipated a favorable reception from what was a largely pro-civil rights political party, but President Johnson, fearful of his upcoming presidential race against ultra-conservative Republican Senator Barry Goldwater, refused to allow the Democratic leadership to give the integrated Mississippians anything beyond honorific status at the convention. That treatment led many of the activists to rethink their expectations that significant progress could be attained by working through the partisan electoral pro-cess. As King and his SCLC colleagues turned their sights toward a major voting rights initiative, many younger activists, particularly those who had worked a year or more in dangerous and intense locations like Mississippi, began to struggle with feelings of "burn out," and some began drifting away from civil rights work.

Voting rights guarantees had been one of the few major omissions from the 1964 Civil Rights Act, and King's desire to stimulate creation and congressional passage of a new act that would mandate tough voting rights enforce-ment took the form of a protest campaign that the SCLC organized in Selma, Alabama. Jim Clark, the county sheriff, was a lawman with a reputation for dramatic and gratuitous violence, and within several weeks of the cam-paign's early 1965 kickoff, Clark began behaving true to form as black protesters marched to the county court-house, seeking fairer and easier voter registration pro-cedures. On Sunday, March 7, when a column of civil rights marchers headed out from Selma toward the state capitol in Montgomery, Clark's "posse" of segregationist deputies, along with a sizable force of Alabama state troopers, attacked the marchers with nightsticks and tear gas. Scores of participants were hospitalized, and as graphic pictures of the assault spread across the country, a vociferous national uproar ensued.

Hundreds of civil rights sympathizers from around the nation headed for Selma, and President Johnson spoke out strongly against the attack. As efforts were made to negotiate safe passage for another—this time peaceful—march from Selma to Montgomery, Johnson went before the Congress to propose a powerful new voting rights bill that fulfilled virtually all of the activists' hopes. A ground-swell of national support greeted both that pro-posal and a triumphal march from Selma to Montgomery that was capped by another memorable King speech, but once again terroristic violence entered the picture as a northern white female participant was murdered by Klansmen while driving from Selma to Montgomery.

By early August 1965 the powerful Voting Rights Act had become law. Only a few days later, the first of the major urban riots of the late 1960s broke out in the Watts section of Los Angeles, California. When the violence

Item 9-12
Warren K. Leffler, Signing of the Civil Rights Act, April 11, 1968. Standing to the president's right, as Lyndon Baines Johnson signs the Civil Rights Act, is Thurgood Marshall.
U.S. News and World Report Photograph Collection, Prints and Photographs Division.

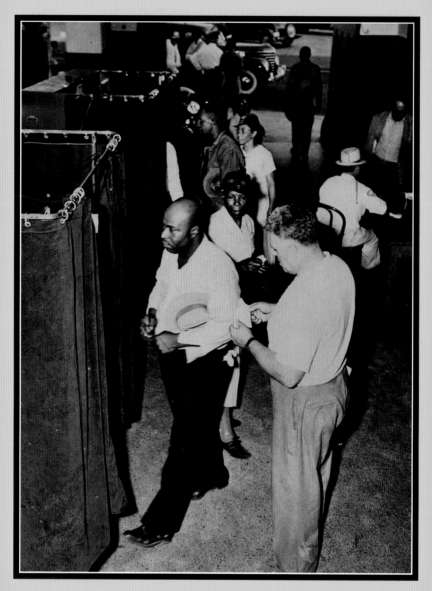

Item 9-17
Voters enter the voting booths. Ca. 1945.
Silver gelatin print. NAACP Collection, Prints and Photographs Division.

finally ended six days later, there were thirty-four people dead and property damage totaling at least $45 million. The Watts rebellion demonstrated to King and others that the struggles and successes of the southern civil rights crusade had been only half of the battle, and that the economic obstacles and forces constraining black equality outside the South as well as within might very well be much harder to overcome than the barriers of formal, legal segregation that had begun to be toppled by court decisions and acts of Congress.

In the years after 1965, significant black electoral progress was registered in many cities and counties all across the South, as the provisions of the 1965 Voting Rights Act led to large increases in black voter registration and to dramatic gains in the number of black candidates elected to public office. In some locales white control remained intact, however, in part because of the relative economic powerlessness of black communities. Particularly in the political arena, however, fundamental change gradually spread across more and more of the South.

The years from 1945 to 1965 witnessed tremendous legal progress for black Americans and supplied the legal foundations that allowed for such dramatic political progress by black communities in the years after 1965. Ensuing decades would highlight again and again how incomplete the gains of the 1945 to 1965 period actually were. Yet the civil rights era represents the greatest leap forward for black Americans since the decade of the Civil War a century earlier.

James Keen, Candid shot of kids listening to a reading at the Louisville Free Public Library, Louisville, Kentucky, June 1963.
U.S. News and World Report Photograph Collection, Prints and Photographs Division. (LC-U9-9936-24)

N o t e s

Preface
Debra Newman Ham

1. Washington: Library of Congress, 1993.

2. A symposium introducing *The African-American Mosaic* took place in February 1997. The presenters were Wesley, civil rights historian and writer David Garrow, historian and museum director John Fleming, author and film historian Thomas Cripps, Africanist Joseph Harris, librarian Jessie Carney Smith, and musicologist Josephine Wright.

3. Washington: Library of Congress, 1969.

4. Washington: Library of Congress, 1970, p.54.

5. Volume 26 (July 1969): 126–40.

6. Participants in these informal seminars and brainstorming sessions included Beverly Brannan, Prints and Photographs Division; Dena Epstein, formerly of the Music Division; Ronald Grim, Geography and Map Division; Ardie Myers, General Collections; Rosemary Plakas, Rare Book and Special Collections Division; Wayne Shirley, Music Division; Debra Newman Ham, Manuscript Division; and Samuel Brylawski, David Parker, and Brian Taves, Motion Picture, Broadcasting, and Recorded Sound Division.

7. *Bearing the Cross* (New York: Vintage Books, 1988).

Introduction
Debra Newman Ham

1. London: A. Bell, 1773.

2. Boston: J.P. Jewett, 1985.

3. *The Interesting Narrative of the Life of Olaudah Equiano, or Gustavus Vassa, the African* (Norwich: The Author, 1794; originally published in 1789), chap. 2.

Chapter 1

Unwilling Immigrants of Sable Hue
Debra Newman Ham

1. Philip Curtin, *The Atlantic Slave Trade: A Census* (Madison: University of Wisconsin Press, 1969); Joseph E. Inikori and Stanley L. Engerman, eds., *The Atlantic Slave Trade: Effects on Economies, Societies, and Peoples in Africa, the Americas, and Europe* (Durham, N.C.: Duke University Press, 1992).

2. Olaudah Equiano, *The Interesting Narrative of the Life of Olaudah Equiano, or Gustavus Vassa, the African* (Norwich: The Author, 1794), chap. 2, passim.

3. John Quincy Adams, *Diary of John Quincy Adams, 1794–1845*, ed. Allen Nevins (New York: Charles Scribner & Sons, 1951), 519.

4. Edwin Morris Betts, ed., *Thomas Jefferson's Farm Book with Commentary and Relevant Extracts from Other Writings* (Princeton, N.J.: Princeton University Press, 1953), 5.

5. Carter G. Woodson Collection, Manuscript Division, Library of Congress, Washington, D.C.

6. For a more complete treatment of this subject, see Debra Newman Ham, ed., *The African-American Mosaic: A Library of Congress Resource Guide for the Study of Black History and Culture* (Washington: Library of Congress, 1993), chap. 1.

7. W. E. B. DuBois, *The Negro Artisan* (Atlanta: Atlanta University Press, 1902), 13–23.

8. Equiano, *The Interesting Narrative*, chap. 2.

9. Nat Turner, *The Confessions of Nat Turner, the Leader of the Late Insurrection in Southampton, Virginia* (Richmond: T. R. Gray, 1832).

10. Carter G. Woodson Collection, Manuscript Division, Library of Congress.

11. Governor John Floyd to Governor James Hamilton, November 19, 1831, John Floyd Collection, Manuscript Division, Library of Congress.

12. Ibid.

13. Ibid.

14. David Walker, *David Walker's Appeal in Four Articles, together with a Preamble, to the Coloured Citizens of the World, But in Particular, and Very Expressly, to Those of the United States of America*, ed. Charles M. Wiltze (New York: Hill and Wang, 1965), 12.

15. Floyd to Hamilton, November 19, 1831.

16. Ibid.

17. Herbert Aptheker, ed., *A Documentary History of the Negro People in the United States* (New York: Citadel Press, 1963), 1–16.

18. Two works relating to African Americans during the Revolutionary war era are Benjamin Quarles, *The Negro in the American Revolution* (Chapel Hill: University of North Carolina Press, 1961), and Sidney Kaplan and Emma Nogrady Kaplan, *The Black Presence in the Era of the American Revolution*, rev. ed. (Amherst: University of Massachusetts Press, 1989).

19. See Ira Berlin, *Slaves without Masters: The Free Negro in the Antebellum South* (New York: Pantheon Books, 1975), and Leon Litwack, *North of Slavery: The Negro in the Free States, 1790–1860* (Chicago: University of Chicago Press, 1961).

20. Joseph E. Harris, "A Comparative Approach to the Study of the African Diaspora," in *Global Dimensions of the African Diaspora*, ed. Joseph E. Harris (Washington: Howard University Press, 1982), 112–13.

21. New York: Arno Press, 1968.

22. Lorenzo J. Greene, *The Negro in Colonial New England* (New York: Anthenum, 1971); Sheldon H. Harris, *Paul Cuffee, Black American and the African Return* (New York: Simon and Schuster, 1972);

Henry Noble Sherwood, "Early Negro-Deportation Projects," *Mississippi Valley Historical Review* 2 (March 1916): 484-508; Henry Noble Sherwood, "Paul Cuffee," *Journal of Negro History* 8 (April 1923): 153–229; Peter Williams, Jr., *A Discourse Delivered on the Death of Captain Paul Cuffee* (New York: Young, 1817).

23. Ibid.

24. Ibid.

25. Paul Cuffee, *A Brief Account of the Settlement and Present Situation of the Colony of Sierra Leone in Africa* (New York: Samuel Wood, 1812).

26. P. J. Staudenraus, *The African Colonization Movement, 1816–65* (New York: Columbia University Press, 1961), 32–34, and Aptheker, ed., *Documentary History,* 70-72.

27. Ibid., 71.

28. Ibid.

29. Staudenraus, *African Colonization Movement,* 140; *African Repository 5* (August 1829): 185; *African Repository 7* (March 1831): 26.

30. "Negroes' Rejection of Colonization," in *The Negro American, A Documentary History,* ed. Leslie H. Fishel, Jr., and Benjamin Quarles (Glenview, Ill.: Scott, Foresman, 1967), 145–46.

Chapter 2

Harsh As Truth
Paul Finkelman

1. In 1860 probably 90 percent of the United States was Protestant. American culture at this time was overwhelmingly Protestant.

2. Jefferson, Madison, Monroe, Jackson, Tyler, Polk, and Taylor.

3. William Henry Harrison.

4. Van Buren, Fillmore, Pierce, and Buchanan.

5. In 1860 blacks had equal suffrage rights in Maine, New Hampshire, Vermont, Massachusetts, and Rhode Island; New York allowed black males to vote if they satisfied a property test; Ohio allowed men who were more than half white to vote; in Michigan black men could vote in school-board elections; and in some places in Ohio blacks could vote in schoolboard elections.

6. During the Civil War Delany would become one of the first black officers in the United States Army.

7. J. Clay Smith, Jr., *Emancipation: The Making of the Black Lawyer, 1844–1944* (Philadelphia: University of Pennsylvania Press, 1993), 96; Paul Finkelman, "Not Only the Judges' Robes Were Black: African-American Lawyers as Social Engineers," *Stanford Law Review* 47 (1994): 161–209; William Cheek and Aimee Lee Cheek, *John Mercer Langston and the Fight for Black Freedom, 1829–65* (Urbana: University of Illinois Press, 1989), 260; Robert J. Cottrol, *The Afro-Yankees: Providence's Black Community in the Antebellum Era* (Westport, Conn.: Greenwood Press, 1982), 93.

8. Irving H. Bartlett, *Wendell Phillips: Brahmin Radical* (Boston: Beacon Press, 1961), 221.

9. *Bailey v. Cromwell,* 3 Scam. (Ill.) 71 (1841).

10. *In re Jane, a Woman of Color,* 5 Western L.J. 202 (1848).

11. Bartlett, *Wendell Phillips,* 222.

12. Leon F. Litwack, *Been in the Storm So Long: The Aftermath of Slavery* (New York: A.A. Knopf, 1979), 102.

13. "Germantown Protest against Slavery," in Kermit L. Hall, William M. Wiecek, and Paul Finkelman, eds., *American Legal History,* 2nd ed. (New York: Oxford University Press, 1996), 35–36.

14. *Somerset v. Stewart,* 98 Eng. Rep. 499 (K.B., 1772).

15. Francis Hargrave, *An Argument in the case of James Sommersette a Negro . . .* (London: W. Otgridge and G. Kearsly, 1772).

16. Quoted in Paul Finkelman, *An Imperfect Union: Slavery, Federalism, and Comity* (Chapel Hill: University of North Carolina Press, 1981), 39.

17. This is Act CII, March, 1661–62; William Waller Hening, ed., *The Statutes at Large; Being a Collection of All the Laws of Virginia from the First Session of the Legislature, in the Year 1619*, 13 vols. (Richmond: Samuel Pleasants, 1809–23), 2:116–17.

18. "An Act directing the trial of Slaves, committing capital crimes, and for the more effectual punishing of conspiracies and insurrections among them; and for the better government of Negros, Mulattos, and Indians, bond or free," Act of May 1723, Hening, *Statutes at Large*, 4:126.

19. St. George Tucker, *A Dissertation on Slavery: With A Proposal for the Gradual Abolition of It, in the State of Virginia* (Philadelphia: Mathew Carey, 1796).

20. Paul Finkelman and David Cobin, eds., *Tucker's Blackstone* (1803; reprinted., New York: Lawbook Exchange, 1996), vol. 2, Appendix, Note H, 31–85.

21. Thomas Jefferson to Edward Coles, August 25, 1814.

22. Quoted from David Walker, *David Walker's Appeal in Four Articles, together with a Preamble, to the Coloured Citizens of the World, But in Particular, and Very Expressly, to Those of the United States of America*, ed. Charles M. Wiltse (New York: Hill and Wang, 1965), 55.

23. It is worth noting that the Garrisonians also promoted and fostered gender equality.

24. Loguen helped organize the famous Jerry Rescue in Syracuse.

25. A white friend in Richmond packed Brown into a wooden box and shipped him to Philadelphia on a railroad freight car. His narrative shows woodcuts of Brown stepping out of his box.

26. Henry Highland Garnet, *Walker's Appeal, with a Brief Sketch of His Life; and Also Garnet's Address to the Slaves of the United States of America* (New York, 1848).

27. Uncle Tom was not, in the common language of today, an "Uncle Tom." He did not sell his people out for his own benefit; on the contrary, he went to a painful death to protect other slaves.

28. They were, respectively, secretary of treasury, secretary of state, and vice president in Lincoln's first administration. Chase later became Chief Justice of the United States.

Chapter 3

Battlefield and Home Front
Ervin L. Jordan, Jr.

1. Charles H. Wesley and Patricia W. Romero, *Negro Americans in the Civil War* (Washington: Publishers Company, 1967), 18–19.

2. Ervin L. Jordan, Jr., *Black Confederates and Afro-Yankees in Civil War Virginia* (Charlottesville and London: University Press of Virginia, 1995), 4, 136.

3. Harry Reed, *Platform for Change: The Foundations of the Northern Free Black Community, 1775–1865* (East Lansing: Michigan State University Press, 1994), 4–5, 47, 76–77, 97, 107, 109, 165, 176, 194, 220.

4. David W. Blight, *Frederick Douglass' Civil War: Keeping Faith in Jubilee* (Baton Rouge: Louisiana State University Press, 1989), 68–69, 148–49; Richard Long, ed., *Black Writers and the American Civil War* (Secaucus, N.J.: Blue & Grey Press, 1988), 261–68.

5. Jordan, *Black Confederates*, 83-84; James M. McPherson, *The Negro's Civil War: How American Negroes Felt and Acted during the War for the Union* (Urbana: University of Illinois Press, 1982), 85-86, 91.

6. Elizabeth Keckley, *Behind the Scenes, or, Thirty Years a Slave and Four Years in the White House* (New York: G. W. Carleton, 1868), 80–88.

7. Lewis C. Lockwood, *Mary S. Peake, The Colored Teacher at Fortress Monroe* (Boston: American Tract Society, 1863), 5–6; Jordan, *Black Confederates,* 102; Long, *Black Writers,* 129–47; Clarence L. Mohr, *On the Threshold of Freedom: Masters and Slaves in Civil War Georgia* (Athens: University of Georgia Press, 1986), 86, 320n.

8. Dudley Taylor Cornish, *The Sable Arm: Negro Troops in the Union Army, 1861–1865* (New York: Norton, 1966), 32, 36, 53.

9. Benjamin Quarles, *The Negro in the Civil War* (Boston: Little, Brown, 1953), 71–74, 91–93, 337; Wesley and Romero, *Negro Americans in the Civil War,* 104–6.

10. Wesley and Romero, *Negro Americans in the Civil War,* 213–16; Abraham Lincoln, *The Collected Works of Abraham Lincoln,* 9 vols., ed. Roy P. Basler (New Brunswick, N.J.: Rutgers University Press, 1953), 5:370–75; McPherson, *The Negro's Civil War,* 91–96.

11. Lincoln, *Collected Works,* 5:388-89.

12. Cornish, *The Sable Arm,* 73–78; George Washington Williams, *A History of the Negro Troops in the War of the Rebellion 1861–1865* (New York: Harper & Brothers, Franklin Square, 1888), 88–89; Peter H. Clark, *The Black Brigade of Cincinnati* (Cincinnati: Joseph B. Boyd, 1864), 3–30.

13. James G. Hollandsworth, Jr., *The Louisiana Native Guards: The Black Military Experience during the Civil War* (Baton Rouge: Louisiana State University Press, 1995), 17, 21; Quarles, *The Negro in the Civil War,* 119; Joseph T. Glatthaar, *Forged in Battle: The Civil War Alliance of Black Soldiers and White Officers* (New York: Free Press, 1990), 122; Cornish, *The Sable Arm,* 77–78.

14. McPherson, *The Negro's Civil War,* 116; Long, ed., *Black Writers,* 151–94.

15. Quarles, *The Negro in the Civil War,* 128–31, 246; Wesley and Romero, *Negro Americans in the Civil War,* 134–37; McPherson, *The Negro's Civil War,* 136-39; Jordan, *Black Confederates,* 88; Joseph P. Reidy, "'Coming from the Shadow of the Past': The Transition from Slavery to Freedom at Freedman's Village, 1863–1900," *Virginia Magazine of History and Biography* 95 (October 1987): 403–28; Olive Gilbert, *Narrative of Sojourner Truth* (1850; reprint, New York: Arno Press, 1968), 182–83; Hertha E. Pauli, *Her Name Was Sojourner Truth* (New York: Appleton-Century-Crofts, 1962), 208–20; Erlene Stetson and Linda David, *Glorying in Tribulation: The Lifework of Sojourner Truth* (East Lansing: Michigan State University Press, 1994), 147.

16. Lincoln, *Collected Works,* 6:28–31; Jordan, *Black Confederates,* 84, 287–88, 255-56, 319–20; Quarles, *The Negro in the Civil War,* 169-82.

17. Glatthaar, *Forged in Battle,* 122; Luis F. Emilio, *A Brave Black Regiment: History of the Fifty-Fourth Regiment of Massachusetts Volunteer Infantry, 1863–1865,* 3rd ed. (Salem, N.H.: Ayer, 1990), 8, 20; Wesley and Romero, *Negro Americans in the Civil War,* 70.

18. "Negroes as Soldiers," *Harper's Weekly,* March 14, 1863, 174; Joseph T. Wilson, *The Black Phalanx: A History of the Negro Soldiers of the United States in the War of 1775–1812, 1861–'65* (Hartford, Conn.: American Publishing, 1888), 125; Cornish, *The Sable Arm,* 130, 208–9; Glatthaar, *Forged in Battle,* 38-39; United States, Adjutant-General's Office, *Official Army Register of the Volunteer Force of the United States Army for the Years 1861, '62, '63, '64, '65: Part 8: Territories of Washington, New Mexico, Nebraska, Colorado, Dakota; Veteran Reserve Corps, U.S. Veteran Volunteers, U.S. Volunteers, U.S. Colored Troops* (Washington: Adjutant General's Office, 1867; reprint, Gaithersburg, Md.: Ron R. Van Sickle Military Books, 1987), 8:169.

19. U.S. War Department, *U.S. Infantry Tactics, for the Instruction, Exercise, and Manoeuvers of the Soldier, A Company, Line of Skirmishers, for the Use of the Colored Troops of the United States Infantry, Prepared under the Direction of the War Department* (Washington: Government Printing Office, 1863), passim; Jordan, *Black Confederates,* 268, 274; Wesley and Romero, *Negro Americans in the Civil War,* 245; Quarles, *The Negro in the Civil War,* 210.

20. U.S. Adjutant-General's Office, *Official Army Register*, 8:176, 284, 246, 248; Quarles, *The Negro in the Civil War*, 328–29; Glatthaar, *Forged in Battle*, 9, 123, 188, 197; Jordan, *Black Confederates*, 218–19, 269; Wesley and Romero, *Negro Americans in the Civil War*, 103, 177–79.

21. Cornish, *The Sable Arm*, 142–45; Wesley and Romero, *Negro Americans in the Civil War*, 83–88; Quarles, *The Negro in the Civil War*, 214-25; Hollandsworth, *Louisiana Native Guards*, 54.

22. Quarles, *The Negro in the Civil War*, 225–27; Wesley and Romero, *Negro Americans in the Civil War*, 106–8.

23. Charles Bernard Fox, *Record of the Service of the Fifty-Fifth Regiment of Massachusetts Volunteer Infantry* (Cambridge: Press of John Wilson and Son, 1868), 85–89; G. W. Williams, *A History of the Negro Troops*, 154–60; Wesley and Romero, *Negro Americans in the Civil War*, 97–100; Glatthaar, *Forged in Battle*, 169-75; James Henry Gooding, *On the Altar of Freedom*, ed. Virginia Matzke Adams (Amherst: University of Massachusetts Press, 1991), 119.

24. Susan Cooper, "Records of Civil War African American Troops Inspire Major Project," *The Record: News from the National Archives and Records Administration 3* (November 1996): 11; Fox, *Fifty-Fifth Regiment of Massachusetts*, 133.

25. Jordan, *Black Confederates*, 272; Wesley and Romero, *Negro Americans in the Civil War*, 88–91; New York, *Report of the Committee of Merchants for the Relief of Colored People Suffering from the Late Riots in the City of New York* (New York: George A. Whitehorne, 1863), 3–10, 14–25, 30; Glatthaar, *Forged in Battle*, 138–41; Quarles, *The Negro in the Civil War*, 12-21; Cornish, *The Sable Arm*, 153–56; Emilio, *Brave Black Regiment*, 70–95; Peter Burchard, *One Gallant Rush: Robert Gould Shaw and His Brave Black Regiment* (New York: St. Martin's Press, 1965), 132–47; Gooding, *On the Altar of Freedom*, 37–38.

26. Lincoln, *Collected Works*, 6:357.

27. Jordan, *Black Confederates;* and "Different Drummers: Black Virginians as Confederate Loyalists," in *Black Southerners in Gray: Essays on Afro-Americans in Confederate Armies*, ed. Richard Rollins (Murfreesboro, Tenn.: Southern Heritage Press, 1994), 57; and "A Negro Preaching Secession Doctrine," *New York Herald*, October 5, 1861, 5, col. 2.

28. G. W. Williams, *A History of the Negro Troops*, 81–84; Jordan, *Black Confederates*, 218–19; Hollandsworth, *Louisiana Native Guards*, 2, 7, 10, 17, 96; Wilson, *The Black Phalanx*, 481.

29. Jordan, *Black Confederates*, 220; U.S. Naval War Records Office, *Official Records of the Union and Confederate Navies in the War of the Rebellion*, Series I–II, 30 vols. (Washington: U.S. Government Printing Office, 1894–1922), 1:8, 113; "Rebel Negro Pickets," *Harper's Weekly*, January 10, 1863, p. 17; Mohr, *On the Threshold*, 286.

30. Frank A. Rollin [Frances Anne Rollin], *Life and Public Services of Martin R. Delany* (Boston: Lee and Shepard, 1868), 183; Gooding, *On the Altar of Freedom*, 54.

31. Wilson, *The Black Phalanx*, 484, 487, 488–96; Jordan, *Black Confederates*, 242, 294–95; U.S. War Department, *The War of the Rebellion: A Compilation of the Official Records of The Union and Confederate Armies*, Series I–IV, 128 vols. (Washington: U.S. Government Printing Office, 1880–1901), Series 1, vol. 49, part 2, p. 1,276.

32. Emilio, *Brave Black Regiment*, 159-73; Cornish, *The Sable Arm*, 267-69.

33. G. W. Williams, *A History of the Negro Troops*, 257–72; Wilson, *The Black Phalanx*, 333; Glatthaar, *Forged in Battle*, 156–57; Wesley and Romero, *Negro Americans in the Civil War*, 92–93; Cornish, *The Sable Arm*, 173–77.

34. U.S. Adjutant-General's Office, *Official Army Register*, 8:339; Jordan, *Black Confederates*, 276–78.

35. Wesley and Romero, *Negro Americans in the Civil War*, 167–68; Jordan, *Black Confederates*, 272–73,

279; U.S. Adjutant-General's Office, *Official Army Register*, 8:338; Quarles, *The Negro in the Civil War*, 305–11.

36. Mohr, *On the Threshold*, 86, 93–95; Wesley and Romero, *Negro Americans in the Civil War*, 151–54.

37. Edward P. Smith, *Incidents of the United States Christian Commission* (Philadelphia: Lippincott, 1871), 360; Wesley and Romero, *Negro Americans in the Civil War*, 130–34.

38. Jordan, *Black Confederates*, 292, 295; R. J. M. Blackett, *Thomas Morris Chester, Black Civil War Correspondent: His Dispatches from the Virginia Front* (Baton Rouge: Louisiana State University Press, 1989), 289, 297, 303–4.

39. William Wells Brown, *The Negro in the American Revolution* (Boston: Lee & Shepard, 1867), 323–25; U.S. Adjutant-General's Office, *Official Army Register*, 8:235, 339; Ralph A. Wooster, *Lone Star Blue and Gray Essays on Texas in the Civil War* (Austin: Texas State Historical Association, 1995), 332–35; Glatthaar, *Forged in Battle*, 257–61.

40. Ira Berlin, Joseph Reidy, and Leslie S. Rowland, eds., *Freedom: A Documentary History of Emancipation, 1861-1867, Selected from the Holdings of the National Archives of the United States*, Series II: The Black Military Experience (New York: Cambridge University Press, 1982), 652; McPherson, *The Negro's Civil War*, 308; Jordan, *Black Confederates*, 296.

41. Randolph B. Campbell, *An Empire for Slavery: The Peculiar Institution in Texas, 1821–1865* (Baton Rouge: Louisiana State University Press, 1989), 231, 249–51; Quarles, *The Negro in the Civil War*, 346.

42. Leonard Sweet, *Black Images of America 1784–1870* (New York: Norton, 1976), 167.

Chapter 4

Forty Acres and a Mule
Kenneth Marvin Hamilton

1. *Quotations of Booker T. Washington*, ed. E. Davidson Washington (Tuskegee, Ala.: Tuskegee Institute Press, 1938), 32, 33.

2. Quoted from the *Harrison County Texas Republican*, June 23, 1865.

3. William H. Baldwin, Jr., "The Present Problem of Negro Education," *Journal of Social Science* 37 (December 1899).

4. Harold D. Woodman, *King Cotton and His Retainers* (Columbia: University of South Carolina Press, 1990), 346.

5. W. E. B. DuBois, *Dusk of Dawn* (New York: Harcourt, Brace & World, 1940), 242–43.

Chapter 5

"If We Must Die"
Charles Johnson, Jr.

1. For the quotation from Col. Howard Donovan Queen, above, see Mary Motley, ed., *The Invisible Soldier: The Experience of the Black Soldier, World War II* (Detroit: Wayne State University, 1975). See also Marvin Fletcher, *The Black Soldier and Officer in the United States Army, 1891–1917* (St. Louis: Columbia University of Missouri Press, 1974), passim; John A. Johnson, "The Medal of Honor and Sergeant John Ward and Private Pompey Factor," *Arkansas Historical Quarterly* 29 (1970): 361–75; William Leckie, *The Buffalo Soldiers* (Norman: University of Oklahoma Press, 1963), passim; Kenneth W. Porter, *The Negro on the American Frontier* (New York: Arno Press, 1971), 472–91; Mary Stubbs and Stanley R. Connor, *Armor-Infantry* (Washington: Office of the Chief of Military History, 1969), 193–209; Frank N. Schubert, *Black Valor* (Wilmington: Scholarly Books, 1997), passim; Frank N. Schubert, *Buffalo Soldiers, Braves, and the Brass* (Shippenburg: White Mane, 1993), passim; and Frank N. Schubert, ed., *On the Trail of the Buffalo* (Wilmington Scholarly Books, 1995), passim.

2. Maurice Matloff, ed., *American Military History* (Washington: Office of the Chief of Military History, 1969), 359, 363–64.

3. Matloff, *American Military History,* 366–67; Charles Johnson, Jr., *African Americans Soldiers in the National Guard* (Westport, Conn.: Greenwood Press, 1992), 101–2.

4. Kenneth R. Janken, *Rayford W. Logan and the Dilemma of the African American Intellectual* (Amherst: University of Massachusetts Press, 1993), 36; Bernard C. Nalty, *Strength for the Fight* (New York: Free Press, 1986), 110; Emmett J. Scott, *Scott's Official History of the American Negro in the World War* (New York: Arno Press, 1969), 81–91, 471–81.

5. Nalty, *Strength for the Fight,* 198; Jack D. Foner, *Blacks and the Military in American History* (New York: Praeger, 1974), 111–12; Benjamin Quarles, *The Negro in the Making of America* (New York: Collier Cooks, 1964), 181, 183.

6. Foner, *Blacks and the Military,* 114–16.

7. Arthur E. Barbeau and Florette Henri, *The Unknown Soldiers: Black American Troops in World War I* (Philadelphia: Temple University Press, 1974), 27–31; Garna L. Christian, *Black Soldiers in Jim Crow Texas, 1899–1917* (College Station: Texas A&M University Press, 1995), 145–72.

8. Robert E. Greene, *Black Defenders of America* (Chicago: Johnson Publishing, 1974), 163; Foner, *Blacks and the Military,* 113; Nalty, *Strength for the Fight,* 111.

9. Charles Johnson, *National Guard,* 99–103.

10. Foner, *Blacks and the Military,* 118; Nalty, *Strength for the Fight,* 112; P. J. Carissella and James W. Ryan, *The Black Swallow of Death* (Boston: Marlborough House, 1972), passim; Robert J. Jakeman, *Divided Skies* (Tuscaloosa: University of Alabama Press, 1992), 56; Lawrence P. Scott and William M. Womack, *Double V* (East Lansing:

Michigan State University, 1994), 6–14, 19–21, 25.

11. Charles Johnson, *National Guard,* 105; Barbeau and Henri, *The Unknown Soldiers,* 72–74.

12. Barbeau and Henri, *The Unknown Soldiers,* 142–47; Charles Johnson, *National Guard,* 105–8; W. E. B. DuBois, "An Essay toward a History of the Black Man in the Great War," *Crisis* 18 (January 1919): 67; W. E. B. DuBois, "Secret Information Concerning Black American Troops," *Crisis* 18 (June 1919): 17; W. E. B. DuBois, "Documents of War," *Crisis* 18 (May 1919): 16–19.

13. Barbeau and Henri, *The Unknown Soldiers,* 70–163; William S. Bradden, *Under Fire with the 370th Infantry (8th ING) AEF* (Chicago: Bradden, c. 1919), passim; Chester D. Haywood, *Negro Combat Troops in the World War: The Story of the 371st Infantry* (New York: Negro Universities Press, 1969), passim; Charles Johnson, *National Guard,* 108–10; Monroe Mason and Arthur Furr, *The American Negro Soldier with the Red Hand of France* (Boston: Cornhill, 1920), passim; Scott, *Scott's Official History,* passim. For additional information, see American Battle Monuments Commission, *92nd Division: Summary of Operations in the World War* (Washington: U.S. Government Printing Office, 1944), passim; American Battle Monuments Commission, *93rd Division: Summary of Operations in the World War* (Washington: U.S. Government Printing Office, 1944), passim.

14. Foner, *Blacks and the Military,* 124.

15. Quarles, *The Negro in the Making,* 186–87; Scott, *Scott's Official History,* passim; Clarence A. Bacote, *The Story of Atlanta University, 1865–1965* (Atlanta: Atlanta University, 1969), 163; William J. Breen, "Black Women and the Great War: Mobilization and Reform in the South," *Journal of Southern History* 44 (August 1978): passim.

16. William H. Harris, *The Harder We Run* (New York: Oxford University Press, 1982), 61–67, 72–94; Charles Johnson, *National Guard,* 119; Allan H. Spear, *Black Chicago* (Chicago: University of Chicago Press, 1967), 129–66.

17. Quarles, *The Negro in the Making,* 199–203.

18. Nalty, *Strength for the Fight,* 128–30.

19. Charles Johnson, *National Guard,* 119–37; Nalty, *Strength for the Fight,* 132–33.

20. *Baltimore Sun,* February 14, 1937; *Washington Afro-American,* February 27, 1937; Foner, *Blacks and the Military,* 130.

21. Foner, *Blacks and the Military,* 126–30.

22. Harris, *The Harder We Run,* 99–106.

23. Danny D. Collum, ed., *African Americans in the Spanish Civil War* (New York: G. K. Hall, 1992), 26, 28–29, 39, 73–74, 81–84; Scott, *Scott's Official History,* 31.

24. Allan R. Millet and Peter Maslowski, *For the Common Defense* (New York: Free Press, 1984), 393–95; Jakeman, *Divided Skies,* 1–157; Scott and Womack, *Double V,* 77–127; Stanley Sandler, *Segregated Skies: All-Black Combat Squadrons of WW II* (Washington: Smithsonian Institution Press, 1992), 1–13.

25. Richard M. Dalfiume, "Military Segregation and the 1940 Presidential Election," *Phylon* 30 (Spring 1969): 42–47; Ulysses Lee, *The Employment of Negro Troops* (Washington: Office of the Chief of Military History, 1966), 84; Florence Murray, ed., *The Negro Handbook, 1942* (New York: Wendell Maliet & Co., 1942), 60.

26. Dalfiume, "Military Segregation," 50–55; Lee, *Employment of Negro Troops,* 75–76; George Q. Flynn, "Selective Service and American Blacks during the World War," *Journal of Negro History* 69 (Winter 1984): 16; Herbert Garfinkel, *When Negroes March* (New York: Atheneum, 1969), passim; Robert Brisbane, *The Black Vanguard* (Valley Forge: Judson Press, 1970), 162, 166, 178, 180–81; Horace R. Cayton and George S. Mitchell, *Black Workers and the New Unions* (College Park, Md.: McGrath Publishing, 1969), 416–21; A. Philip Randolph, "A. Philip Randolph Tells . . .Why I Would Not Stand for Reelection as President of the National Negro Congress," *American Federationist* 48 (July 1940): 24–25; A. Philip Randolph, "Why We Should March," *Survey Graphic* 31 (November 1942): 488–89; Philip S. Foner, *Blacks and the Military, Organized Labor and the Black Worker* (New York: Praeger, 1974), 172–73, 210–11; *New York Age,* October 19, 26, 1940; Neil A. Wynn, *The Afro-American and the Second World War* (Holmes & Meier, 1976), 40–42.

27. Lee, *Employment of Negro Troops,* 36, 38, 41–43, 46; *Annual Report of the Chief of the National Guard Bureau, 1941,* 15, 85, 93, 95; *Annual Report of the Secretary of War, 1941,* 71–72; Charles Houston to Major Sidney P. Simpson, September 27, 1940, Robert P. Patterson Papers, Manuscript Division, Library of Congress; Walter White to Governor Herbert H. Lehman, June 10, 1940; Memorandum from NAACP Secretary, June 10, 1940, Governor Lehman to W. White, July 27, 1940, NAACP Papers, Manuscript Division, Library of Congress; Charles Johnson, "The Army, the Negro and the Civilian Conservation Corps, 1933–1942," *Military Affairs* 26 (October 1972): 86; *Washington Afro-American,* January 18, 25, March 1, 8, 15, 1941; *Chicago Defender,* December 7, 21, 1940, March 29, 1941.

28. Jakeman, *Divided Skies,* 132–316. Also see Alan M. Osur, *Blacks in the Army Air Corps during World War II* (Washington: Office of Air Force History, 1977), passim; Sandler, *Segregated Skies,* passim; Scott and Womack, *Double V,* passim.

29. Millet and Maslowski, *For the Common Defense,* 397-400.

30. Motley, ed. *The Invisible Soldier,* 39–40.

31. Charles Wollenberg, "Blacks vs. Navy Blue," *California History* 58 (Spring 1979): 62–79; Foner, *Blacks and the Military,* 169.

32. Paul Stilwell, ed., *The Golden Thirteen* (Annapolis: Naval Institute Press, 1993), xx–xxv.

33. Foner, *Blacks and the Military,* 170–71.

34. Henry I. Shaw, Jr., and Ralph W. Donnell, *Blacks in the Marine Corps* (Washington: Marine Corps History and Museums Division, 1988), 1–46.

35. Charles Johnson, Jr., "Pea Island: The Coast Guard's Black Lifesaving Station, 1880-1900," *Journal of the Afro-American Historical and Genealogical Society* 3

(Summer 1982): 67–72; Foner, *Blacks and the Military,* 173–74; John Beecher, *All Brave Sailors* (New York: L. B. Fischer, 1945), passim.

36. Martha S. Putney, *When the Nation Was in Need* (Metuchen: Scarecrow Press, 1992), 1, 13, 41, 52–53, 99; Foner, *Blacks and the Military,* 165; Charity Adams Early, *One Woman's Army* (College Station: Texas A&M University Press, 1989), passim.

37. Putney, *When the Nation Was in Need,* 61–64.

38. Foner, *Blacks and the Military,* 174.

39. Darlene Clark Hine, *Black Women in White* (Bloomington: Indiana University Press, 1989), 164–83; Robert V. Piemonte, *Highlights in the History of the Army Nurse Corps* (Washington: U.S. Army Center of Military History, 1989), 13.

40. John Cash et al., *The Exclusion of Black Soldiers from the Medal of Honor in World War II* (Jefferson: McFarland & Co., 1997), 69–92.

41. Ibid., 93-138; Hondon B. Hargrove, *Buffalo Soldiers in Italy: Black Americans in World War II* (Jefferson: McFarland & Co., 1985), passim.

42. Lawrence J. Paszek, "Negroes and the Air Force, 1939-1949," *Military Affairs* 31 (Fall 1967): 6; Scott and Womack, *Double V,* 226; Foner, *Blacks and the Military,* 163.

43. Cash, *The Exclusion,* 139–65.

44. Ibid., 167–84.

45. Lee, *Employment of Negro Troops,* 123–25, 291, 474; Phillip McQuire, ed., *Taps for a Jim Crow Army: Letters from Black Soldiers in World War II* (Lexington: University Press of Kentucky, 1983), 75–76; Stubbs and Connor, *Armor-Infantry,* 193–209.

ALLEN TEMPLE AFRICAN M. E. CHURCH; Cor. Broadway and Sixth Street, Cincinnati, O. Feb. 8, 1874.

Item 5-3
Allen Temple, AME Church, Broadway and 6th, Cincinnati, Ohio. From *Proceedings of the Semi-centenary Celebration of the African Methodist Episcopal Church of Cincinnati, February 8th, 9th, and 10th, 1874,* edited by Rev. B. W. Arnett (Cincinnati: H. Watkin, 1874).
Rare Book and Special Collections Division.

Further Reading

Akers, Regina. "Female Naval Reservists during World War II: A Historiographical Essay," *Minerva* (Summer 1990).

Ashe, Arthur. *A Hard Road to Glory: A History of the African-American Athlete*. New York: Warner Books, 1988; 3 vols.

Bell, Howard H., ed. *Minutes of the Proceedings of the National Negro Conventions, 1830–1964*. New York: Arno Press, 1969.

Bennett, Lerone, Jr. *Before the Mayflower: A History of Black America*. New York: Penguin Books, 1993.

Berlin, Ira, ed. *Freedom: A Documentary History of Emancipation, 1861–1867*. New York: Cambridge University Press, 1982–90; 3 vols.

Berlin, Ira. *Slaves without Masters: The Free Negro in the Antebellum South*. New York: Pantheon Books, 1975.

Blackett, R. J. M. *Thomas Morris Chester, Black Civil War Correspondent: His Dispatches from the Virginia Front*. Baton Rouge: Louisiana State University Press, 1982.

Blassingame, John W. *The Slave Community: Plantation Life in the Antebellum South*. New York: Oxford University Press, 1979.

Blassingame, John W. *Slave Testimony: Two Centuries of Letters, Speeches, Interviews, and Autobiographies*. Baton Rouge: Louisiana State University Press, 1977.

Blassingame, John W., and Mae G. Henderson. *Antislavery Newspapers and Periodicals*. Boston: G. K. Hall, 1980–84; 5 vols.

Blight, David W. *Frederick Douglass' Civil War: Keeping Faith in Jubilee*. Baton Rouge: Louisiana State University Press, 1989.

Blockson, Charles L. *The Underground Railroad*. New York: Prentice Hall Press, 1987.

Bracey, John H., Jr., August Meier, and Elliott Rudwick, eds. *Free Blacks in America, 1800–1860.* Belmont, Calif.: Wadsworth Publishing Co., 1971.

Brown, William Wells. *The Negro in the American Revolution.* Boston: Lee and Shepard, 1867.

Burchard, Peter. *One Gallant Rush: Robert Gould Shaw and His Brave Black Regiment.* New York: St. Martin's Press, 1965.

Carson, Clayborn, David J. Garrow, Gerald Gill, Vincent Harding, and Darlene Clark Hine, eds. *The Eyes on the Prize Civil Rights Reader.* (New York: Viking Penguin, 1991).

Carver, George Washington. *George Washington Carver in His Own Words*, edited by Gary R. Kremer. Columbia: University of Missouri Press, 1987.

Catterall, Helen H., ed. *Judicial Cases Concerning American Slavery and the Negro.* Washington: Carnegie Institution of Washington, 1926–37. 5 vols.

Chalmers, David. *And the Crooked Places Made Straight.* Baltimore: Johns Hopkins University Press, 1991.

Clark-Lewis, Elizabeth. *Living In, Living Out: African American Domestics in Washington, D.C., 1910–1940.* Washington: Smithsonian Institution Press, 1994.

Cornish, Dudley Taylor. *The Sable Arm: Negro Troops in the Union Army, 1861–1865.* New York: Norton, 1966.

Cripps, Thomas. *Black Film as Genre.* Bloomington: Indiana University Press, 1978.

Delany, Martin. *The Condition, Elevation, Emigration, and Destiny of the Colored People of the United States.* New York: Arno Press, 1968.

Donnan, Elizabeth, ed. *Documents Illustrative of the History of the Slave Trade to America.* Washington: Carnegie Institution of America, 1930–35. 4 vols.

Douglass, Frederick. *The Frederick Douglass Papers*, edited by John W. Blassingame et al. New Haven: Yale University Press, 1979–92+.

DuBois, W .E. B. *The Correspondence of W. E. B. DuBois*, edited by Herbert Aptheker. Amherst: University of Massachusetts Press, 1973–78.

Epstein, Dena. *Sinful Tunes and Spirituals: Black Folk Music to the Civil War.* Urbana: University of Illinois Press, 1977.

Finkelman, Paul. *The Atlantic Slave Trade and American Courts: The Pamphlet Literature.* New York: Garland Publishing Co., 1988. 2 vols.

Finkelman, Paul, ed. *Slavery in the Courtroom: An Annotated Bibliography of American Cases.* Washington: Library of Congress, 1985.

Foner, Eric. *Freedom's Lawmakers: A Directory of Black Office Holders during Reconstruction.* Baton Rouge: Louisiana State University Press, 1966.

Fox, Charles Bernard. *Records of the Service of the Fifty-Fifth Regiment of Massachusetts Volunteer Infantry.* Cambridge: Press of John Wilson and Son, 1868.

Franklin, John Hope. *Reconstruction after the Civil War.* Chicago: University of Chicago Press, 1994.

Franklin, John Hope, and Alfred A. Moss, Jr. *From Slavery to Freedom: A History of Negro Americans.* New York: McGraw-Hill, 1994.

Frey, Sylvia R. *Water from the Rock: Black Resistance in a Revolutionary Age.* Princeton: Princeton University Press, 1991.

Garrow, David J. *Bearing the Cross: Martin Luther King, Jr. and the Southern Christian Leadership Conference.* New York: Vintage Books 1988.

Garrow, David J., ed. *The Montgomery Bus Boycott and the Women Who Started It: The Memoir of Jo Ann Gibson Robinson.* Knoxville: University of Tennessee Press, 1987.

Gates, Henry Louis, ed. *The Schomburg Library of Nineteenth Century Black Women Writers.* New York: Oxford University Press, 1988+.

Gatewood, Willard B. *"Smoked Yankees" and the Struggle for Empire: Letters from Negro Soldiers, 1898–1902*. Urbana: University of Illinois Press, 1971.

Greene, Lorenzo J. *The Negro in Colonial New England*. New York: Atheneum, 1968.

Gutman, Herbert G. *The Black Family in Slavery and Freedom, 1750–1925*. New York: Pantheon Books, 1976.

Ham, Debra Newman, ed. *The African-American Mosaic: A Library of Congress Resource Guide for the Study of Black History and Culture*. Washington: Library of Congress, 1993.

Hamilton, Kenneth M. *Black Towns and Profit: Promotion and Development in the Trans-Appalachian West, 1877–1915*. Urbana: University of Illinois Press, 1991.

Hampton, Henry, and Steve Fayer. *Voices of Freedom*. New York: Bantam Books, 1990.

Harlan, Louis R. *Booker T. Washington: The Wizard of Tuskegee, 1901–1915*. New York: Oxford University Press, 1983.

Harlan, Louis R., and Raymond W. Smock. *The Booker T. Washington Papers*. Urbana: University of Illinois Press, 1972–89; 14 vols.

Harris, Joseph E. *Global Dimensions of the African Diaspora*. Washington: Howard University Press, 1993.

Henri, Florette. *Bitter Victory: A History of Black Soldiers in World War I*. Garden City, N.Y.: Doubleday, 1970.

Higginbotham, A. Leon, Jr. *In the Matter of Color: Race and the American Legal Process, The Colonial Period*. New York: Oxford University Press, 1978.

Higginbotham, Evelyn Brooks. *Righteous Discontent: The Women's Movement in the Black Baptist Church, 1880–1920*. Cambridge, Mass.: Harvard University Press, 1993.

Hill, Robert, ed. *Marcus Garvey and the Universal Negro Improvement Association Papers*. Berkeley: University of California Press, 1983–95+.

Hine, Darlene C., ed. *"We Specialize in the Wholly Impossible": A Reader in Black Women's History*. New York: Carlson Publishers, 1995.

Holt, Thomas C. *Black over White: Negro Political Leadership in South Carolina during Reconstruction*. Urbana: University of Illinois Press, 1977.

Jones, Howard. *Mutiny on the "Amistad:" The Saga of a Slave Revolt and Its Impact on American Abolition, Law, and Diplomacy*. New York: Oxford University Press, 1987.

Jones, Jacqueline. *Labor of Love, Labor of Sorrow: Black Women, Work, and the Family from Slavery to the Present*. New York: Vintage Books, 1986.

Jordan, Ervin L. *Black Confederates and Afro-Yankees in Civil War Virginia*. Charlottesville: University Press of Virginia, 1995.

Jordan, Winthrop D. *White over Black: American Attitudes toward the Negro, 1500–1812*. Chapel Hill: University of North Carolina Press, 1968.

Katz, William Loren. *Black Indians*. New York: Alladin, 1997.

Katz, William Loren. *The Black West*. New York: Simon & Schuster, 1996.

Kellogg, Charles Flint. *NAACP: A History of the National Association for the Advancement of Colored People, 1909–1920*. Baltimore: Johns Hopkins Press, 1967.

Kluger, Richard. *Simple Justice*. New York: Vintage Books, 1977.

Lawson, Sandra. *Generations Past: A Selected List of Sources for Afro-American Genealogical Research*. Washington: Library of Congress, 1988.

Leckie, William H. *The Buffalo Soldiers: A Narrative of the Negro Cavalry in the West*. Norman: University of Oklahoma Press, 1963.

Lee, Ulysses. *The Employment of Negro Troops.* Washington: Office of the Chief of Military History, U.S. Army, 1966.

Levine, Lawrence W. *Black Culture and Black Consciousness: Afro-American Folk Thought from Slavery to Freedom.* New York: Oxford University Press, 1978.

Lewis, David Levering. *When Harlem Was In Vogue.* New York: Vintage Books, 1981.

Litwack, Leon F. *Been in the Storm So Long: The Aftermath of Slavery.* Boston: Skinner House Books, 1991.

Litwack, Leon F. *North of Slavery: The Negro in the Free States, 1790–1860.* Chicago: University of Chicago Press, 1961.

Locke, Alain, ed. *The New Negro: An Interpretation.* New York: Atheneum, 1992.

Logan, Rayford. *The Betrayal of the Negro: From Rutherford B. Hayes to Woodrow Wilson.* New York: Collier Books, 1968.

MacGregor, Morris J., Jr., and Bernard C. Nalty. *Blacks in the Military: Essential Documents.* Wilmington, Del.: Scholarly Books, 1981.

McGuire, Philip. *Taps for a Jim Crow Army: Letters from Black Soldiers in World War II.* Santa Barbara, Calif.: ABC-Clio, 1983.

Meier, August. *Negro Thought in America: 1880–1915: Racial Ideologies in the Age of Booker T. Washington.* Ann Arbor: University of Michigan Press, 1988.

Meyer, Walter Dean. *Now is Your Time: The African American Struggle for Freedom.* New York: HarperCollins, 1991; Juvenile Literature.

Miller, Richard. "The Golden Fourteen, Plus: Black Navy Women in World War One," *Minerva* 13 (Fall/Winter 1995).

Moss, Alfred A., Jr. *The American Negro Academy: Voice of the Talented Tenth.* Baton Rouge: Louisiana State University Press, 1981.

Nalty, Bernard C. *Strength for the Fight: A History of Black Americans in the Military.* New York: Free Press, 1986.

Nell, William C. *The Colored Patriots of the American Revolution.* New York: Arno Press, 1968.

Painter, Nell Irvin. *Exodusters: Black Migration to Kansas after Reconstruction.* Lawrence, Kansas: University of Kansas Press, 1986.

Painter, Nell Irvin. *Sojourner Truth: A Life, A Symbol.* New York: Norton, 1996.

Patterson, Orlando. *Slavery and Social Death: A Comparative Study.* Cambridge, Mass.: Harvard University Press, 1982.

Payne, Charles M. *I've Got the Light of Freedom: The Organizing Tradition and the Mississippi Freedom Struggle.* Berkeley: University of California Press, 1995.

Porter, Dorothy B. *Early Negro Writing, 1760–1837.* Boston: Beacon Press, 1971.

Quarles, Benjamin. *Black Abolitionists.* New York: DaCapo Press, 1991.

Quarles, Benjamin. *The Negro in the American Revolution.* Chapel Hill: University of North Carolina Press, 1996.

Quarles, Benjamin. *The Negro in the Civil War.* Boston: Little, Brown, 1953.

Reagon, Bernice Johnson, ed. *We'll Understand It Better By and By: Pioneering African American Gospel Composers.* Washington: Smithsonian Institution Press, 1992.

Rose, Willie Lee. *Rehearsal for Reconstruction: The Port Royal Experiment.* Indianapolis: Bobbs-Merrill, 1964.

Sammons, Vivian O. *Blacks in Science and Medicine.* New York: Hemisphere Publishing Co., 1990.

Scott, Emmett J. *Official History of the American Negro in the World War.* Chicago: Homewood Press, 1919.

Shick, Tom W. *Behold the Promised Land: A History of Afro-American Settler Society in Nineteenth Century Liberia.* Baltimore: Johns Hopkins University Press, 1980.

Southern, Eileen. *Biographical Dictionary of Afro-American and African Musicians.* Westport, Conn.: Greenwood Press, 1982.

Stampp, Kenneth M. *The Peculiar Institution: Slavery in the Ante-bellum South.* New York: Vintage Books, 1989.

Staudenraus, P. J. *The American Colonization Movement, 1816–1865.* New York: Octagon Books, 1980.

Terborg-Penn, Rosalyn. *Women in the African Diaspora: A Reader.* Washington: Howard University Press, 1996.

Trotter, Joe William, Jr., ed. *The Great Migration in Historical Perspective: New Dimensions of Race, Class, and Gender.* Bloomington: Indiana University Press, 1991.

Washington, Booker T. *Up from Slavery.* New York: Doubleday, 1998.

Weisbrot, Robert. *Freedom Bound: A History of America's Civil Rights Movement.* New York: Plume/Penguin, 1991.

Weiss, Nancy J. *The National Urban League, 1910–1940.* New York: Oxford University Press, 1974.

Wesley, Charles H., and Romero, Patricia W. *Negro Americans in the Civil War.* Washington: Publishers Company, 1967.

Williams, Eric. *Capitalism and Slavery.* Chapel Hill: University of North Carolina Press, 1994.

Williams, George Washington. *A History of the Negro Troops in the War of the Rebellion, 1861–1865.* New York: Harper & Brothers, 1888.

Woodson, Carter G. *The History of the Negro Church.* Washington: Associated Publishers, 1921.

Woodson, Carter G. *The Miseducation of the Negro.* New York: AMS Press, 1977.

Woodward, C. Vann. *The Strange Career of Jim Crow.* New York: Oxford University Press, 1955.

```
                    -3-          Act I. Scene I.

Chorus    (Addressing Mr. Williams)  Speech!  Speech!
Williams  Friends and citizens of Jimtown. - - It is
          useless for me to attempt to tell you what
          kind of a man Harry Walton is and that he IS
          the right man for the Mayor, for no doubt, you all
          know him as well as I.  In fact, we have watched
          him grow from boyhood.
Chorus    (Interrupting) He is the man.
Williams  (Continuing) His honesty, integrity and efficiency
          make him the logical man for the office and it is
          the solemn duty of each and every citizen of
          Jimtown to vote for him for he's all right.
Citizen   What's the matter with Harry Walton?
Chorus    He's all right.
Williams  Who's all right.
Chorus    Harry Walton's all right.
          Hooray!  Hooray!  Hooray!
             Song, Dance and Exit of Chorus.
          We're for Harry Walton, here we come,
          We'll vote for Harry Walton, our favorite son,
          And with banners blowing, we will soon be showing,
          If we keep step with the hep hep and rattle of the
                                drum,
          Honor is our motto, bright and brand,
          Justice is the platform on which we stand,
          And since we are in it, we are going to win it,
          Harry Walton is the man.
```

Item 7-18
Eubie Blake. *Shuffle Along.* Lyrics by Noble Sissle. The musical show *Shuffle Along* opened on May 23, 1921, and ran for over five hundred performances. Eubie Blake (1883–1983) wrote the music and Noble Sissle (1889–1975) the lyrics. The principals included Adelaide Hall and Florence Mills. Both Josephine Baker and Ethel Waters played in the chorus line, and Paul Robeson was briefly a member of the cast as part of a barbershop quartet. "Harry Walton," whose mayoral campaign is celebrated on this page of the libretto, is the subject of the show's biggest hit, "I'm Just Wild about Harry."
Carbon copy of typescript by Authors' Typing Service, [1922]. Music Division.

(a.) Constans et perpetua voluntas, jus _Suum_ cuique tribuendi.
The constant and perpetual will to secure to every one, <u>his own</u>
right.

To every one <u>his own</u>!

(b.) ∧ for himself alone

(c.) At an early period of my life, it was my fortune to witness the representa-
-tion upon the Stage of one of the tragic masterpieces of the great drama-
-tist of England, or I may rather Say of the great dramatist of the world;
and in that Scene which exhibits in action the sudden, the instan-
-taneous fall from unbounded power into irretrievable disgrace, of
Cardinal Wolsey, by the abrupt declaration of displeasure and dismission
from the service of his king made by that Monarch in the presence of
Lord Surry and of the Lord Chamberlain; at the moment of Wolsey's
humiliation and distress, Surry gives vent to his long Suppressed re-
-sentiments for the insolence and injuries which he had endured from
the fallen favourite while in power, and breaks out into insulting and
bitter reproaches, till checked by the Chamberlain who Says

        "Oh! my Lord;

"Press not a falling man too far: 'tis "Virtue"
the repetition of that single line in the relative position of the parties,
struck me as a moral principle, and made upon my mind an impression
which I have carried with me through all the changes of my life, and
which I trust I shall carry with me to my grave.

(d.) The charge ~~that~~ I make against the present Executive administration
that
is in all their proceedings relating to these unfortunate men, instead of
that _Justice_ to which they were bound not less than this honourable Court
itself to observe, they have substituted _Sympathy_! — Sympathy, with
one of the parties in this conflict of Justice ~~and~~ _Antipathy_ to the other
Sympathy, with the white — Antipathy to the black — And in proof of
this charge I adduce the admission and avowal of the Secretary of State
himself — In the Letter of Mr Forsyth to the Spanish Minister d'Argaiz
of 13. December 1839. [Document H. R. U. S. 185] defending the course of the
Administration against the reproaches utterly groundless but not the less
bitter of the Spanish Envoy, he Says

Checklist of the Exhibition

CARROLL JOHNSON

A reproduction number with the prefix LC-USZ indicates that a black-and-white negative exists or with the prefix LC-USZC2 or C4 that a color transparency exists. Copyprints of items not restricted by copyright can be ordered directly from the Photoduplication Service, Library of Congress, Washington, D.C. 20540–5230 (telephone 202 707-5640). If no reproduction number is cited, contact the division holding the item described.

Part One: Slavery—The Peculiar Institution

1-1   A slave revolt aboard the Brigantine *Hope,* March 17, 1765. Holograph transcript. Peter Force Collection, Manuscript Division.

1-2   "To be sold . . . a cargo of 170 prime young likely healthy Guinea slaves." Savannah, July 25, 1774. Photograph of a broadside. Prints and Photographs Division. (LC-USZ62-16876)

1-3   Jupiter Hammon. *An Address to the Negroes in the State of New York.* New York: Samuel Wood, 1806. Rare Book and Special Collections Division.

1-4   Michael Shiner. Diary, 1813–69. Holograph manuscript. Manuscript Division.

1-5   *Guinea propia, nec non Nigritiae vel Terrae Nigrorum maxima pars* . . . . Nuremberg: Homann Hereditors, 1743. Engraved, hand-colored map. Geography and Map Division.

1-6   Lionel H. Kennedy and Thomas Parker. *An Official Report of The Trials of Sundry Negroes, Charged with an Attempt to Raise an Insurrection in the State of South Carolina* . . . . Charleston, S.C.: James R. Schenck, 1822. Rare Book and Special Collections Division.

1-7   John Floyd, governor of Virginia, to James Hamilton, governor of South Carolina, November 19, 1831. Holograph letter, discussing the Nat Turner revolt. Manuscript Division.

1-8   *The Confessions of Nat Turner, the Leader of the Late Insurrection in Southampton, Virginia...*1832. Richmond: Thomas R. Gray, 1832. Rare Book and Special Collections Division.

1-9 John Rutherford to William B. Randolph on the slave mutiny at "Chatsworth," Richmond, Virginia, September 1, 1833. Manuscript Division.

1-10 Romare Bearden. *Roots Odyssey.* Screen print, 1976. Ben and Beatrice Goldstein Foundation Collection, Prints and Photographs Division.

1-11A "A Chart of the Sea Coasts of Europe, Africa, and America . . . ." From John Thornton, *The Atlas Maritimus or the Sea Atlas.* London, 1700?. Geography and Map Division.

1-12 John Quincy Adams. A draft of a brief delivered before the U.S. Supreme Court, 1840–1841. Lewis Tappan Papers, Manuscript Division.

1-13 Affidavit of an *Amistad* African, 1839. Holograph transcript. Tappan Papers, Manuscript Division.

1-14 Romare Bearden. *Prince Cinque.* Screen print, 1971. Ben and Beatrice Goldstein Foundation Collection. Prints and Photographs Division.

1-15 William E. Channing. *The Duty of the Free States, or Remarks Suggested by the Case of the Creole.* Boston: William Crosby & Company, 1842. Rare Book and Special Collections Division.

1-16 "$200 Reward. Ranaway from the subscriber . . . Five Negro Slaves." St. Louis, 1847. Broadside. Rare Book and Special Collections Division. (LC-USZ62-62797)

1-17 Billy G. Smith and Richard Wijtowicz. *Blacks Who Stole Themselves; Advertisements for Runaways in the Pennsylvania Gazette, 1728–90.* Philadelphia: University of Pennsylvania, 1989. General Collections.

1-18 *David Walker's Appeal in Four Articles, together with a Preamble, to the Coloured Citizens of the World* ...(September 1829). Edited by Charles M. Wiltse. New York: Hill and Wang, 1965. General Collections.

1-19 *An Account of Some of the Principal Slave Insurrections. . . .* Compiled by Joshua

Coffin. New York: The American Anti-slavery Society, 1860. Rare Book and Special Collections Division.

1-20 "Africans on Board the Slave Bark Wildfire," April 30, 1860. From *Harper's Weekly,* June 2, 1860. Wood engraving made from a daguerreotype. Prints and Photographs Division. (LC-USZ62-19607)

1-21 *"Long Time Ago Negro Song . . . As sung by M. T. Rice in the Ethiopian Opera."* Baltimore: John Cole, 1833. Sheet music. Music Division.

1-23 "Jump Isabel, slide water." Sung by ex-slave-owner Isabel Barnwell and recorded by Stetson Kennedy. Jacksonville, Florida, August 1939. American Folklife Center.

1-24 "Monologue on plantation experiences." Spoken by Irene Williams and recorded by John A. and Ruby T. Lomax. Rome, Mississippi, October 1940. American Folklife Center.

Part Two: Free Blacks in the Antebellum Period

2-1 Olaudah Equiano. *The Interesting Narrative of the Life of Olaudah Equiano, or Gustavus Vassa, the African.* Norwich: The Author, 1794. Rare Book and Special Collections Division. (LC-USZ62-54026)

2-2 Certificate of Freedom of Harriet Bolling, Petersburg, Virginia, 1851. Carter G. Woodson Collection, Manuscript Division.

2-3 [Northwest part of Montserrado County, Liberia, in ten-mile squares]. Manuscript map. [1800?] Geography and Map Division.

2-4 George H. Moore. *Historical Notes on the Employment of Negroes in the American Army of the Revolution.* New York: C.T. Evans, 1862. General Collections.

2-5 Revolutionary War documents for Juba Freeman. State of Connecticut, June 1, 1782. Gladstone Collection, Manuscript Division.

2-6 Black seaman Samuel Fox's certificate of citizenship, August 12, 1854. Black History Collection, Manuscript Division.

2-7 Paul Cuffee. *A Brief Account of the Settlement and Present Situation of the Colony of Sierra Leone in Africa.* New York: Samuel Wood, 1812. Rare Book and Special Collections Division.

2-8 Andrew Ellicott. [Territory of Columbia.] Surveyed by Benjamin Banneker. Manuscript map, [1793]. Geography and Map Division.

2-9 *Freedom's Journal,* March 16, 1827. John B. Russwurm and Samuel Cornish, founders. Humanities and Social Sciences Division.

2-10 *North Star,* June 2, 1848. Frederick Douglass, Founder. Serial and Government Publications Division.

2-11 William Still. *The Underground Railroad: A Record of Facts, Authentic Narratives, Letters. . . .* Philadelphia: People's Publishing Co., 1879. Rare Book and Special Collections Division.

2-12 Leonard Black. *The Life and Sufferings of Leonard Black, a Fugitive from Slavery.* Providence, Rhode Island: L. Black, 1847. Rare Book and Special Collections Division.

2-13 Henry Bibb. *Narrative of the Life and Adventures Henry Bibb, an American Slave.* New York: The Author, 1849. Rare Book and Special Collections Division.

2-14 *Benjamin Banneker's Pennsylvania, Delaware, Maryland, and Virginia Almanack and Ephemeris, for the Year of Our Lord 1792 . . . .* Baltimore: William Goddard and James Angell, [1791]. Rare Book and Special Collections Division.

2-15 Phillis Wheatley. *Poems on Various Subjects: Religious and Moral.* London: A. Bell, 1773. Rare Book and Special Collections Division.

2-16 David Ruggles. *The "Extinguisher" Extinguished or David M. Reese, M.D., "Used Up."* New York: D. Ruggles, 1834. Markoe Pamphlet Collection. Rare Book and Special Collections Division.

2-17 *Proceedings of the Colored National Convention, Held in Rochester July 6th, 7th, and 8th, 1853.* Rochester: Frederick Douglass, 1853. Susan B. Anthony Collection, Rare Book and Special Collections Division.

2-18 Charles White. *Frederick Douglass.* Lithograph, 1951. Ben and Beatrice Goldstein Foundation Collection, Prints and Photographs Division.

2-19 Prince Hall. *A Charge Delivered to the African Lodge, June 24, 1797, at Menotomy.* Boston: Members of the Said Lodge, 1797. Hazard Pamphlet Collection, Rare Book and Special Collections Division.

2-20 J. H. Daniels. *Bishops of the AME Church.* Boston: J.H. Daniels, 1876. Lithograph. Prints and Photographs Division. (LC-USZ62-15059)

2-21 Alfred Hoffy. *Mrs. Juliann Jane Tillman, Preacher of the A.M.E. Church.* Philadelphia: Peter S. Duval, 1844. Lithograph. Prints and Photographs Division. (LC-USZ62-54596)

2-22 Francis Johnson. *Boone Infantry Brass Band Quick Step.* Philadelphia: Osbourn's Music Saloon, 1844. Sheet music. Music Division.

2-23 Francis Johnson. "Recognition March of the Independence of Hayti. . . ." Philadelphia: F. Willig, [1825]. Sheet music. Music Division.

Part Three: Abolitionists, Antislavery Movements, and the Rise of the Sectional Controversy

3-1 Anthony Benezet. *Observations on the Inslaving, Importing and Purchasing of Negroes.* Germantown, Pennsylvania: Christopher Sower, 1760. American Imprints Collection, Rare Book and Special Collections Division.

3-2 Jonathan Edwards, D.D. *The Injustice and Impolicy of the Slave Trade, and of the Slavery of the Africans . . . A Sermon.* New Haven, Connecticut: Thomas and Samuel Green, 1791. Rare Book and Special Collections Division.

3-3 "Declaration of the Anti-Slavery Convention Assembled in Philadelphia, December 4, 1833." Broadside. Rare Book and Special Collections Division.

3-4   *Mission to Fugitive Slaves in Canada: Being a Branch of the Operations of the Colonial Church and School Society . . . 1858–9.* [London]: Society's Offices, 1859. Pamphlet. Rare Book and Special Collections Division.

3-5   S. M. Africanus. "The Fugitive Slave Law." Hartford, Connecticut, [ca. 1850]. Broadside. Rare Book and Special Collections Division.

3-6   John Brown. "Address of John Brown . . . Sentence of Death; For his heroic attempt at Harpers Ferry . . . ." Boston: C.C. Mead, n.d. Broadside. Rare Book and Special Collections Division.

3-7   William H. Johnson. *On a John Brown Flight.* Screen print, ca. 1945. Harmon Foundation Collection, Prints and Photographs Division. (LC-USZC4-1865)

3-8   Frederick Douglass. "A Lecture on John Brown." Typescript with autograph corrections and autograph drafts, 1860. Frederick Douglass Papers, Manuscript Division.

3-9   Anthony Burns. Boston: R. M. Edwards, 1855. Wood engraving with letterpress. Prints and Photographs Division. (LC-USZ62-9075)

3-10   Palmer's "Uncle Tom's Cabin." 1882. Buffalo, N.Y.: Courier Litho. Co., c. 1899. Color lithograph. Prints and Photographs Division.

3-11a   "Sojourner Truth." Portrait. Albumen print, carte de visite, 1864. Gladstone Collection, Prints and Photographs Division.

3-11b   "Sojourner Truth." Portrait, seated. Carte de visite, 1864. Gladstone Collection, Prints and Photographs Division.

3-12   "The Negro Woman's Appeal to Her White Sisters." Leaf. [London]: Richard Barrett, [1850]. Broadside. Printed Ephemera Collection, Rare Book and Special Collections Division.

3-13   *The Child's Anti-Slavery Book: Containing a Few Words about American Slave Children . . . .* New York: Carlton &

Porter, 1859. Rare Book and Special Collections Division.

3-14   *A northern view of slavery in the United States.* Chicago: Orcutt Lithographing Company, 1888. Geography and Map Division.

3-15   John G. Whittier. "The Branded Hand." Philadelphia, 1845? Leaflet. Rare Book and Special Collections Division.

3-16   *The Anti-Slavery Harp: A Collection of Songs for Anti-Slavery Meetings.* Compiled by William Wells Brown. Boston: Bela Marsh, 1848. Music Division.

3-17   George W. Clark. *The Liberty Minstrel.* New York: Leavitt & Alden [et al.], 1844. Music Division.

3-18   "Harriet Beecher Stowe." Copyprint of engraving. Prints and Photograph Division. (LC-USZ62-10476)

3-19a   William L. Garrison. "Sonnet to Liberty." Manuscript, December 14, 1840. Manuscript Division.

3-19b   William L. Garrison. "Song of the Abolitionist." Manuscript, 1841. Manuscript Division.

3-20   William Reynolds. *Reynolds's Political Map of the United States . . . .* New York: Wm. C. Reynolds, 1865. Geography and Map Division.

3-21   Sarah H. Bradford. *Harriet, the Moses of Her People.* New York: J.J. Little & Co., 1901. Susan B. Anthony Collection, Rare Book and Special Collections Division.

3-22   Benjamin Lay. *All Slave-Keepers that Keep the Innocent in Bondage . . . .* Philadelphia: Printed for the Author, 1737. Franklin Collection, Rare Book and Special Collections Division.

Part Four: The Civil War

4-1   Alfred Waud. *Contrabands Coming into Camp.* Chinese white on brown paper. Drawing for publication in *Harper's Weekly,* January 31, 1863. Prints and Photographs Division.

4-2   William R. Pywell. "Slave Pen in Alexandria, Va." Copyprint, [1862]. Prints and Photographs Division. (LC-B8171-2296)

4-3 First African Church, Broad Street, Richmond Virginia, 1865. Copyprint. Prints and Photographs Division. (LC-B8171-3368)

4-4 Fugitive African Americans fording the Rappahannock River, Virginia, August 1862. Copyprint. Prints and Photographs Division. (LC-B8171-0518)

4-5 "1st South Carolina Volunteers on review to hear the reading of Lincoln's [Emancipation] Proclamation, January 1, 1863." Copyprint. Prints and Photographs Division. (LC-BH82201-341)

4-6 107th U.S. Colored Infantry Band at Fort Corcoran. Arlington, Virginia, November 1865. Copyprint. Prints and Photographs Division. (LC-B8171-7861)

4-7 Regimental flags of the 6th U.S. Colored Troops. Carte de visite. Gladstone Collection, Prints and Photographs Division.

4-8 "Wounded Colored Troops at Aikens Landing." Stereograph. Gladstone Collection, Prints and Photographs Division.

4-9 "Camp Brightwood, D.C. Contrands in 2nd R.I. camp," ca. 1863. Carte de visite. Gladstone Collection. Prints and Photographs Division.

4-10 "Unidentified sailor," n.d. Carte de visite. Gladstone Collection. Prints and Photographs Division.

4-11 F. Deilman. *"Celebration of the abolition of slavery in the District of Columbia, by the colored people in Washington, April 19, 1866."* Wood engraving. From *Harper's Weekly,* May 12, 1866. Copyprint. Prints and Photographs Division. (LC-USZ62-33937)

4-12 Benjamin Tucker Tanner (A.M.E. bishop). Diary, 1860–61. Holograph manuscript. Carter G. Woodson Papers, Manuscript Division.

4-13 Sojourner Truth (written by Cockrane) to Mary Gale, Feburary 25, 1864. Letter concerning the emancipation of her children and her son's Civil War service. Manuscript Division.

4-14 Christian A. Fleetwood. Diary, September 24, 1864. Holograph manuscript. Christian A. Fleetwood Papers, Manuscript Division.

4-15 "Christian A. Fleetwood in uniform." Albumen print, carte de viste, 1884. Manuscript Division. (LC-USZ62-44731)

4-16 C. W. Foster, U.S. War Department, to Frederick Douglass, August 13, 1863. Typed letter. Manuscript Division.

4-17 Charles Douglass [son] to Frederick Douglass, July 6, 1863. Autograph letter. Frederick Douglass Papers, Manuscript Division.

4-18 "Down in the Lonesome Valley: A Shout Song of the Freedmen of Port Royal." Boston: Oliver Ditson, 1864. Music Division.

4-19 Albert H. Campbell. *Map of the Vicinity of Richmond and Part of the Peninsula.* Department of Northern Virginia, Topographical Department, 1864. Baltimore: T. Swell Ball, 1891. Photolithograph facsimile reproduction. Geography and Map Division.

4-20 Julia Ward Howe. "Battle Hymn of the Republic." Supervisory Committee for Recruiting Colored Regiments. Broadside. Rare Book and Special Collections Division.

4-21a Heard and Moseley. "Waiting for the hour [Emancipation], December 31, 1862." Photograph, carte de visite. Washington, 1863. Gladstone Collection, Prints and Photographs Division.

4-22 After David G. Blythe. "President Lincoln, Writing the Proclamation of Freedom, January 1st, 1863." Cincinnati: Ehrgott and Forbriger, 1864. Lithograph. Prints and Photographs Division. (LC-USZ62-2069, LC-USZC4-1425)

4-23 Charlotte L. Forten. *The Journal of Charlotte L. Forten.* Introduction and notes by Ray Allen Billington. New York: Dryden Press, 1953. General Collections.

Part Five: Reconstruction and Its Aftermath

5-1 Alfred R. Waud. *Mustered Out.* Little Rock, Arkansas, April 20, 1866. *Harper's Weekly,* May 19, 1866. Drawing, Chinese white on green paper. Prints and Photographs Division. (LCUSZ62-175)

5-2 "Sea-island School, no. 1,—St. Helena Island. Established April 1, 1862." *Education among the Freedmen,* ca. 1866–70. Rare Book and Special Collections Division. (LC-USZ62-107754)

5-3 *Proceedings of the Semi-centenary Celebration of the African Methodist Episcopal Church of Cincinnati . . . February 8th, 9th, and 10th, 1874.* Edited by Rev. B. W. Arnett. Cincinnati: H. Watkin, 1874. Daniel Murray Pamphlet Collection, Rare Book and Special Collections Division.

5-4 *The Wilberforce Alumna: A Comprehensive Review of the Origin, Development, and Present Status of Wilberforce University.* Compiled by B. W. Arnett and S. T. Mitchell. Xenia, Ohio: Gazette Office, 1885. Daniel Murray Pamphlet Collection, Rare Book and Special Collections Division.

5-5 James E. Taylor. "The Freedmen's Union Industrial School, Richmond, Va." From *Frank Leslie's Illustrated Newspaper,* September 22, 1866. Copyprint. Prints and Photographs Division. (LC-USZ62-33264)

5-6 *The First Colored Senator and Representatives, in the 41st and 42nd Congress of the United States.* Washington: Currier & Ives, 1872. Color lithograph. Prints and Photographs Division. (LC-USZC2-2325)

5-7 J. Hoover. *Heroes of the Colored Race.* Philadelphia, 1881. Color lithograph. Prints and Photographs Division. (LC-USZ62-10180)

5-8 *Standard Atlas of Graham Co. Kansas, Including a Plat Book of the villages, cities, and townships.* Lithograph maps. Chicago: A. Ogle, 1906. Geography and Map Division.

5-9 Thomas Nast. *Emancipation.* Wood engraving. Philadelphia: S. Bott, 1865. Prints and Photographs Division. (LC-USZ62-2573)

5-10 George F. Crane. *Distinguished Colored Men.* New York: A. Muller, 1883. Hand-colored lithograph. Prints and Photographs Division. (LC-USZC4-1561)

5-11 "Radical Members of the First Legislature after the War, South Carolina." South Carolina, 1878. Photograph. Prints and Photographs Division. (LC-USZ62-28044)

5-12 Henry L. Stephens. [Elderly black man with spectacles reading by candlelight.] Watercolor, ca. 1863. Prints and Photographs Division. (LC-USZC4-2442)

5-13 "Ho for Kansas!" Nashville, Tennessee, March, 18, 1878. Copyprint of broadside. Historic American Buildings Survey. Prints and Photographs Division. (HABS KSFN-6/KS-49-14)

5-16 "I Am the Door." From *Songs of the Jubilee Singers from Fisk University.* Cincinnati: John Church & Co., 1884. Sheet music. Music Division.

5-17 *Laws in Relation to Freedmen, U.S. Sen. 39th Congress, 2nd Sess. Senate Executive Doc. No. 6.* Washington: War Department, Bureau of Refugee Freedmen and Abandoned Lands, 1866–67. Pamphlet. Law Library.

5-18 *Statistical Atlas of the United States based on the Results of the Eleventh Census.* Plate 11. Washington: U.S. Government Printing Office, 1898. Lithograph. Geography and Map Division.

5-20 Hampton Plantation Account Book, 1866–68. South Carolina. Holograph manuscript. Miscellaneous Collection, Manuscript Division.

5-21 Alfred R. Waud. [Black Men Casting Ballots.] From *Harper's Weekly,* November 16, 1867. Copyprint of wood engraving. Prints and Photographs Division. (LC-USZ62-19234)

5-22 Elizabeth White. *All God's Chillun's Got Wings!,* ca. 1933. Soft-ground etching and aquatint. Ben and Beatrice Goldstein Foundation Collection. Prints and Photographs Division. (LC-USZC4-6164)

5-23   "Monologue on post-bellum experiences."
        Spoken by Wallace Quarterman and
        recorded by Alan Lomax, Zora Neale
        Hurston, and Mary Elizabeth Barnicle.
        Frederica, Georgia, June 1935. American
        Folklife Center.

Part Six: The Booker T. Washington Era

6-1   *Afro-American Monument.* Chicago: Goes
        Lithograph Company, 1897. Color litho-
        graph. Prints and Photographs Division.
        (LC-USZ62-22397)

6-2   "Booker T. Washington." [Copyright by
        C. M. Battery, 1917.] Prints and Photographs
        Division. (LC-USZ62-25624)

6-3   Frances Benjamin Johnston. "Tuskegee
        history class." Copyprint, 1902. Prints and
        Photographs Division. (LC-USZ62-64712)

6-4a,   *Elizabeth City County, Va.* Hampton Normal
6-4b   and Agricultural Institute, sheets 5, 6. New
        York: Sanborn Perris Map Co., 1891. Hand-
        colored lithographs. Geography and Map
        Division.

6-5   Booker T. Washington. "Atlanta Exposition
        Speech," September 18, 1895. Typescript
        draft, with autograph corrections. Booker T.
        Washington Papers, Manuscript Division.

6-6   W. E. B. DuBois to Booker T. Washington,
        September 24, 1895. Autograph letter.
        Booker T. Washington Papers. Manuscript
        Division.

6-7   Paul Laurence Dunbar to Booker T.
        Washington, January 23, 1902. Typed
        letter. Booker T. Washington Papers,
        Manuscript Division.

6-8   Platform adopted by the National Negro
        Committee, 1909. Document. NAACP
        Collection, Manuscript Division.

6-9a   National Negro Committee. A call for
        a national conference, 1909. NAACP
        Collection, Manuscript Division.

6-9b   William G. Walling to Ray Stannard Baker,
        February 6, 1909. Typed letter. NAACP Collection,
        Manuscript Division.

6-10a   "A Man Was Lynched Yesterday." Flag, ca. 1930.
        NAACP Collection, Manuscript Division.

6-10b   "A Man Was Lynched Yesterday." Flag flying above
        Fifth Avenue, New York City, ca. 1938. Photograph.
        NAACP Collection, Prints and Photographs Division.
        (LC-USZ62-33793, LC-USZC4-4734)

6-11   Ida B. Wells-Barnett. *Lynch Law in Georgia.*
        Chicago: Chicago Colored Citizens, 1899. Daniel
        Murray Pamphlet Collection, Rare Book and
        Special Collections Division.

6-12   Rev. Alexander Crummell. *Incidents of Hope
        for the Negro Race in America: A Thanksgiving
        Sermon, November 26, 1895.* Washington, 1895.
        Daniel Murray Pamphlet Collection, Rare Book
        and Special Collections Division.

6-13   *Preliminary List of Books and Pamphlets by Negro
        Authors for Paris Exposition and Library of Congress.*
        Compiled by Daniel A. P. Murray. Washington:
        Library of Congress, 1900. Pamphlet. Rare Book
        and Special Collections Division.

6-14   "First Commencement Exercise." National Training
        School for Women and Girls, Lincoln Heights,
        Washington, D.C. Photograph, June 9, 1911.
        Nannie H. Burroughs Collection, Prints and
        Photographs Division.

6-15   Mary Church Terrell. *The Progress of Colored
        Women.* Washington: Smith Brothers, 1898. Daniel
        Murray Pamphlet Collection, Rare Book and
        Special Collections Division.

6-16   George Carver. *Help for the Hard Times.* Alabama:
        Tuskegee Institute, ca. 1916. General Collections.

6-17   Charles Barthelmess. "Buffalo Soldiers, Ft. Keogh,
        Missouri, 25th Infantry," n. d. Cabinet card,
        photograph. Gladstone Collection, Prints and
        Photographs Division.

6-18   "24th Infantry Leaving Salt Lake City, Utah,
        for Chattanooga, Tennessee." April 24, 1898.
        Photograph. Gladstone Collection, Prints and
        Photographs Division.

6-19   Madame C. J. Walker's House (Villa
       Lewaro). Irvington-on-the-Hudson,
       New York, ca. 1987. Historic American
       Buildings Survey, Prints and Photographs
       Division. (HABS no. NY-5618-1)

6-20   [John] Rosamond Johnson. "The Old Flag
       Never Touched the Ground." Words by
       Bob Cole and J. W. Johnson. New York:
       Jos. W. Stern & Co., 1901. Sheet music.
       Music Division.

6-21   Booker T. Washington. *Atlanta Exposition
       Speech,* 1895. Recorded by Booker T.
       Washington, 1908. Motion Picture,
       Broadcasting, and Recorded Sound
       Division.

6-22   Committee on Urban Conditions among
       Negroes, Minutes of the First Meeting.
       New York, N.Y., September 29, 1910.
       National Urban League Collection,
       Manuscript Division.

6-23   "Camp Lincoln." Cabinet card, photograph,
       1897. Gladstone Collection, Prints and
       Photographs Division.

6-24   "Horse-drawn Carriage in Front of Corner
       Drugstore." Georgia, ca. 1900. Photograph.
       W. E. B. DuBois Collection, Prints and
       Photographs Division. (LC-USZ62-76771)

6-25   William J. Swaidner. "Jack Johnson and
       James Jeffries at the World Championship
       Battle." Reno, Nevada, July 4, 1910.
       Photograph. Prints and Photographs
       Division (LC-USZ62-91059)

Part Seven: World War I and Postwar Society

7-1   Charles Gustrine. "True Sons of Freedom."
       Chicago, Chas Gustrine, 1918. Color offset
       poster. Prints and Photographs Division.
       (LC-USZC4-2426)

7-2   Emmett J. Scott. *Scott's Official History
       of the American Negro in the World War.*
       1919; reprinted by Arno Press, New York,
       1969. Humanities and Social Sciences
       Division.

7-3   Cosby's Studio. "Sunshine Laundry." National
       Training School for Women and Girls, Washington,
       D.C. 1920–1930. Photograph. Nannie H. Burroughs
       Collection, Prints and Photographs Division.
       (LC-USZ61-2219)

7-4   Rayford Logan. Diary, May 10–11, 1943. Holograph
       manuscript. Rayford W. Logan Papers, Manuscript
       Division.

7-5   "803rd Pioneer Infantry Band, No. 16," July 18,
       1919. Photograph. Gladstone Collection, Prints
       and Photographs Division.

7-6   Mary Church Terrell. *What the National Association
       [of Colored Women] Has Meant to Colored Women.*
       Typescript, undated. Mary Church Terrell Papers,
       Manuscript Division.

7-7   Report of Anti-Lynching Committee, January 21,
       1921. Typescript. NAACP Collection, Manuscript
       Division.

7-8   Langston Hughes. "Booker T. Washington." Poem,
       second and final drafts, 1941. Manuscript Division.

7-9   Wingold Reiss. "A Photograph of Wingold Reiss's
       drawing of Countee Cullen." June 1, 1941. Silver
       gelatin print. Harmon Foundation Records,
       Manuscript Division.

7-10   Countee Cullen to George H. Haynes, December 7,
       1926, thanking the Harmon Foundation for its liter-
       ary award. Holograph letter. Harmon Foundation
       Records, Manuscript Division.

7-11   "Claude McKay," n. d. Silver gelatin print. Harmon
       Foundation Records. Manuscript Division.

7-12   Alan Lomax. [Zora Neale Hurston. Eatonville,
       Florida, 1935.] Silver gelatin print. American
       Folklife Center. (LC-USZ61-1859)

7-13   Langston Hughes, n. d. Silver gelatin print. Harmon
       Foundation Records, Manuscript Division.

7-14   Nella Larson, n. d. Silver gelatin print. Harmon
       Foundation Records, Manuscript Division.

7-15   *Lynching in the United States, 1889–1922.* New
       York: American Civil Liberties Union, 1923. NAACP
       pamphlet. Geography and Map Division.

7-16   *Map of Anne Arundel [and] Prince Georges Counties, Maryland, and District of Columbia.* [Chicago]: Rand McNally and Company, [1917]. Color printed map. Geography and Map Division.

7-17   Noble Lee Sissle. *Memoirs of "Jim" Europe.* Carbon copy of typescript, ca. 1942. Music Division.

7-18   Eubie Blake, *Shuffle Along.* Lyrics by Noble Sissle. Carbon copy of typescript by Authors' Typing Service, [1922]. Music Division.

7-19   *Guinn v. United States,* board minutes, June 3, 1913. Typescript. NAACP Collection, Manuscript Division.

7-20   *In the Supreme Court of the United States, October term, 1916 [no. 231]. Charles H. Buchanan v. William Warley.* Pamphlet. NAACP Collection, Manuscript Division.

7-21   *Black 15th Regiment Returning to a Hero's Welcome.* Gaumont Graphic, February 1919. Film. Donald Nichol Collection, Motion Picture, Broadcasting, and Recorded Sound Division.

7-22   *The Negro Soldier.* Directed by Frank Capra and produced by the U.S. War Department Special Service Division, Army Service Forces. February 1944. Film. U.S. Government Film Collection, Motion Picture, Broadcasting, and Recorded Sound Division.

Part Eight: The Depression, the New Deal, and World War II

8-1   *The Negro Speaks of Rivers.* Words by Langston Hughes and Margaret Bonds. Sheet music. New York: Handy Brothers Music Company, 1942. Music Division.

8-2   William Grant Still. *Afro American Symphony.* Composer's holograph manuscript, 1930. Music Division.

8-3   Marion Post Wolcott. "Hotel Clark: The Best Service for Colored Only." Memphis, Tennessee, 1939. Copyprint. Farm Security

Administration/Office of War Information Collection, Prints and Photographs Division. (LC-USF33-30637-M3)

8-4   John Vachon. "Colored Men Room." Manchester, Georgia, 1938. Photograph. Farm Security Administration/Office of War Information Collection. Prints and Photographs Division. (LC-USF33-1172M4)

8-5   "European Theater of Operations, Nurses in England," 1944. Photograph. NAACP Collection, Prints and Photographs Division.

8-6   Toni Frissell, "Tuskegee Airmen,"1945. Photograph. Prints and Photographs Division.

8-7   "Airmen with Lena Horne and Noel Parrish," 1940. Silver gelatin print. Noel Parrish Collection, Manuscript Division.

8-8   "Why Should We March." March on Washington, fliers, 1941. A. Philip Randolph Papers, Manuscript Division.

8-10   "'Above and Beyond the Call of Duty': Dorie Miller Received the Navy Cross at Pearl Harbor, May 27, 1942." Color offset poster, 1943. Prints and Photographs Division. (LC-USZC4-2328)

8-11   Gordon Parks. "Duke Ellington at the Hurricane Club." New York, May 1943. Copyprint. Farm Security Administration/Office of War Information Collection, Prints and Photographs Division. (LC-USW3-23953)

8-12   "Marian Anderson receives the Congressional Medal of Honor from Eleanor Roosevelt, 1939." Silver gelatin print. NAACP Collection, Prints and Photographs Division.

8-13   William H. Johnson. *Training for War,* ca. 1941. Screenprint. Harmon Foundation Collection, Prints and Photographs Division. (LC-USZC4-1779)

8-14   Tuskegee Institute, Research Department, *Lynchings by State and Counties in the United States, 1900–1931.* New York: American Map Company, [1931]. Geography and Map Division.

8-15   "Birmingham, Alabama, Block Statistics." *Sixteenth Census of the United States,* 1940, pages 16–17. Washington, 1943. Geography and Map Division.

8-16 Thurgood Marshall to the NAACP, Tuskegee Institute, Research Department. November 17, 1941. NAACP Collection, Manuscript Division.

8-17 Arthur Herzog, Jr., and Billie Holiday. "'God Bless' the Child,' a swing-spiritual based on the authentic proverb God Blessed the Child That's Got His Own.'" Sheet music. New York: Edward B. Marks Music Corporation, 1941. Music Division.

8-18 Prentiss Taylor. *Scottsboro Limited (P.T. VII)*, inscribed for Langston Hughes, November 1931. Lithograph. Prints and Photographs Division. (LC-USZC4-4717)

8-19 Charles White. *The Return of the Soldier*, 1946. Pen-and-ink on illustration board. Prints and Photographs Division. (LC-USC4-4886)

8-20 "Songs of the PWA." Sung by Will Wright and recorded by Sidney Robertson. Clinton, Arkansas, December 1936. American Folklife Center.

8-21 "I'm Making Records for the WPA." Sung by Clyde (Kingfish) Smith and recorded by Herbert Halpert. New York, N.Y., November 1939. American Folklife Center.

8-22 *Cabin in the Sky.* Produced by Metro-Goldwyn-Mayer, 1943. Film. Turner Entertainment Company Collection, Motion Picture, Broadcasting, and Recorded Sound Division.

8-23 A. Philip Randolph. "The Negro Worker." From *Freedom's People.* Broadcast recording. Motion Picture, Broadcasting, and Recorded Sound Division.

8-24 Walter White to Jesse Owens, December 4, 1935. Unsent, typed letter, concerning participation by black athletes in the 1936 Olympic Games. NAACP Collection, Manuscript Division.

8-25 *Spalding's Official Athletic Almanac, 1937.* New York: American Sports Publishing Co., 1937. General Collections.

8-26 "Thirteenth Spingarn Medal awarded to Paul Robeson, October 18, 1945." Photograph. NAACP Collection, Prints and Photographs Division. (LC-USZ62-119112)

8-27 *The Jackie Robinson Story.* Jewel Pictures Corporation, May 19, 1950. Lobby card, no. 50/330. Motion Picture, Broadcasting, and Recorded Sound Division.

8-28 [Althea Gibson, of New York, reaching high for shot during women's singles semifinal match against Christine Truman, of England, in All England Lawn Tennis Championships at Wimbledon, England, July 4, 1957.] Copyprint. New York World-Telegram and Sun Newspaper Collection, Prints and Photographs Division.

8-29 [Fred Palumbo. Wilt Chamberlain, three-quarter-length portrait, wearing uniform of the Harlem Globetrotters basketball team, 1959.] Copyprint. New York World-Telegram and Sun Newspaper Photograph Collection, Prints and Photographs Division. (LC-USZ62-115428)

8-30 "The Brown Bomber Fights His Greatest Fight against Crime: Joe Louis in *The Fight Never Ends.*" Toddy Picture Co., [1949]. Poster. Prints and Photographs Division. (LC-USZ62-115428)

8-31 Library of Congress. *An Exhibit of Books, Manuscripts, Music, Paintings, and Other Works of Art Commemorating the 75th Anniversary of the Thirteenth Amendment to the Constitution, December 18, 1940.* Brochure. Interpretive Programs Office.

Part Nine: The Civil Rights Era

9-1 Press release for Executive Order No. 9981, Establishing the President's Committee on Equality of Treatment and Opportunity in the Armed Forces, July 26, 1948. Typescript document. NAACP Collection, Manuscript Division.

9-2 "By Executive Order President Truman Wipes Out Segregation in Armed Forces." *Chicago Defender*, July 31, 1948. Copyprint from microfilm. Serial and Government Publication Division.

9-3 "5,000 at Meeting Outline Boycott; Bullet Clips Bus." *Montgomery Advertiser*, December 6, 1955.

Copyprint from microfilm. Serial and Government Publication Division.

9-4   *Background Map: 1961 Freedom Rides.*
       [New York]: Associated Press (AP)
       Newsfeature, [1962]. Printed map and
       text. Geography and Map Division.

9-5   Warren K. Leffler. "Bayard Rustin," n. d.
       Copyprint. U.S. News and World Report
       Photograph Collection, Prints and
       Photographs Division. (LC-U9-103332-9)

9-6   Max Roach. *We Insist! Max Roach's
       Freedom Now Suite.* New York: Columbia,
       1960. Record jacket. Motion Picture,
       Broadcasting, and Recorded Sound Division.

9-8   "James Meredith, Oxford, Mississippi,
       1962." Copyprint. New York World-
       Telegram and Sun Newspaper Photograph
       Collection, Prints and Photographs
       Division. (LC-USP-8556-24)

9-9   "Lunch Counter Sit-in," Greensboro,
       North Carolina, 1960. Copyprint NAACP
       Collection, Prints and Photographs Division.
       (LC-USZ62-114749)

9-10   *Ebony.* May 1965. Cover. General
       Collections.

9-11   "Thurgood Marshall, James Nabrit, and
       Others on the Supreme Court Steps after
       Announcement of *Brown* Decision, 1954."
       Copyprint. New York World-Telegram
       and Sun Newspaper Photograph Collection,
       Prints and Photographs Division.
       (LC-USZ62-111236)

9-12   Warren K. Leffler. Signing of the Civil
       Rights Act, April 11, 1968. Copyprint.
       U.S. News and World Report Photograph
       Collection, Prints and Photographs
       Division. (LC-USZ62-95480)

9-13   "March on Washington." U.S. News and
       World Report Photograph Collection,
       August 28, 1963. Copyprint. Prints and
       Photographs Division. (LC-U9-10360-23)

9-14   Martin Luther King. "I Have a Dream."
       August 28, 1963. Manuscript Division.

9-15   Kenneth B. Clark. *The Genesis of Racial
       Identification and Preferences in Negro
       Children, 1940.* K. B. Clark Papers,
       Manuscript Division.

9-16   "Mahalia Jackson at the May 17, 1957, Prayer
       Pilgrimage for Freedom in Washington, D.C."
       Photograph. NAACP Collection, Prints and
       Photographs Division.(LC-USZC4-6177,
       LC-USZ62-119977.

9-17   "Voters at the Voting Booths," ca. 1945.
       Photograph. NAACP Collection, Prints
       and Photographs Division.

9-18a Daisy Bates to Roy Wilkins, December 17,
       1957, on the treatment of the Little Rock Nine.
       Holograph letter. NAACP Collection, Manuscript
       Division.

9-18b [The Little Rock Nine, ca. 1957–60.] Copyprint.
       NAACP Collection, Prints and Photographs
       Division. (LC-US62-119154)

9-19   Silphia Horton, Frank Hamilton, Guy Carawan,
       and Pete Seeger. "We Shall Overcome." New York:
       Ludlow Music, Inc., 1963. Sheet music. Music
       Division.

9-20   "Signing the Voting Rights Act, August 6, 1965."
       U.S. News & World Report, August 16, 1965,
       p. 8. General Collections.

9-21   Gordon Parks. *The Stranger,* 1958. Color
       photograph. Gordon Parks Archives, Prints
       and Photographs Division.

9-22   Brumsic Brandon, Jr. "The Weary Picket," 1977.
       Ink and tonal film overlay over pencil on paper.
       Gift of Brumsic Brandon, Jr. Prints and Photographs
       Division.

9-23   "Wilma Rudolph winning the U.S. women's 400-
       meter with relay team, 1960." Copyprint. New
       York World-Telegram and Sun Newspaper
       Photograph Collection, Prints and Photographs
       Division. (LC-USZ62-113285)

9-24   "Who Wouldn't Love a Man Like That." Sung by
       Mable John and produced by Berry Gordy, G.
       Gordy, and R. Davis. 1960. Sound recording.
       Motion Picture, Broadcasting, and Recorded
       Sound Division.

9-25   William C. Green. Willie Mays, standing, with his arm around Roy Campenella, 1961. Copy-print. New York World-Telegram and Sun Newspaper Photograph Collection, Prints and Photographs Division.

9-26   Richard Scott Rennert. *Hank Aaron.* New York: Chelsea House Publishers, 1993. General Collections.

9-27   Arthur Ashe, Jr. *A Hard Road to Glory: A History of the African-American Athlete 1619–1918.* With the assistance of Kip Branch, Ocania Chalk, and Francis Harris. New York: Warner Books, 1988. Volume 1. General Collections.

9-28   Oliver W. Harrington. *Dark Laughter.* "My Daddy said they didn't seem to mind servin' him on the Anzio beach-head . . . . " *Pittsburgh Courier,* April 2, 1960. Crayon, ink, blue pencil, and pencil on paper. Prints and Photographs Division.

Item 8-2
William Grant Still, *Afro American Symphony* (1930), second revision, ca. 1935. First performed in 1931, the Still symphony symbolized the African American composer's right to be heard in the concert hall and continues in repertory today. The English horn melody in the opening, evocative of Paul Laurence Dunbar's pastoral poem "All my life long," metamorphoses into a driving blues tune, the symphony's unifying motif.
Composer's holograph manuscript. Music Division. Used by permission of Novello & Company, Ltd. Music Sales Corporation, exclusive agent.

Index

Page numbers for illustrations are given here in boldface type.

"Grand Concert! of Vocal & Instrumental Music, and Exhibition Drill, Metropolitan A. M. E. Church, M bet. 15th and 16th Sts., N.W., Friday Evening, February 15th, '89, Testimonial to Major C. A. Fleetwood by the Citizens of Washington."
Broadside. Christian A. Fleetwood Papers, Manuscript Division.

Contributors

Paul Finkelman is the Baker & Hostetler Visiting Professor at the Cleveland-Marshall College of Law at Cleveland State University. He is the author of numerous articles and books on African American history, including *Dred Scott v. Sandford: A Brief History* (1997); *Slavery and the Law* (1997); *Slavery and the Founders: Race and Liberty in the Age of Jefferson* (1996); and *The Law of Freedom and Bondage* (1985). His book *Slavery in the Courtroom: An Annotated Bibliography of American Cases* was published by the Library of Congress in 1985 and won the Joseph C. Andrews Award from the American Association of Law Librarians. He has held numerous fellowships from, among others, the Library of Congress, the American Historical Association, the American Philosophical Society, the National Endowment for the Humanities, and the American Council of Learned Societies.

David J. Garrow is Presidential Distinguished Professor at Emory University School of Law and is the author of *Liberty and Sexuality: The Right to Privacy and the Making of Roe v. Wade* (1994). His book *Bearing the Cross: Martin Luther King, Jr., and the Southern Christian Leadership Conference* (1986) won the 1987 Pulitzer Prize in Biography and the seventh annual Robert F. Kennedy Book Award. He is also the author of *The FBI and Martin Luther King, Jr.* (1981) and *Protest at Selma* (1978), as well as editor of *The Montgomery Bus Boycott and the Women Who Started It: The Memoir of Jo Ann Gibson Robinson* (1987) and coeditor of *The Eyes on the Prize Civil Rights Reader* (1987). He served as a senior adviser for "Eyes on the Prize," the award-winning PBS television history of the American black freedom struggle.

Debra Newman Ham, professor of history at Morgan State University in Baltimore, Maryland, is editor of *The African-American Mosaic: A Library of Congress Resource Guide for the Study of Black History and Culture* (1993). She served as specialist in African American history and culture in the Manuscript Division at the Library of Congress from 1986 to 1995 and as the black history specialist in the National Archives and Records Administration from 1972 to 1986. At the National Archives, Ham compiled *Black History: A Guide to Civilian Records in the National Archives* (1984). Both *The African-American Mosaic* and *Black History* received awards from the Mid-Atlantic Regional Archives Conference; *Black History* was awarded the 1985 Coker Finding Aid Award from the Society of American Archivists. Ham has a Ph.D. degree in African history from Howard University.

Kenneth Marvin Hamilton, associate professor of history and director of the Ethnic Studies Program at Southern Methodist University in Dallas, Texas, has been a student of the life and work of Booker T. Washington for many years. He is currently working on two books about Washington. One investigates Washington's political, economic, and educational philosophies and the other analyzes the National Negro Business League, the organization Washington founded. Hamilton is an active member of the Executive Council of the Association for the Study of Afro-American Life and History and is the author of *Black Towns and Profit: Promotion and Development in the Trans-Appalachian West,*

1877–1977 (1991). He has a doctoral degree from Washington University in St. Louis, Missouri.

Charles Johnson, Jr., assistant professor of history at Morgan State University in Baltimore, Maryland, has researched African American military history for more than two decades. He served for many years as the president of the Afro-American Historical and Genealogical Society and published numerous articles in the society's journal. His book *African-Americans in the National Guard: Recruitment and Deployment during Peacetime and War* (1992) documents many of the problems of racism and discrimination faced by soldiers of color in the defense of the nation. Johnson is a retired lieutenant colonel in the U.S. Army and received his Ph.D. degree in history from Howard University.

Ervin Jordan is associate professor and curator of technical services, Special Collections Department, at the Alderman Library, University of Virginia, in Charlottesville. His study *Black Confederates and Afro-Yankees in Civil War Virginia* (1995) was the History Book of the Month Club selection in February 1995 and the recipient of the Kirkland Book Award Certificate of Meritorious Excellence in Confederate History. An active leader in the Mid-Atlantic Regional Archives Association, he has pioneered new approaches to the use of African American documentation in the Alderman Library and numerous other archival repositories throughout the State of Virginia and elsewhere.